"Teddy Bears to Dangerous Missions"

An Autobiographical Journey from Teddy Bears to
Submarines and Beyond!

Dennis Robertson

Fulton Books, Inc.
Meadville, PA

Published by Fulton Books 2021

ISBN 978-1-64952-717-2 (paperback)
ISBN 978-1-64952-718-9 (digital)

Printed in the United States of America

DEDICATION

This book is dedicated to my amazing wife, Diane Dolores, my life partner and true Rock of our family. She's been standing by me and supporting me for over fifty-six years now, through the good times (and there were many) and the *dark days*, as she calls them. Without her love, encouragement, and support, this book would never have been written.

During my adult life, when telling stories about my life to family members, my children would always say, "Hey, Dad, can you tell us some more?"

And I'd reply, "Try to be patient. It'll all be in MY BOOK." As it turns out, COVID-19 came along, which inspired me to get started. I enjoyed writing about my life, and the more I wrote about it, the more I remembered. So here it is. I hope you enjoy *Teddy Bears to Dangerous Missions*!

Note: Most of the names that appear in this book are that person's actual name; however, some fictitious names have been substituted for the person's real name to protect that person or their family.

PROLOGUE

On the eighth of April 1948, a brother and sister were quietly married by a justice of the peace in Pittsburgh, Pennsylvania. More about them later, but this story isn't only about the brother and sister. It's about me, Dennis Alan Robertson (a.k.a. Dennis Alan Holt), and my life of eighty-one-plus years.

CHAPTER ONE

GROWING UP IN PRE-WWII MIAMI

I was born in Jackson Memorial Hospital in Miami, Florida, on February 1, 1939. My mother was Edith Louise Kirk Holt, whose family was from Bethel, Maine. And my father, John Lawrence Holt, grew up in Berlin, New Hampshire. He never liked the name John, so he went by Lawrence J.

I don't remember too much of the early years, except the baby pictures I've seen and later pictures with me on my tricycle with lush tropical plants and shrubs in the background. Life in pre-WWII Miami was simple. The United States was just recovering from the Great Depression, and the mood was upbeat. We didn't have a lot of money, but life was good. The music of the big bands and jazz played from the floor console or table model AM radios along with stories told about adventures of the Shadow ("the Shadow knows, ha, ha, ha!"), Green Hornet, and other fictional heroes.

My first remembrances of a home was an apartment above a garage in the NE section of Miami a few avenues west of Biscayne Boulevard. The address was 226 NE 21st Street. My father and mother never owned a home; they always rented.

My mother was very health conscious, and I remember walking with her south along Biscayne Boulevard to the Burdine's department store where they offered nutrition classes. She'd bring crayons and paper to keep me occupied while I sat patiently on the floor, coloring with my paper on a chair seat during the class. Being very healthy, Mother had a very trim figure. She liked to tell the story of "being in the movies." Apparently, a Hollywood crew was in Miami shooting a film. There was one scene where Barbara Stanwyck was getting out of a car, and the camera zoomed in, getting a tight shot of Barbara's legs as she stepped onto the street. They needed a stand-in for that scene. Mother interviewed for the part and got it! She was always very proud of being on the "silver screen!" Other memories of the time that we lived in Miami was a very small live Christmas tree sitting on a table in the apartment with a few sparse presents scattered around it. About once a week, when we lived in the apartment above the garage, a large black lady would push her vegetable cart around the neighborhood. She'd hawk her fresh vegetables with a loud, "'Um got carrots. 'Um got turnips. 'Um got collard greens," or whatever the fresh vegetables of the day were! Life was simple. Life was good!

I was probably three when we moved to 740 SW 10th Street. It was a small single-family home in a cul-de-sac of about eight new homes. The house even had an attached porte cochère or carport! We didn't have a car initially, but we would later. I remember one unfortunate event that happened while living there. My mother and I were going to make a slingshot, so we went to the vacant lot next door to find a bush with a nice *Y* branch. When we found one, Mother said, "Here's one," and waded right into the large bush, cutting out the appropriate piece! We finished attaching the rubber sling with its leather pouch for the projectile, and it worked fine! Later that evening, my mother developed a terrible rash on her arms, hands, and face. Come to find out, the large bush was a poison oak, and Mom was deathly allergic to poison ivy and oak! She suffered terribly for days, all for a slingshot for her son.

One innocent incident that sticks out in my memory later while living there involved Lila Jean, a young girl my age who lived across the street. It seems my mother looked out of her kitchen door and into the back seat of our car that was parked in the porte cochère. There, Lila Jean and I were in the back seat with our pants off and checking out each other's private parts. Mother scolded me, but the strongest consequences came when my father got home from work that evening! Lila Jean's father was a Florida State Trooper, and apparently my father was concerned about some sort of family arrest for molestation or something.

Streets in Miami run east and west, and avenues run north and south. SW Tenth Street in the southwest section of Miami is two blocks south of what is today known as Calle Ocho, or Eighth Street (also called the Tamiami Trail), and occupied currently by Cubans who fled from Castro in the early 1960s. I grew up in what is now Little Havana.

WWII had ratcheted up quite intensely while we were living at 740 SW 10th Street. Almost everything was scarce and rationed. We would receive ration stamps periodically for things like meat, sugar, gasoline, etc., and everyone could only purchase those items in quantities equal to their ration stamps. I recall butcher shops would sell horsemeat as an alternative to beef. Yummy! We bought war bonds and saved old tin cans and other reusable items for the war effort. Life was not so simple anymore.

During this time, my father was drafted, selected the Navy, and went away to the war. Fortunately for our family, he was classified with a Navy Storekeeper rating or SK and was not deployed to a war-zone but instead to Sampson, New York, to a Navy Supply Depot. We only saw him occasionally when he'd come home on leave.

It's much different today, but when we lived at *740*, there were no houses on either side of the cul-de-sac nor across Tenth street, only empty lots with palmetto (and poison oak!) bushes. I remember walking down to the end of the cul-de-sac where there were kumquat bushes and eating the kumquats, which were delicious.

Our local grocery store was located nearby on SW Eighth Street and one of the Carl's Market chain of stores in Miami. It was the same store that sold ground horsemeat hamburger. One month, they were running a "Name Your Bike" contest. The winners would receive a nice new Schwinn bicycle. My mother entered the name "Breeze Bender," and we were subsequently notified that I had won a bike! We went to the store for a presentation by the store manager, and a photographer took our picture. Mother liked to write poems and was, in general, good with words.

Our driveway sloped slightly down onto SW Tenth Street. My mother would hold on to the back of my new bike's seat, steadying me as I tried to keep my balance going down the driveway. One day, as she was doing that, I reached the street and continued across the seldom traveled road. When I stopped at the other side, I realized Mother had let go of my seat a while ago, and I could now ride a bike!

On the left side of our house and behind the porte cochère, my mother had planted a victory garden. She had some tomato plants and other vegetables that we'd supplement our meals with. Miami has more than its share of bugs, so to keep the tomato plants from being eaten up, Mother would get some cheap Cuban cigars, soak them in water until the tobacco leaves turned the water brown, and then she'd spray that juice on the tomato plants. It did the trick, and the plants and fruit weren't eaten up by insects.

My mother and I became good buddies. We'd sometimes ride the bus into downtown Miami where there was a myriad of things to do. One was visiting a juice bar in an open-front shop right off the sidewalk. They sold freshly squeezed orange, grapefruit, papaya, and other juices. My favorite was coconut milk; it was delicious! We'd occasionally go to movies at the Paramount Theater on E. Flagler Street downtown. Besides movies, the Paramount also featured stage acts. One time, Mother took me to see a new skinny singer named Frank Sinatra. He was just getting started and not yet well-known.

Before they were married, my father was Catholic and my mother Protestant. My father wanted to be married in the Catholic church, so Mother converted to Catholicism. When we moved to 740 SW Tenth Street, our parish was Sts. Peter and Paul Church. I made my First Communion at Sts. Peter and Paul.

In the fall of 1946, I started first grade at Sts. Peter and Paul Catholic School which was about two miles from home. There were no school buses, so Mom installed a child's seat on her bicycle and would peddle me to and from school. One sad day, my wirehaired terrier, Whiskers, dashed out the door as we were leaving for school. He was extremely evasive, and we didn't have time to catch him and put him back in the house. He followed us to school, or at least partway, until he ran into the road. He was struck by a car and killed instantly. I cried all day in school and recall the nuns teaching my class weren't very sympathetic regarding my loss. The nuns were strict disciplinarians. I must have been a cutup in school, as I remember being told to hold out my hands palms up so one of the nuns could discipline me by whacking my palms with a ruler. I also spent my share of time facing a corner of the classroom, another favorite punishment of the nuns. The girls sat on one side of the classroom and the boys on the other. A third favorite punishment, this usually for talking, was for me being told to sit with the girls on their side, which I actually didn't mind at all!

For fun on weekends, Mom and I would get on a Miami city bus at the nearest stop on SW Eighth Street and transfer in downtown Miami to a *jitney* (like a shared cab) that would take us to Miami Beach for the day. I loved the beach! Life was good. The beach we went to is now called South Beach. In those days, the big hotels that are now above Thirteenth Street and higher north were all private oceanfront estates. For example, where the Fountainebleau Hotel is at Forty-Fourth Street and Collins Avenue now was then the large Firestone family estate.

Occasionally, while at the beach, we would see a plume of thick dark smoke originating from just over the horizon out in the Atlantic. It was only later that I learned these were our merchant ships that had been torpedoed by German U-boats patrolling off our coast. Miami life during the war was also filled with frequent air raid drills when sirens would sound and everyone would be required to turn out all unnecessary lights. Also mandatory was pulling shut the blackout shades covering all windows inside the house. We had an old car by then. The headlights were in pods sticking out from the engine compartment and over the separate front fenders. It was a law that black tape be placed over the headlight lenses so only a small rectangle remained to let light shine through while driving. The idea was to create a *blackout* in the event that an enemy tried to bomb the city at night from the air. Life was getting more complicated, not less.

Miami, FL: Pre-WWII

Father and Mother,
Miami, 1939

226 NE 21st St., Miami, FL 1939

Dennis in Miami,
FL 1939

740 SW 10th St, Miami, 1941
(Little Havana now)

Dennis, Miami,
Florida, 1941

Dennis, Miami,
Florida, 1941

CHAPTER TWO

MY FAMILY BACK IN NEW ENGLAND

Air-conditioned homes in those times were very rare, so over a period of one, and sometimes two, of the hot summer months in Miami, my mother and I would go visit her mother, my Nana, Mabel Flora Bean Robertson, in Maine. We'd board the Florida East Coast *Champion* in Miami for the twenty-five-hour train ride to New York City. Trains then all had coal-fired steam engines that billowed nasty smelling smoke. You couldn't open a window as the smoke trailed back from the engine and enveloped the passenger cars. In fact, even with the windows closed, some smoke and soot would seep into the car anyway. Sleeping in a coach seat overnight was a challenge, and the rancid smell of half-eaten box lunches didn't add positively to the experience!

Once arriving at New York's Penn Station the next morning, we'd take a cab to Grand Central Station then board another train to Portland, Maine. Upon arriving in Portland, the next leg of the long journey would be by bus. My grandmother, always Nana to me, lived on Route 26 in Bethel, and the bus route conveniently went right by her house. The bus would stop in front of Nana's house, and Mom and I would hop off on our Maine summer adventure.

As I indicated earlier, Nana's maiden name was Mabel Flora Bean. My great-grandfather Vear Bean's family were longtime residents of Bethel, and at one time Vear owned 160 acres around Waterspout Mountain up on Chandler Hill. The first time I came up from Miami and met him, he lived alone in a small trailer in Locke Mills, Maine. He was sitting at his kitchen table having *supper* and eating peas balanced on a dinner knife! I'd never seen anyone do that, and it was amazing to this young child!

My great-great-grandfather, Ira Wesley Bean, fought in the Civil War with the 10th Maine Brigade. He'd received that large parcel of property up on Chandler Hill in Bethel as a land grant under a federal government program of the time. Included with the photos of this book is a stern-faced photo of Ira in his *Yankee* Civil War uniform sitting beside his beautiful young wife, Georgiana. Basically, they lived off the land in the best way they could, planting crops and supplementing protein by harvesting partridge and venison, which were abundant around Chandler Hill. This was in no way the trophy hunting one sees today. It was for survival. I still have great-great-grandfather Ira's Marlin rifle with eleven notches in the wooden grip, proudly tallying the number of deer he shot with it.

My maternal grandfather was Robert H. Kirk, born on February 21, 1886, in Oskaloosa, Iowa. His paternal grandfather had migrated from Ireland and settled in Pennsylvania before moving west to Iowa. His maternal grandmother and grandfather were both born in Scotland and settled in Ohio before moving west to Iowa. In the mid-1800s, people that landed on our eastern shores were moving west with expectations of establishing a new life and prosperity in the new world. Life was promising! I don't know the exact date, but by the early 1910s, my grandfather Kirk had moved back east to Bethel, Maine, and at the outbreak of WWI, joined the Navy. He enlisted as a cook, as he always said, "If anyone can read a cookbook, they can cook!"

When I was a senior at Gould Academy in Bethel, the (required) Grandfather's Theme for English IV that I wrote was about him, and I learned a lot about his life from my mother. During the war, a light cruiser he was serving aboard was torpedoed and sank. He survived that disaster, but later, over the period of his naval career, he became a Chief Warrant Officer, having gone into a *very* new rating called *radioman*. You might Google "heterodyne receiver" to see how primitive radio transmission was at the time. It consisted of an oscillating crystal with a "cat's whisker" touching the crystal to generate the signal—very primitive early radio communication method, no voice or video, only Morse code. He must have had a technical inclination to have become much more than a cook!

My grandfather Kirk and Nana had four children—Edith, Robert, David, and Richard. David was killed on Chandler Hill on November 25, 1939, in a hunting accident over a Thanksgiving holiday. He was pulling his rifle up by the barrel into a tree stand when it accidentally discharged. He was only sixteen years old. I got to know my other uncles, but unfortunately not David. Mom was born on May 26, 1916, while Grandfather Kirk was still in the Navy. Nana was pregnant with my mother during a transfer in duty stations for Grandfather Kirk. He had selected Hawaii on his *dream sheet* but was assigned to Charleston, South Carolina, where my mother was born. She always lamented that she wished she could have been born in Hawaii. Sadly, Mom never made it to those exotic shores. Life is not always fair.

My father, Larry Holt, was born in Berlin, New Hampshire, on April 1, 1916. He never knew his mother, Margurite Holt (née) Butler, who died as a result of childbirth. My paternal grandfather, Ernest Holt, was a callused-hand, gentle, working man who was employed by the Brown Paper Company in Berlin, New Hampshire. I recall that he had a prominent Roman nose, and there were always several abandoned cars on the side of his property that I would climb on and pretend I was driving when Mother and I came to visit. He worked in that paper mill in Berlin most of his life. The relatives of my father's mother came to America from Prince Edward Island, Canada, while Ernest Holt's parents also came here from Canada, but from the province of New Brunswick. Their parents immigrated to New Brunswick from England and Ireland (during the Potato Famine there).

Shortly after his wife died, Grandfather Ernest was looking for a housekeeper, primarily to take care of his young son, Larry, while he was working his shift at the paper mill. He found and hired Mildred Young, who soon moved in with her four children. Ernest and Mildred were subsequently married and had *six* children of their own! My father continued living at home during high school years, where he was an excellent ski jumper and loved winter sports.

However, upon graduation, and especially considering there were *ten* half brothers and sisters living under the same roof, he moved to Miami, entered the hotel business as a bellman, and never lived outside Miami again!

While he was always good to me, what I heard from Nana and my mother was that my grandfather, Robert Kirk, became a changed unpleasant man after being discharged from the Navy. After the Navy, he bought a home on Chandler Hill in Bethel. That's where my mother grew up most of her life. Robert Kirk became verbally and physically abusive to both women in his life. Finally, Mabel Bean Kirk couldn't take it any longer and left him, later obtaining a final divorce. My mother was then the primary caregiver for her two remaining siblings, but as soon as she got old enough, she left home also. Her father was furious and shut her out of his life from then until his death in 1957. If he saw Mom on the street in Bethel, he'd cross to the other side to avoid her. I remember one time we were up from Miami visiting Nana, and Mom brought me up to his Chandler Hill home to meet my grandfather Kirk. About two and a half miles from the main road, over the dirt Chandler Hill Road, there is a tee in the road. Grandfather Kirk's house was just to the left. As soon as he saw us, I remember him saying to Mom, "I'm not interested in seeing you. It's this young man here that I want to meet." I think that hurt her a lot, but she was a strong woman and was trying to do the right thing and not deprive me of meeting one of my grandfathers.

CHAPTER THREE

LIFE AFTER MIAMI

My mother, Edith Kirk, had met my father, Larry Holt, while they were both working at summer resort hotels in the White Mountains of New Hampshire. These hotels were mostly occupied by well-to-do families from the Boston and New York City areas. I believe Mother and Father even spent one summer working at Pinehurst in North Carolina. My father was a bellman, and my mother waited on tables in the dining room.

It's a wonder my father and mother ever became man and wife! Their personalities were diametrically opposed. My mother was more of a country girl, as influenced by her upbringing in rural Maine. She loved to cook, sew, can vegetables, make jelly, and other such domestic pastimes. She was very health conscious and would walk a couple miles a day or more whenever she could. She also loved to be outdoors doing gardening, getting some sun, or simply enjoying the fresh air. My father, on the other hand, could have been happy never being outdoors and wasn't particularly fond of the beach, probably partially because he had fair skin that burned very easily. I never knew him to have any specific hobbies, and he wasn't very handy at fixing things when they broke. This isn't to be derogatory or disrespectful; that was just his personality. He enjoyed the nightlife, and having a beer or two (or sometimes a CC and ginger) with friends at a local bar was his idea of having a good time.

Sometime, after he returned home from WWII, the personality differences between my mother and father started to become more apparent. We were now living in a nice house in the NW section of

Miami. I remember the orange trees and lemon trees growing on the property. They bore more fruit than we could consume, so we'd give the excess to friends and neighbors. I still had my bike that I rode all around the neighborhood. Life for me was still good, but not so much so for my mother. My father would stay out late and sometimes not come home at all. My mother found out he had a female friend and finally had had enough. She filed separation papers and was awarded custody of me, her only son. One day, Mom packed our bags and we left Miami, taking one last ride north on Florida East Coast's train, the Champion. We moved in with Nana and Frank Robertson in their house on Rt. 26 in Bethel, Maine. The divorce became final during our stay with Nana and Frank.

The year was 1946, and WWII had been over almost a year! As fall approached, it was time for me to start second grade. Just a short distance down Rt. 26, toward Locke Mills, Maine, was a one-room schoolhouse. It was the typical *schoolhouse red* outside. As I recall, I was one of two kids in second grade. We had one teacher for all the first through eighth grade students. The older kids would help the teacher and assist by tutoring the younger class students after finishing their own lessons. As colder weather approached, which it does early in Maine, the teacher would build a fire in the potbelly stove that resided in the very center of the single-room building. Once the fire was going, it was the job of the older students to add wood whenever necessary. The school itself backed up to a large lumber sawmill. At recess, we'd all climb on the lumber piles, and it was great fun! I didn't realize it at the time, but this experience in a one-room schoolhouse would be a rather unique event in my life, and the one in Bethel was only the first of two that I would attend while growing up. To this day, I don't know very many people who received an education in a one-room schoolhouse!

Roughly halfway through the second grade school year, Mother and I moved to Swampscott, Massachusetts, to live with Jack and Leona Jackman. I'm not sure how the arrangements were made, but Leona was a distant relative of my grandmother Mabel's. I called them Uncle Jack and Auntie. Jack was a stockbroker who took the train into Boston five days a week to his office. He was a very friendly and outgoing man. Auntie was a homemaker and a very short serious woman. Their home was at *the S-curve* on Burrill St. in Swampscott. My mother took a job at a dry-cleaning shop just around the corner from the Jackman's home. The shop was called Paramount Cleansers.

Approximately a mile walking distance from Auntie and Uncle Jack's home was my new school. My mother walked me down the next school day after we arrived in Swampscott to check me in. Transferring midyear during the school year was daunting for me, but apparently I adjusted to the new school sufficiently enough that I didn't have any trouble scholastically. It *was* different coming to a class with many students after having spent half the year in a one-room schoolhouse environment, but I'd been in a similar class size while attending first grade at Sts. Peter and Paul in Miami. This was the one school where I was bullied by an upperclassman. About half-way on the long walk to school, there was a bigger kid who liked to cross the street and start giving me a hard time, blocking my way, pushing, and just being a pain. He seemed to be waiting for me to come by as this happened frequently. I'd never encountered this before, and at first I didn't know how to handle it. I initially wanted to avoid conflict and even dreaded my walk to school in the morning. My mother and Uncle Jack told me the only way to remedy this was to push the kid back, punching him if necessary. On the next encounter, I took their advice, and the kid never bothered me again. I have an appreciation of how children feel today, although today the bullying is much worse with social media.

Auntie was a strict disciplinarian from the old school! When my mother was at work, Auntie felt free to dispense punishment for whatever when she deemed it necessary. When I did something against the rules or disrespectful to my mother, she would tell me, "Take off your belt, Denny." And I'd never get any more than three whacks on the butt. Looking back, the anticipation of removing my belt and waiting for the next event to occur was actually worse than the sting of the belt itself! With Auntie, I'd get three or more whacks, but with the buckle end of the belt, which my mother never used. This may sound extreme by today's standards, but back then, reasonable physical punishment was a norm in many families.

Life in Swampscott with mother and Auntie and Uncle Jack was actually enjoyable for me. I didn't have any close friends my age, but I had my bike and would ride all over the North Shore of Boston just observing an area that was *so* different from Miami. Of course, there was very little traffic in those days compared with now. I would ride past the docks and fishermen's boats along the way to Marblehead. I remember nets drying in the warm sea breeze and fishermen busy mending their nets that had been damaged on their last trip out to sea. The smell of salt air was almost intoxicating. Marblehead itself was a beautiful place and usually my final destination north on my biking adventures. When I wanted a change on my bike forages, I'd ride south from Swampscott to Revere Beach. It, too, was a beautiful spot, and of course I had an inborn love of beach places from our days in Miami.

WWII Years, Before and After

Ira (10th Maine Brigade)
and Georginna Bean

Larry Holt, US Navy
SK2, 1941

Dennis, Bethel, Maine, 1942

Uncle Jack, Dennis, and
Father—Swampscott, 1946

Dennis Swampscott, 1948

CHAPTER FOUR

THE STORY OF THE BROTHER AND SISTER WHO MARRIED

This gets a little complicated, so please follow me closely, but circa 1917, there was a home at the corner of Main and Elm Streets in *downtown* Bethel, Maine, occupied by Frank O'Neil Robertson and his wife, Mabel Scribner Robertson. They would later have two sons—Frank O'Neil, born 1918, and Edward Neil, born 1920. Frank owned and operated a gasoline and service station a few blocks away down Main St., and Mabel was a homemaker. Frank O'Neil (Neil, the son) became a medical doctor, and after internship, he opened a practice in Kittanning, Pennsylvania, caring for coal miners. Edward Neil (Ed) became a civil engineer and served in WWII in France, seeing horrific action with the loss of the lives of many of his men. When he returned home after the war, Ed had a severe case of *shell shock*, known today as PTSD. He'd wake up in the middle of the night screaming after reliving some of his horrible wartime memories in his dreams. Ed was a 1ˢᵗ Lieutenant in the Army Corps of Engineers. It was their job to be in front of the main body of troops and rebuilding bridges that the Nazis had destroyed behind them. It was a very precarious position to be out front and between the enemy and our main Army units. He didn't talk about it, but I learned at one point Ed was just stepping off a pontoon bridge the Corps was building so the US Army could advance across that French river when the Germans attacked. Many enlisted engineers were killed instantly, but others who were badly injured were calling for Lieutenant Robertson to help them. Memories like that and worse were causing the PTSD, bad dreams, and memories that he was trying to suppress. He struggled a lot during that period.

Frank O'Neil Sr. and Mable Scribner were divorced at some point. Then in September 1944, Frank married my then single grandmother, Mabel Bean Kirk, making her new name Mabel Bean Kirk Robertson! They initially lived in the home on Route 26 in South Bethel where the bus used to drop my mother and me off when we were visiting from Miami.

Several times, when Mom and I were visiting Nana in Bethel and years after my parents were divorced, we'd tag along with Nana and Frank when they were driving to Rockwood, Maine, to visit Frank's son Edward. Ed was managing a set of sports camps on Moosehead Lake. It was a beautiful place, and I loved going up there! Moosehead Lake is located in about the geographic center of the state of Maine. It's forty miles long and ten miles wide at its widest point. In the north/south center of the lake on the east bank is Mount Kineo. Opposite on the west side of Mount Kineo is the small town of Rockwood. There were about two hundred full-time residents in Rockwood, but the town swelled to around two thousand during the summer months, counting tourists. Moosehead Lake is a great recreation spot, attracting boaters and fishermen from all over New England.

Mom and Ed were attracted to each other, and a relationship soon developed. There's more that I'll fill in in subsequent chapters, but when Mom and Ed were married in Pittsburg, a brother and a sister (by marriage) were joined in holy matrimony!

Bean, Kirk, Robertson Family Tree

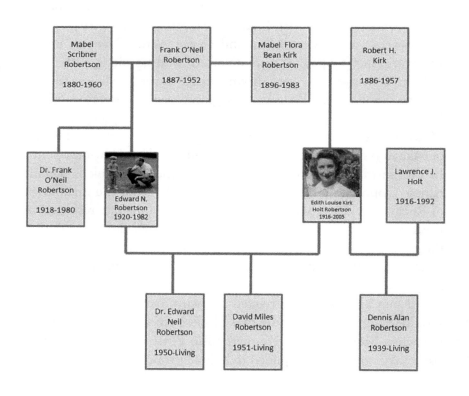

How a Brother & Sister (by Marriage) Were Legally Married!

CHAPTER FIVE

MULTIPLE GRAMMAR SCHOOLS DAZE

In the early part of the summer of 1947, after I'd completed second grade in Swampscott, Mother and I moved back to Maine. Nana and Frank had sold their home on Rt. 26 in Bethel and moved to a house in Bryant Pond, Maine, on Church St. We moved in with them. Bryant Pond was a typical rural Maine town run by a group of selectmen chosen from town residents. It had a couple of grocery stores, a hardware store, a drugstore, and several gas stations. Residential homes were mixed with the businesses on both sides of the length of Main Street. The drugstore sold bundles of *licorice root*, which consisted of natural root sections of the plant itself. I thought they were delicious, and whenever I had a couple of spare pennies, I would go over to the store and buy some!

There were several ponds around town that were used by the residents for swimming and fishing during summer months. I also recall a small baseball field with bleachers used occasionally by adults for semi-organized games. Neighborhood kids would form *pickup* teams and use the field when it was available. I had a baseball glove and played sometimes, but I wasn't very good, so I usually ended up in the outfield when my team wasn't at bat.

Nana, Frank, Mother, and I did a lot of traveling by car in those days. Uncle Bob, the older of mother's younger brothers, was an electrician and lived in Mechanic Falls, Maine, with his wife, Carolyn, and children, Cassie and Bobby. I *really* disliked visiting them as shortly after we arrived, Uncle Bob would send Bobby and me out to the garden to pull weeds in the hot summer sun! There was no time to talk or play with Bobby and Cassie.

The summer soon passed, and it was time to go back to school. My mother had enrolled me in the Bryant Pond Elementary School for my third-grade year. The school was conveniently located off Church St., very near Nana's house. I was enjoying the school, teachers, and classmates when about halfway through the school year, Mother made the decision to leave Bryant Pond, and we moved to Rockwood, Maine! Ed Robertson was still working there, and I think they missed seeing each other and were tired of trying to conduct a long-distance relationship. In Rockwood, I started attending what was my second one-room schoolhouse. It was the same situation as the first one I attended in Locke Mills, Maine. The older students would assist the teacher and tutor the younger ones after they finished their own lessons. Our young teacher was very pleasant and enthusiastic but inexperienced as she had just graduated from normal school in Madawaska, Maine, located in northern Aroostook County. Ron Rancourt, who became my buddy, and I made up the third grade. This time, the midyear transition wasn't quite as smooth. Third grade studies in Bryant Pond were *way* ahead of the curriculum taught in Rockwood. I was bored going over the same material I'd already learned until studies in Rockwood caught up with where I'd left off before the move.

I didn't see my father, Larry Holt, very much after Mother and I left Miami. He did have some visitation rights as part of the divorce, but I think my mother was always concerned that I would leave her and would want to be with my father on a more permanent basis. One previous summer, he was working at a seasonal hotel on Saranac Lake in Upstate New York. He made arrangements with mother and sent a round-trip airline ticket for me. I remember boarding a DC-3 for the flight, my first time on a commercial airliner. My uncle Bob had been in the Army Air Corps during WWII and had a pilot's license. He kept a small Piper Cub tied down at Bethel's grass field airstrip and would take me up on occasion, but I'd never been on a commercial airplane. DC-3s had no nose wheel and were *tail draggers*, so when on the ground, they had only the main landing gear and a tail wheel touching the ground. I vividly remember boarding that aircraft bound for Saranac Lake, saying hello to the stewardess at the rear door (flight attendants hadn't been invented yet) and walking *up* the aisle, which was at least at a fifteen-degree angle to my seat!

In 1948, after completing third grade in Rockwood, Maine, I again made a visit to my father, this time to Miami. He was now married to his *female friend*, Evelyn Middleditch, the same person from the period when he was married to my mother. Again, he sent a round-trip plane ticket, this time on Eastern Airlines, for my travel from Maine to Miami. For the first leg of my journey, I boarded another DC-3 in Portland, Maine. I walked up the sloped aisle to my seat, and the plane took off for New York City. In New York, I changed planes to an Eastern Airlines propeller-driven, four-engine Constellation or *Connie* made by Lockheed. Aircraft in those days didn't have the range jetliners have today, so the flight had to make a stop in Jacksonville, Florida, to refuel on the way to Miami.

I had a pleasant enough visit, as I recall. My father drove me around Miami and Miami Beach to show me the changes to the area since WWII's end. We even went to a local pool a couple times during my visit. I was a bit uncomfortable around Evelyn, particularly due to my mother's negative feelings about her and simply due to the fact that I didn't know her very well. I learned later that Evelyn's initial impression of me was that I was a spoiled brat, and she couldn't wait for me to leave! Evelyn was a very candid person.

Sometime during early 1948, Dad, Ed Robertson, had applied for and accepted a job offer from the Pittsburgh and Lake Erie (P&LE) Railroad as a draftsman. The position was in Pittsburgh, Pennsylvania, and Dad accepted. While I was in Miami, Mom and Dad packed their modest belongings in their car and drove to Pittsburgh. I'm not sure why Pittsburgh was chosen, but Dad's older brother, Neil, had his medical practice well established in Kittanning, Pennsylvania, by then and maybe that was an influencing factor as Kittanning is not too far north of Pittsburgh(?). When I returned north from visiting my father, I flew into Pittsburgh to join them. I learned later that Mom and Dad had it a bit rough financially until he started getting paychecks from the P&LE Railroad. Apparently, they supplemented some meals with dandelion greens picked from a nearby park. Dandelion greens were all they had for dinner on some evenings. It was during their time in Pittsburgh that Mom married her second husband, her brother by marriage, Ed Robertson!

Late summer of 1948 found me living in the Swissvale area of Pittsburgh. It was a very blue-collar part of the city with a mixture of residences and factories interspersed together. The Union Switch and Signal Corporation was just down the street from our third-floor walk-up apartment. I remember the challenge of helping to carry groceries up all those steep flights of stairs. The apartment had a porch in the rear with a long rope clothesline stretching between two pulleys to dry our clothes, sheets, etc. Pittsburgh was one of the first cities in the USA to have a television station. It was station KDKA. TV receivers were *very* expensive then, but the neighbors just below us had one. The picture was about twelve inches in diameter and round. The table-mounted case was very deep as it had to accommodate the cathode ray tube (or CRT) that created the picture and was the main element of the receiver. KDKA was the *only* TV station available, and programs like *The Lawrence Welk Show* and *Ed Sullivan Show*, comedy by Milton Berle, and kids' shows such as *Howdy Doody* were not broadcast continuously. When regular programs weren't being broadcast, there was a *test pattern* on the screen. Perhaps some of you remember that?

Pittsburgh today is a relatively clean city. However, in 1948, it was the steel producing capital of the USA. Surrounding the downtown area were many steel mills that would billow smoke and dump chemicals at an unregulated rate. Companies were free to pollute the air or dump into the Ohio River whatever byproducts of steel making that they desired. Depending upon the direction of the wind, Swissvale could be an unpleasant place to be anywhere in the outdoors! There was a park south of our home, within walking distance and near the Monongahela River, that Mother and I would go to on nice days when Dad was at work. I remember the warm sun, open grassy areas, lush vegetation, and just enjoying the companionship of a son and his mother being together.

One day, while we were living in Swissvale, my mother came to me and said, "Den, Ed is a jealous person, and every time he hears the name Holt, it makes him think of your father, Larry. If he adopted you, your last name would be Robertson, and the reminder would be gone. Would you have any problem with that?" I really didn't, and if it would contribute to peace in the family, I was okay with it. The adoption proceedings went ahead, and a number of months later, I was Dennis Alan Robertson. I'm not sure whether or not this hurt my father, as in the years later, he never said anything to me about it.

That fall, I attended the fourth grade in Pittsburg, but I don't really recall any details, so the year must have been relatively uneventful. I do remember joining Cub Scouts and going to den meetings that I really enjoyed. One sad event that happened in 1948 while we were living in Swissvale was that Mother had a miscarriage. The first son of Ed and Edie didn't make it into this world.

In 1949, Dad and my mother bought a house in Rockwood, Maine, and left Pittsburg, both going back to the state they knew best and both loved. They bought the house from Reddy McNeil, a local carpenter. The house had been moved by Reddy to a foundation he had built on a lot on Rockwood Rd. in the town itself and just before the start of the dirt road that led to Moose River and Jackman, Maine. When we left Pittsburgh, Dad had a 1940s vintage Chrysler product of some sort (Dodge, Plymouth, etc.). It was a four-door sedan with a stick shift on the floor.

Dad had accepted a job with the Great Northern Paper Company. He was a GNP clerk and responsible for managing the company's wood pulp logging operations in very remote regions of the Great Northern's vast forests north of Moosehead Lake. Initially, Mother lived in the Rockwood house, and Dad was at one of the remote logging camp operations during the week but would come home on weekends. I was living in the Rockwood house with my mother and Dad during the summers and non-school months, also coming home on school holidays whenever possible.

Shortly after we first moved to Maine, I was intrigued by the Mainer accent. When Mother and I would visit Nana as a child, I guess I was too young to notice, but the local accents in Maine are very different and sometimes hard to understand. One very common word was *a-yuh* for "yes". Others that come to mind are *no-suh* for

33

"no, sir" and *ubet* (all one word) for "you bet." There are many *Down East* stories, but one of my favorites is the one about the traveling salesman who was lost on an old Maine country road. He saw a farmer up ahead and stopped to get directions. In the course of the conversation, the salesman asked the farmer, "Say, old codger, you lived here all your life?" The farmer paused for a while and then finally replied, "No, not chet!"

During the school months of my fifth- and sixth-grade years, 1949 through 1951, I boarded with Ed's mother, Mabel Scribner Robertson. She was still living in the home at the corner of Main and Elm Streets in Bethel, Maine, where Dad had been born. The Bethel elementary school was nearby on Elm Street. I remember walking into that fifth grade classroom on the first day and seeing two cute classmates, Myrna Blake and Roberta Bean. I knew going to school in Bethel was going to be okay!

Grandmother Mabel Scribner also boarded two to three high school students each year who attended Gould Academy, which was just a couple blocks from her home. I thought it was cool and some-how felt a bit more grown up living in the same quarters as high school guys and enjoyed hearing their stories about Gould Academy life!

As mentioned, I would return to Rockwood during the sum-mers to live with Mother and Dad. In 1949, when they purchased it, the house had no running water or bathroom. That summer, one of Dad's friends, known for his skill of finding in-ground water with a *witching stick*, came by. A *witching stick* was basically a freshly cut forked branch from a willow tree that would be held on the forked ends with palms reversed and fists down. The person with that talent would walk over the property, *witching for water*. Water was found when the long base end of the *Y* would be *pulled* toward the ground in a series of *tugs*, indicating the perfect spot for a well. By the way, I learned not everyone had this talent. I tried using the same *witching stick* over the same spot where Dad's friend had found water and didn't feel any downward tug on the stick! Good thing I never tried to go into that business.

Later that day, Dad and I grabbed two spade shovels and started digging a well in the same spot. The witched well location was adjacent to a protruding slate ledge near the house. This slate ledge became one side of our well. At approximately four to five feet below the surface, we struck water. I was amazed (and surprised)! We kept digging through the mostly clay soil until the well was approximately four by six feet at the top and around six feet deep. We built a wooden cover to keep debris out of the well and installed a trapdoor for access to the well with a bucket. Dad later dug a trench and laid a galvanized pipe from the well to the house. He installed an electric pump on the basement end of the pipe and a check valve in the water on the well side. The next phase of the installation was to connect the pump output in the basement to a faucet in the kitchen sink directly above the electric pump. We then had running water!

We still had the outhouse in the back of the house for a while, however. I'll never forget going out to that outhouse in the Maine winter with cold wind blowing up through the toilet seat hole. My mother kept it as clean as possible and well stocked with toilet paper (*no* rough Montgomery Ward catalog pages for wiping for us!), but it was still quite primitive.

During one of the summers that I spent in Rockwood, I built a tree house that was supported by three trees in the backyard. It consisted of four two-by-four floor joists in a rectangle shape about eight feet above the ground. The tree house was constructed with two-by-four framing and a single, slanted, shingled roof. The sides were plywood with small windows on three of the sides. Access was via a wooden ladder and a trap door in the floor. I had built a shelf inside and brought up a couple of folding chairs for seating. It was a place to just hang out alone, especially if it was raining outside, or to have *secret meetings* with my friends.

My brothers Ned and Dave were born while Mother and Dad lived in our Rockwood house: Edward Neil (or Ned) on March 3, 1950, and David Miles on August 11, 1951. There was a hospital in Greenville, Maine, about twenty miles south at the far end of Moosehead Lake. However, Mother and Dad decided the facilities for birth were likely much better at the Rumford, Maine, hospital, so she traveled down to Bethel just before the birth of both boys.

Rumford is thirty minutes from Bethel where Nana and Frank were then living on Chandler Hill.

I believe it was sometime in 1950 when I was eleven years old and living with my grandmother Mabel Scribner that I developed an interest in Boy Scouts. I joined troop 217 in Bethel, Maine. We met in a room above the firehouse just off the Bethel Commons at the head of Main St. Troop 217 was part of the BSA Pine Tree Council. I enjoyed Scouts, worked on advancement, and enjoyed the campouts, even though those were limited because of the cold Maine winters. During a subsequent summer, I went to Camp Hines in Raymond, Maine. I learned Scout skills and earned merit badges like swimming, canoeing, basket weaving, etc. After living in the Maine woods, it was a natural for me, and I loved it! During my week at Camp Hines, the council was offering a ten-day trip to Mount Katahdin in northern Maine. I had money in the bank saved from previous summer jobs and called Mother, telling her I would like to go on the Mt. Katahdin adventure. I'd pay for it from my own money. Happily, she agreed! It was the most thrilling adventure I'd been on to date. We camped at Roaring Brook, climbed Mt Katahdin, camped at Chimney Pond, climbed to the summit, and walked across the Knife Edge. What a trip! I was hooked! I continued in Scouting whenever I was living in Bethel during school years and reached the rank of Star Scout. Sadly, I had to drop out after eighth grade when my ninth-grade year took me to the town of Greenville, Maine, where there was no Scout troop.

One of the summers, when I was back home in Rockwood, Dad and I built a bathroom in the Rockwood house. We ran a line from the electric water pump in the basement to the new bathroom then through the walls as necessary to feed a toilet and sink. Dad would cut the galvanized pipe to the correct lengths, and I used a pipe threader to thread the ends. It was nice to be able to *retire* the outhouse!

Across Moosehead Lake from Rockwood was a hotel, a golf course, and a beautiful mountain known as Mount Kineo, described briefly in a previous chapter. There had been a number of hotels on that property. The original Mount Kineo House was built in 1848 and burned down in 1868. Two additional hotels, each iteration larger than the one before it, were built on the site of the first hotel and years later burned to the ground. The New Mount Kineo House was built in 1910 and still standing when we lived there. It catered to wealthy guests from as far away as Boston and New York City. Henry Ford didn't start producing his Model-T until 1908, so travel by automobile didn't exist initially. The guests came into the area by train. There was a train station in Greenville Junction at the foot of Moosehead Lake. The twenty-mile trip to Kineo by the guests was done over the water by a fleet of medium-size steamboats. During the years I lived in Rockwood, only one of the steamboats remained; it was called *The Mount Katahdin*. The *Katahdin* didn't carry passengers anymore (although I got to ride on it several times while living there). It was used to haul *booms* of logs from the source where they were felled *up the lake* and hauled down Moosehead Lake within a *boom* to one of the sawmills lining the shore.

Mount Kineo itself is quite unusual. It presents different shapes depending upon where you are viewing it from around the lake. From Rockwood, it looks something like the profile of an old Indian chief's head starting at the bottom of his nose and extending upward. He's looking south, down the lake, and his feathered headdress flows north, disappearing gradually into Moosehead Lake. Mt. Kineo rises about 750 feet above the lake. The mountain is said to contain one of the largest formations of rhyolite in the world. Rhyolite is an igneous rock, hard but similar to quartz.

While living in Rockwood, I became interested in geology and Native America lore. The native Abenaki Indians, an Algonquian speaking tribe that populated the region many years ago, valued that rock (today more commonly known as Kineo flint) for making arrows, spearheads, chisels, and other utensils. Other tribes would come from miles around to trade their goods for Kineo flint. I once found a piece of jasper on the shore, which is not native to the region. It looked like it had been shaped by the chipping process the Abenaki's used for making arrowheads. A geologist friend of mine told me, "The jasper piece was probably brought into the area by another tribe to trade for Kineo flint." Striking steel against Kineo flint would also make sparks to start fires.

Oliver Bernard was an experienced Indian guide who lived across the street from our Rockwood house. He had many tales, and one of them was how the local tribe made their arrowheads. First the piece of Kineo flint being shaped would be heated in a fire and, when at just the right temperature, was removed, and cold water from a feather would be strategically dropped on the flint. The flint being crystalline and layered would flake off at an edge. That process was repeated carefully until the arrowhead shape was achieved. Unfortunately, sometimes the flint edge being shaped would flake off in the wrong direction or a larger proportion and the arrowhead would be ruined. Per Oliver, there had been an Indian village where Moose River enters Moosehead Lake just above Rockwood. One of our summers in Rockwood, the lake was lowered around four feet so a new damn could be built at West Outlet south of Rockwood. That exposed the former Indian village. I would spend days just exploring it. I could imagine the smell of the sweetgrass Oliver told me had grown there in those days and the Indian women weaving sweetgrass baskets from it. There were occasional groupings of pieces of flint scattered in small areas of the old village. These were locations of fires used to make the arrowheads and implements. The pieces I found were mostly fragments that had been flaked off by the feather's cold water, but I did find several half or mostly completed arrowheads that had chipped off the wrong way and had to be discarded. I was lucky enough to find two arrowheads that were nearly perfect!

On the back or northeast side of Mt. Kineo is a sheer cliff dropping into one of the deepest parts of Moosehead Lake. That sheer drop off is called Lover's Leap. Legend has it that a disappointed Indian princess couldn't gain the love of a young buck she desired, so in desperation, she jumped off the cliff to her death. Mount Kineo is an interesting climb, and there are several trails starting at an old railroad bed along the lake to the summit. The Indian trail is .9 miles long and climbs steeply along the open ledge of the mountain on the Rockwood side. It leads to what was at one time a manned fire warden's seventy-foot watchtower. Other less steep trails are the Bridal trail and the Carriage trail, which are a bit longer, but both end up at the old fire tower.

I believe it was as early in the summer of 1951 when I started caddying at the Mount Kineo House's golf course. I was twelve years old. In the mornings when I'd caddy, I'd board Mount Kineo's employee boat and travel the mile from Rockwood across the lake to Kineo, walk over to the golf pro shop, and wait outside on a bench until needed. The course was only nine holes, with some playing up a grass slope to the base of Kineo where the flint rock rose vertically. Holes one and two were level, but then holes three, four, and five played up that steep grass fairway to the base of Kineo itself. There was one par five coming all the way down, hole six. The remaining three holes were on the flat part of the Kineo peninsula all the way back to the clubhouse. I didn't play golf then, but I recall having to remember such club names as *mid-iron, mashie, mashie-niblick, spoon,* etc. If I recall correctly, the caddy fee for nine holes was $0.75. *Carrying double* was $1.50. Going up those steep holes with one bag was hard enough, but carrying double was a real challenge for me at my young age. I was able to save some money by working that summer, however.

Other summer memories at our Rockwood house were when I built a flat-bottom boat. Our house was on the Rockwood Road in the main part of this tiny town of two hundred year-round residents and upward of two thousand in the summer, including tourists, fishermen, etc. There was a large lot directly down the hill and behind ours. One of its boundaries was the Moosehead Lake shoreline. The owners of the property were very friendly and didn't mind sharing their lake access. I constructed my boat, probably twelve feet long, four feet wide, and with a twelve inches freeboard near the lakeshore so I could launch it easily. I covered the outside of the boat's wooden hull with canoe canvas then sealed and painted it for waterproofing. Dad had a small 3 hp Evinrude outboard motor that I attached to the stern, and I had great fun exploring the Rockwood shores during calm weather. Moosehead can get rough very quickly, so I never took that small boat far from shore.

I really don't recall which summer it was while we were living in Rockwood, but I purchased a used Old Town wooden canoe for fifty dollars. The canvas wasn't in perfect shape, but I gave it a new coat of marine paint on the outside and clear shellac for the wood inside, and it was now in fine shape to go out on Moosehead Lake. My friends and I, or just me solo, were able to paddle it more places than my primitive, homemade boat, so I got many summers of use from it.

My mother was quite artistic. She would make jewelry out of natural material. For example, she'd cut leather into a shape, paint it, and glue it to metal clasp to make a pin. She'd then place the pieces in cellophane sleeves and sell them to local souvenir stores. I liked to draw and do charcoal sketching. One day in Rockwood, Mother said, "Let's both do a watercolor of this moose in a pond and compare the results." We did, and I think she was quietly a bit disappointed as she felt my watercolor was better than hers, but she praised me. I was doing oil painting of scenes then too.

One summer, when we were living in Rockwood, Nana and Frank drove up from Bethel, Maine. Dad had to work, but Mother and I joined Nana and Frank on a trip to Quebec City. It was only about a 3.5-hour drive from Rockwood. We went through Jackman, Maine and through customs at the US-Canada border and on to Lévis, Canada. From Lévis, we took a ferry across the St. Laurence River to Quebec City. Driving through Quebec was very different as none of the French residents spoke much English at all! I don't recall all the details, but we stayed in Quebec a couple of nights visiting the Plains of Abraham, the Chateaux Frontenac, and drove up to the Cathedral at St. Anne du Beaupre. I vividly remember within the cathedral that there were crutches and leg braces mounted everywhere. These were from crippled people who had been healed by prayers and the holy waters of the spring above the cathedral! We drove back to our Rockwood house after several days in Canada. It was my first time out of our country and very exciting.

CHAPTER SIX

MIDDLE SCHOOLS IN BETHEL AND GREENVILLE, MAINE

Sometime during the early 1950s timeframe, the Town of Bethel had funded and subsequently built a new middle school building at the upper end of Chapman St., actually on Crescent Lane. It was named Crescent Park School. Dad and Mother were still living forty miles north of Rockwood in the Great Northern Paper Co. woods. So when the fall of 1951 rolled around and I was ready to start seventh grade, I went to live with Aunt Elsie, who lived on Chapman St. in Bethel. She was widowed and had been married to Grandfather Frank Robertson's brother, Fred.

Aunt Elsie was a strong but extremely kind woman and a die-hard Boston Red Sox fan! She would religiously watch all the Red Sox's televised games and knew all the players. Her house was very comfortable, and I remember a large farm sink in her kitchen, which would be quite fashionable in a renovated kitchen today! Aunt Elsie's bedroom was on the first floor, and I basically had the whole second floor to myself.

Crescent Park School was quite current and modern. A lot of my classmates from the fifth and sixth grades at the elementary school on Elm St. now attended this new school. Myrna Blake, Roberta Bean, Art Mills, Howard Gunther, and Walt Kittridge, with whom I would become good friends. Walt's family lived on Chapman St. across from Aunt Elsie's house.

During recess at Crescent Park School, a favorite pastime of many of my classmates was to go out to the woods behind the school and smoke a cigarette. I tried it but didn't really enjoy smoking. I would still go back to the woods and hang out with my classmates during these brief sessions, but I didn't feel I had to participate to be one of *the group*. I wasn't really that self-confident in those days, but somehow I felt that if people didn't accept me for what I am, so be it!

I must have had a lot of spare time when I was living with Aunt Elsie, because it seems I was always working on some sort of a project. I had an inexpensive Kodak Kodachrome camera and took a lot of color slide pictures. However, I didn't have a slide projector to show them projected larger, so I made one. It was on a wooden base and had an inverted no. 10 tin can, vented on the top, to house the projection bulb. A juice size tin can connected horizontally to a hole in the larger no. 10 can. There was a lens in there somewhere to amplify the light before it hit the slide itself. The slide holder was two slotted pieces of wood where a single slide dropped in upside down. Next in line was another tin juice can on the outboard side of the slide holder, and lastly a cardboard tube holding the projection lens that telescoped into the last juice can. Moving the cardboard tube and lens in and out of the last juice can focused the picture. It was primitive, perhaps, but it worked!

I'd always enjoyed skiing since living in Maine. My earliest memories were skiing on Chandler Hill near Nana's house when I was younger. I didn't have a pair of regular skis, but someone outfitted me with two curved barrel staves that were held onto my boots by several jar rubbers (the seal between the glass lid and its Mason jar). I couldn't go very fast, but this introduction to skiing was fun! Later, while living with Aunt Elsie, Walt Kittridge and I would go out to the ski slope a short distance out Vernon St. in Bethel. There was a single rope lift that skiers would grab onto, right hand behind your back and grabbing the rope and left hand holding onto the rope from in front of you. Novice skiers could get off the rope lift halfway up the slope or stay on to the summit for a longer ride down. By then, I had regular ski boots and my own skis. It could be cold, but I enjoyed it!

Between the seventh and eighth grades of living with Aunt Elsie, I went home to spend the summer at our Rockwood house. Both Ned and Dave had been born by then, so they were with Mother in Rockwood. Dad had an office in one of GNP's Pittston Farm's buildings, twenty miles north of Rockwood, and would come home some evenings and on weekends. I had expanded my interest in photography and was developing black-and-white pictures. I built a darkroom in one corner of the basement and had a sign on the road advertising a two-hour turnaround to develop people's film. For a modest fee per roll, I'd develop the film and make prints. Having no enlarger, I could only print pictures the actual size of the negative, but at least this would give the tourists an idea of the quality of their shot and whether or not to retake it while they were still on vacation. Enlarged pictures of selective shots could be made when they returned home.

Earlier that year, I had also started tying fishing flies. I bought a fly tying vice, a heavy bobbin to hold down the thread during the fly tying process, and some exotic feather material not available locally, like peacock herl. Other materials were available in the local area and were free! I would tie some standard wet and dry flies like a Royal Coachman, Caddis, Black Gnat, and various tandem hook flies for lake fishing. When I got a little more experienced, I'd package some of my flies and sell them at a discount to Rockwood and Moose River tackle and bait stores. My most fun part of fly tying was to go to a local pond or brook, capture an insect the fish were feeding on, and go home and replicate it. The real thrill was when I'd go back to the same spot and catch a fish with the replica fly I'd just tied!

My brother Ned was two years old that summer, and my brother Dave was still an infant. I wanted to do something special for Ned while I was home, so I decided to make him a miniature 1952 Cadillac Coupe Deville! I don't recall the source, but we had a peddle powered, single-seat child's car at the Rockwood house that summer. It was older, and the metal body was not in good shape. I removed the metal body from the chassis and made a wooden replica of the 1952 Cadillac from pictures I had obtained. Dad had a nice set of woodworking hand tools that had been passed down from his grandfather, Edward Norris Robertson. I used those and crafted the

Cadillac grill and fenders for the front then connected the wooden sides to the finlike tail section and lights on the back of the car. It turned out looking quite authentic, I thought, and I could tell that Ned was pleased by the smile on his face! (Of course, he was always smiling then!)

When the fall of 1952 came around, it was back to Bethel and Aunt Elsie's for the eighth grade. Prior to me leaving for school, Dad was reassigned to another remote logging camp about forty-five miles north of Pittston Farm, which is twenty miles north of Rockwood, Maine. Mom and the two boys went up to join Dad at the new camp. The following is an excerpt from my mother's diary, which I've included here as it paints a good picture of the woods camp itself, their living quarters, and life in that remote Great Northern Paper Company environment in general:

St. John's Pond—Northern Maine. August 22, 1952, Friday

"The Great Northern Paper Company has a logging operation here—100 French Canadian woodcutters and three of their wives, the G.N.P. Clerk (Ed) plus his helper (the assistant clerk) and the scaler (Norm Hodgekins). Ed's assistant (Harold Robbins) has his wife "Lil" here, too. The woods crew built us a snug camp all lined with new matched boards. We have a good sized kitchen, living room and two bedrooms. A well out back supplies water for drinking from a pump in the kitchen sink. Water for washing is hauled by the pail full from the river. The "outhouse" is further out back. The Robbins have a camp next to ours. Cousin Bud Coolidge is coming up to help in the office.

We love our camp—it is surrounded by trees and the St. John River is beautiful out in front of the camp. There are deer tracks all over the place and we often watch one deer in particular as he drinks very near our camp.

There is no radio, but we do have electricity because the camp has a generator. At the old camp we had kerosene lamps. We are 65 miles from a grocery store and 85 miles from a doctor. We call our grocery order in to Tessier's Store in Rockwood and the G.N.P. tote truck delivers to us when they bringing the camp supplies."

I must have always enjoyed making things. Here is another excerpt from the same diary and made on September 11, 1952:

"Den built a hand rail down to the river and a nice seat—also a few steps to make it easier to get down there."

Getting back to the first day of eighth grade at Crescent Park School, I learned that my teacher was Libby Kneeland. Libby was a relative of Dad's, and her family had been longtime residents of the Bethel area. It wasn't too far into the school year that I must have gotten to her. Apparently, I was as quick with quips as I was with answers to questions. I don't think I was doing it on purpose, but I *was* getting under her skin. I had a bad habit of randomly tapping the eraser of my pencil on the desk. One day, Libby got so frustrated with me that she told me to come up and start teaching the class. I did. I continued on with the lesson where she had left off, and the teacher took my seat. Immediately, Libby started tapping her pencil on my desktop! Of course, I couldn't tolerate distractions like that in *my* classroom, so I took action. I admonished her, told her she needed to stop or we'd have to make a trip to the principal's office! When the pencil tapping started again, I admonished her several more times and finally said, "Okay, Mrs. Kneeland, you're going to have to leave the classroom. We're going to visit the principal." It was a little awkward because the ending wasn't exactly as she had intended, but we exchanged seats, and Libby continued teaching. Again, I don't think it was on purpose on my part, but guess I was a little bit of a smart ass.

Walt Kittridge and/or other school friends and I would hang out on weekends and sometimes after school. Aunt Elsie continued to be the caring lady that she always was and took good care of me. Life was still good! At the end of the school year of 1953, I returned to live with Dad, Mother, and the boys at the St. John's Pond camp. Typically, Nana, who was now living with Frank at the old family farm on Chandler Hill, would take me part way north when I was traveling to Dad and Mother's home in Rockwood or one of the GNP camps farther north. Dad would come down to meet us halfway. Ed Robertson was a saint of a man and always treated me as if I was his natural son. I loved and respected him so much.

Mother's younger brother, Richard Kirk, and his girlfriend, Stella, lived in Providence, Rhode Island, then. We'd drive down to visit them once or twice during the summer. Uncle Dick had been in the Navy during WWII and served aboard the aircraft carrier USS *Bunker Hill* in the Pacific. He'd seen action aboard the *Bunker Hill* later in the war, and once during a kamikaze attack, he was wounded by shrapnel while pushing a burning Navy aircraft over the side. He was awarded the Purple Heart. I'm not going to go into details, but later in life, Richard turned into a not-so-good person and black sheep of the family.

Now it was time for the family and me to think about high school. It would be coming up this fall, September of 1953, and of course there were no high schools in the Great Northern woods! I'm not sure what thinking went into the final decision, but the family moved back from the far GNP north and again called the Rockwood house their home. I enrolled in Greenville Consolidated School twenty miles south in Greenville, Maine, at the foot of Moosehead Lake. There were two older students that lived up Moose River that attended Greenville High School. They had a pickup truck and traveled back and forth to school five days a week. Mother made arrangements for me to ride with them.

I was yet again entering a new environment with new classmates and new academic curriculums. Life was constantly changing and challenging. At the new school in Greenville, I chose a college prep curriculum. However, for one elective class, I chose *shop*. The school had an excellent woodworking shop in the school's basement, and I loved to build things! The school shop had every electric woodworking machine one could imagine, and the instructor was awesome. There were a couple of forms for making wooded canoes in the shop, and each year two of the seniors made wooded Old Town-style canvas-covered canoes. I was amazed by the things that could be crafted! I did several projects during the year, one of which was a small half-round end table that we still have in our home today.

I wanted to play football, so I discussed it with my parents and signed up. The only drawback was the team practiced after school each afternoon, and neither of the high school guys I rode to school with played football. My only available option was to hitchhike home the twenty miles after practice. There wasn't that much traffic on the Greenville to Rockwood road, so some nights it would be dark by the time I arrived home, and I still needed to do homework! I tried hitchhiking for several weeks, but it was obvious that wasn't going to work out, so I had to quit football.

Just before basketball season began, I was again interested in playing a sport. However, the same transportation issue existed. Somehow, Mother and Dad made arrangements for me to board in Greenville, Maine, with Louisa Wooster. Louisa was a single mother with a daughter several years younger than I was. Louisa already had another ninth grader, Lloyd Wooster, Louisa's nephew as I recall, boarding with her. Her home was right on Moosehead Lake in Greenville. It was a location with dozens of small planes configured with pontoons nearby. There was a charter flying service just across the lake that ferried fishermen and campers to spots north. A game warden lived in the next house up lake from Louisa's. He kept his state-owned single-engine pontoon plane (Cessna, I believe) moored in the lake next to his house. At any rate, I joined the JV basketball team and got to play that season.

I did learn some lessons growing up that year. One was not to be unkind or mock other people. One of my classmates who I didn't know previously was Urban Graham. He was a little on the heavy side, but probably not a bad person. The guys from Moose River that I rode to school with seemed to pick on Urban and call him Slob Gut Graham. Being with the older group and under their *protection*, I would chime in with "Slob Gut" when I was with them. My lesson came to a head when Urban and I were on the JV basketball team together. He obviously remembered my taunts and was out for revenge. When we were sitting on the bench listening to Coach give us instruction, Urban would always sit next to me. The next thing I knew, he was poking me in the ribs with his elbow. I'd poke right back, but he didn't stop. At one practice early in the season, Coach noticed what was going on and said, "Okay, we're going to settle this thing right here and now. You two are going to put on the gloves and duke it out!" A pair of boxing gloves was produced, and Urban and I got on the basketball court and started circling each other. Remember, Urban was a relatively big kid, and I was a skinny one. I felt I was in deep trouble. We traded glancing, harmless blows for a short time, and then he landed a hook squarely on my cheek that stung like hell and made me pause for a short time to get my bearings. When we started back at it, I was fortunate to get a right hander straight into his nose, which started to bleed profusely, and Coach stopped the fight. (Whew!) I never apologized to Urban, which I probably should have, but we never had any problems with each other after that.

Greenville, Maine, was an interesting town. Much like Rockwood, it swelled in population in the summer with tourists and *died* in the winter when only the residents were left. The largest popular spot with tourists was the Indian Store. It sold authentic Native American Indian feathered headdresses, clothing, artifacts, and trinkets—a number of them made in Japan! There was also a malt shop on one corner of the center of town. It was the typical malt shop with a soda fountain and everything you've seen on the old sitcoms. The store had a speaker, outside and I'll never forget hearing songs by the Platters, the Chordettes, the Drifters, Del Vikings, and other *rock 'n rollers* of the time.

There were a few interesting girls in my class. One in particular, Lisa Wortman, stands out in my memory as a really nice person. Her parents owned Wortman's Store, which was just a short distance up Lily Bay Rd. Lisa had two older brothers who were very protective. They would *interview* and admonish any boy who asked their sister out. Because I came from Rockwood and was unknown, I got *the treatment*! I must have passed muster as I took Lisa out on occasion after that. Later during the school year, Lloyd and I were dating two of our classmates who lived in Greenville Junction, which was about a mile from Louisa's house in Greenville. Greenville and Greenville Junction are at the foot of Moosehead Lake, and in the winter, the wind furiously whips down the lake from the north, and Maine winters can be very cold. I'll never forget walking that mile to Greenville Junction and then back after the double date. We must have been a little nuts!

In 1953, the minimum age to obtain a Maine driver's license was fourteen. I believe that was mainly because young family members were expected to help out with farm work, including driving tractors, and some family's acreage was divided by state roads. Instead of ignoring the kids driving farm equipment illegally without a license, the state lowered the minimum age to drive. In summers past when living in Rockwood, Dad had taken me to a less traveled dirt road near the West Outlet dam and taught me how to drive the family stick-shift car. The road was once an old railroad bed, but by then the tracks and ties had been removed. It was narrow but smooth and level. I had the usual issues with achieving the correct pressure on the clutch and gas pedals (sputter, sputter, stall) at first, but I mastered it with Dad's unending patience! In the second half of ninth grade, I enrolled in a driver's ed class at school. My hard-ass basketball coach was the driver's ed instructor. Actually, he was demanding but fair, and I respected him for expecting the best of everyone he instructed or coached. I was able to pass the state written and driving tests and got my driver's license. All I needed now was *wheels* to set me free!

One of my friends while living in Rockwood was GM Whitten or Guy Morton Whitten III. His grandfather was Guy Morton Whitten I or Guy. Guy owned and operated Whitten's Store and a separate hotel and restaurant in Rockwood. GM's father was Guy Morton Whitten II. His mother was a pleasant lady with a bubbly personality as I remember her. The Whittens had a new 1953 Buick Roadster. It was a luxurious car and rode very smoothly. They would frequently invite me to join them, GM, and his younger sister when they went on day trips around that area of Maine.

Sometime after ninth grade graduation, Mother or Dad contacted Uncle Dick in Providence, Rhode Island, to be on the lookout for a used vehicle for me. He found a black 1939 Plymouth Coupe in decent shape for a hundred dollars! We drove down to pick it up. I filled the gas tank with gas ($0.25 a gallon!) and drove it back to Bethel. Over the course of the summer, I made a mail-order purchase of a paint sprayer and automobile paint. The sprayer worked by removing a spark plug from the car's engine and screwing in one end of the sprayer's hose. I painted the top part white and lower half (which included sides, fenders, and trunk) a pleasant yellow color. The paint job had a bit of an *orange peel* finish due in part to the inefficiency of the paint sprayer design and in part my inexperience at spray-painting cars. I replaced the headliner inside with a red fabric and purchased red and yellow seat covers to finish off the interior. The final touch was to stick 3M reflective letters in a scrolling wave pattern on the rear bumper. The reflecting red letters spelled out *Rock and Roll*.

I enjoyed that Plymouth Coupe most of the summer, driving it from Bethel to Rockwood, probably a couple of round trips. My summer job after ninth grade was at a sawmill in Rockwood near the West Outlet of Moosehead Lake. There was a big boom of pine logs in the lake next to the mill. These were logs in the boom that the Katahdin had towed down from farther north up Moosehead Lake. I remember walking on the logs in the boom during breaks while working there. You'd have to be careful and go quickly when stepping on some of the smaller logs as they'd sink under your weight. The solution was to quickly find a larger log to stop on and get your balance before continuing the adventure.

The cutting process for making boards involved pulling one log at a time from the boom in the lake, up a cogged chain, and into the mill. Then each log was positioned horizontally on a moveable *carriage* that fed the giant six-foot diameter saw. The logs would be cut lengthwise into boards as the carriage was moved into the giant saw by the operator. Subsequent cuts would be made by moving the carriage back then ratcheting it and the log one inch closer to the saw. That created boards of various widths with an uneven layer of bark on each side. The next step was to feed these one-inch slabs of timber through another set of saws that would trim the boards to a specific width. The rough boards would then be cut to length, marked by a scaler according to length and quality, and dropped into an acid preservative bath. Finally, they would be lifted from the acid bath container and out of the mill by a dual chain driven conveyer belt. The conveyer belt traversed a table about fifty feet long where one worker on each side would pull the boards off the belt and into carts according to the scale marks, length, width, etc. I was one of those workers. I wore elbow-length rubber gloves, a rubber apron, and rubber boots. The acid bath was irritating to my skin, and I soon developed painful rings where the tops of my boots and ends of the rubber gloves would rub against my skin. Interesting experience, but I was making money over the summer!

Dad and Mother were living in the Great North Woods with the boys at the time, and I lived in the Rockwood house by myself. After all, I was fifteen years old and felt capable of taking care of myself. My friend Ron Rancourt and a couple of the Teriault and Tessier boys were also working at the mill that summer. The Teriault and Tessier families lived about three miles from our Rockwood home up Moose River. Both families were of French Canadian descent, were good people, and their sons were friends of mine. As I was the only one with a car, I drove us all to and from work. I've only been fired from a job twice in my life, and this ended up being one of the times! I'd leave Rockwood with Ron Rancourt in tow in plenty of time and travel to Moose River to pick up the other three. One or more of the Teriault or Tessier boys *usually* overslept or were otherwise late. It was frustrating to me, but the end result was we'd *all* arrive at the sawmill late. Our mill supervisor just couldn't put up with that many of his morning shift people being late for work, and because I was the

51

driver, I got the warnings. Finally, one morning, after a month or so, he'd had enough, called me into his office, and fired *me*. There went my revenue-producing job for that summer.

I spent the rest of the summer up in GNP country with Dad, Mother, and my brothers. I did some fly fishing in the nearby ponds, brook fishing in the streams, and just enjoyed time spent with my family, who I didn't get to see all year-round.

When it came time for my sophomore year, Mother had enrolled me in Gould Academy. I drove my trusty Plymouth coupe to Bethel, put it on blocks in Nana's barn on Chandler Hill, and drained the radiator. As I've mentioned, Maine winters were brutal then, and I didn't have the budget to purchase snow tires and antifreeze for the car, so it had to hibernate like a Maine bear.

CHAPTER SEVEN

MY SOPHOMORE YEAR AT GOULD ACADEMY, BETHEL, MAINE

Gould Academy was founded in 1836 and today is a private, co-ed, college preparatory boarding school located in Bethel, Maine. It was originally incorporated as Bethel Academy and accepted both locals and boarders. Reverend Daniel Gould left his $842 fortune to the school when he died in 1843. Reverend Gould stipulated that the school be named for him, and from then on it was known as Gould's Academy, or today simply as *Gould Academy*. My grandmother Mabel Bean; my mother, Edith Kirk; my dad, Ed Robertson; Dad's brother Neil; their father, Frank Robertson; my brother Ned; and I all graduated from Gould. It was a family tradition!

Gould today is, and really always was, a quality New England college prep secondary school. Approximately 250 students attend each year now, and of those 99 percent of the graduating class matriculates at four-year colleges and universities. The 2020–2021 tuition for resident students is $64,200, which includes room and board! For day students, the annual cost is only $39,600. Today, Gould operates on a trimester schedule and leaves several half days a week open for sports electives. Alpine sports are especially emphasized in the winter trimester and have developed many talented Olympic-class skiers over the years.

In the mid-1950s, when I attended Gould Academy, there were only two semesters. Students consisted of *dorm students* and *townies*. I was a *townie*. As the Town of Bethel had relied upon Gould

53

as its public high school for over a hundred years, all local children were educated at Gould and paid for from the town's budget. A couple years before my brother Dave was scheduled to graduate, Gould notified the town that in the fall of 1969, it would no longer be accepting Bethel students under the current arrangement. The town started building Telstar High School, where Dave later graduated from. Dave was deprived of continuing the Gould Academy alumni family tradition.

The Gould campus is very beautiful and located in the western part of the Town of Bethel on both sides of Church St. In 1954, the campus consisted of the main building, which was located on the site of the original building. It was named Hanscom Hall after Frank Hanscom, who was headmaster from 1897 to 1936. Other buildings are Bingham Hall, which is the girl's gym; Gehring Hall, the girl's dormitory and main dining hall for boarding students; Holden Hall, the boy's dormitory; and finally, a large complex for sports, the Farnsworth Field House. When I attended Gould, there was a football field and a surrounding track just adjacent to Gehring Hall. The school many years ago now discontinued their football program, substituting soccer instead.

As Dad and Mother were still in the Great Northern Paper Co. woods, they made arrangements for me to board with a local couple, Robert and Patricia Baker, for my sophomore year. Robert was a dairy farmer, but the Bakers' home was within Bethel *proper*. I had been enrolled in Gould Academy and was anxious to start a new adventure at yet another new school. This time, it was different, however, as many of my former classmates from Crescent Park School were fellow Gould sophomores—Walt Kittridge, Art Mills, Howard Gunther, Myrna Blake, Roberta Bean, Ronnie Willard, Carla Grover, and others. Probably because of my mother talking with GM's mother while we were still living in Rockwood, Maine, the Whittens had checked out Gould Academy over the summer and enrolled GM as a freshman boarding student at Gould. The year was 1954.

The academic atmosphere at Gould Academy was markedly different from that at Greenville Consolidated School. The majority of students at Gould weren't just completing mandatory state education requirements; they were there to learn and follow already established future goals they had set for themselves. The dorm students especially seemed focused, and rightfully so, as their parents were paying a lot of money for them to attend Gould. Some, like my friend Russell Patterson, were preparing themselves to follow the professions of their fathers or mothers. Russ's dad, for example, was an MD. Russ became a successful medical doctor too. The academic atmosphere at Gould was an inspiration for me to try harder, yet some of the subjects were challenging for me. I loved the math, science, and English classes and received good grades as those subjects were logical to me. I wasn't that enthusiastic about foreign language classes, as there was more memorization of illogical verb conjugations, idioms, nouns, adjectives, etc., and I didn't find it logical at all. There was a requirement in the college prep curriculum to complete three years of one language or two years of two different languages. I'd already completed one year of Latin at Greenville, so in my sophomore year at Gould, I signed up for Latin II and Spanish I. Teachers make a huge difference too. Our Spanish I teacher was Mrs. Richardson. She had studied in Spain, spoke fluent Spanish, and had a knack for teaching languages that generated student interest! I did well in her class. In my junior year, I took Spanish II. Mrs. Richardson started the year, but due to a pregnancy, she stopped teaching after the first semester to have a baby. The substitute teacher that took over her class in the second semester was, in my opinion, not so good. She had little passion for the language, mechanically went through the lessons, and was candidly boring. I almost flunked the second semester!

Although I didn't realize it at the time, Gould Academy was the first influencing factor that put me on the path of shaping my future career(s). (The US Navy would later be the second influencing factor.) While I was optimistic about my future, I really had no general idea what profession I wanted to go into later in life or even a specific field of interest. The academic atmosphere at Gould Academy that I mentioned earlier encouraged me to dig deeper into areas that did interest me, and there were school resources, both human and reference, available that allowed me to go as deeply into a particular area of interest as I could absorb.

As I could walk to school at Gould, I finally got to play football! Robert Scott was the head football coach. He was sort of a Vince Lombardi type of person, demanding of his players, very stoic, and serious. I liked him a lot, however. Looking back on my life, I always had the most respect for people who demanded the most from me. Coach Scott also taught history, as most Gould Academy teachers were required to have dual roles in academics and sports. There was no JV football team at Gould, only the varsity team, so I sat on the bench quite a bit my sophomore year, but still enjoyed the sport and the team. I made new friends. Life was okay!

Later in the year, when basketball season came along, I signed up and made the JV team. Basketball was by far my favorite sport, but I wasn't very good at it. I was lucky to make two to four points a game. The head basketball coach was Odell Anderson. He had been at Gould so long that he'd been Dad's (Ed Robertson's) coach! We had an awesome place to play basketball, the Farnsworth Field House. There was a basketball court and bleacher seating setup in the middle of this huge stadium-like building. We probably played about half of our games at home and the others by traveling in the Gould bus to neighboring towns. I recall coming back from one away game at South Paris or maybe Norway, Maine, in the winter. On the bus were the basketball team, our cheerleaders, and coaches. It was after dark and snowing lightly. Just before reaching Bryant Pond and still over ten miles from Bethel, the bus broke down! The bus driver couldn't get it restarted, so he walked to the nearest farmhouse to use their phone. Remember, there were no cell phones in those days! It probably wasn't much more than an hour or two, but I remember getting pretty cold sitting in that bus, waiting to be *rescued*.

I started dating a quiet and sweet local girl named Ruth Rugg during this time. She lived just outside town with her family. I'd take her to a movie at the Bethel Theater or go out to Abner's on a Saturday night to dance. Abner's was a local dance hall on Songo Pond Rd. It was *the big* weekly event around Bethel, and everyone from old to young came out to dance to a live band. Intermissions found many people taking a break in their cars or pickup trucks to pull on a cigarette, a beer, or something stronger. Of course, my trusty Plymouth coupe was up on blocks in Nana's barn on Chandler Hill, so I'd ask the Bakers if I could borrow their 1952 Chevy for the evening. They were very generous, and it wasn't usually a problem. Strangely, on occasion, Pat Baker would want to come with Ruth and me when I was taking Ruth home. On the way back to Bethel, Pat would have me pull over into a secluded spot. She never went as far as hanky-panky, but there was enough petting going on that the insides of the windows would get steamed up in the cold Maine winter. I always wondered what Pat told Robert regarding why she had to chaperone us when I was taking Ruth home. This happened more than once during my sophomore year. Guess Pat liked fifteen- to sixteen-year-old high school boys? Life was becoming puzzling at times.

Academically, I was doing okay at Gould Academy as a *B average* student. When the spring season rolled around, I signed up for the Gould varsity track team. I had never participated in any track type of events, but I soon found myself running the high and low hurdles and the 440-yard dash. We trained hard, and it was probably the most physically demanding sport I had ever attempted. I was glad that I never smoked, as I probably wouldn't have been able to complete those track events. My better events were the high hurdles and the 440-yard dash. The Gould Huskies held multiple dual or triple meets during that spring season and won the majority of them. We had superstars in several events that broke Gould school records. My very best event was the 440. I exerted *all* my energy into the short race and at the end had nothing left in the tank as my coaches, Joe Roderick and Bob Scott, had taught us. Just after the race, it was common to see me walk over to the nearest bush off the track and throw up. I'd expended it all! Throughout the season, Jimmy Murphy, Paul Stevens, and I would generally finish first, second, and third for Gould in that order. At more than one meet, we were in that same order ahead of the first man on the other team or teams. Jimmy Murphy won the Maine State title in the 440-yard dash that year! I lettered in track and was awarded the coveted Gould G.

I finished my sophomore year at Gould Academy without any other significant events and returned to Rockwood for the summer. Dad had lined up a job for me with the Great Northern Paper Co.

All the roads throughout their vast acres of forest lands were paved with gravel. Periodically, these roads would need to be re-graveled and graded smooth. One project that summer was to lay new gravel north from Rockwood to Ten Mile.

Two background items here:

1. In the days before gasoline-powered trucks and cars, food and supplies were transported to the remote logging camps by horse pulled *tote wagons*. The maximum distance a two-horse and wagon rig could travel in a day was ten miles, so there were rest and overnight stations every ten miles. From Rockwood north, there was Ten Mile, and next was Pittston Farm, which was ten miles above that. Pittston Farm could have been named Twenty Mile if it hadn't been such a major operational center for GNP operations in that area.

2. Many years ago, Maine had been covered by the Continental Glacier. One of the features that remained after the glacier receded was the eskers. Eskers had been formed by an underground stream flowing beneath the glacier where it met the earth's hard surface.

   When the glacier receded, a long narrow mound of sand, gravel, and boulders was left where the under-ice stream bed had been. This was a great source of gravel for use on roads and other purposes.

The road crew that I became part of consisted of four to five Mack dump trucks and drivers, a Caterpillar swing-blade grader, and a Caterpillar D8 bulldozer with a front blade, and me. I wanted to be a truck driver, but I was only sixteen years old and needed to be eighteen to drive a GNP truck. Consequently, I was the person who climbed up on the driver's side running board, and once the dump truck had tilted its bed upward with its gravel load, I would trip the lever, opening the rear gate. At that point, the driver would move forward, spreading the load over a short area of the road. The next step was for the D8 to spread that load until it covered the road with about three to five inches of new gravel. The grader waited until several loads of gravel were spread and put a final leveling on the road. A couple of the drivers and I discovered that by timing their stepping on the gas pedal and my releasing of the dump lever, we could bring the front wheels of the truck off the ground during the dumping process. Of course, it lifted me up in the air with the truck's front end, and I would hang on for dear life! Later in the summer, the D8 driver would let me drive the bulldozer and level a load of gravel or two. It was more difficult than it looked as the operator had to be able to anticipate the D8's up-and-down movements as it went over the rough newly graveled surface. Controlling the blade's "raise or lower" movement with the hydraulic lever was a talent I didn't acquire that summer, but it was fun!

CHAPTER EIGHT

MY JUNIOR AND SENIOR YEARS AT GOULD ACADEMY

Just prior to my junior year at Gould, I moved in with Nana on Chandler Hill in Bethel, Maine. Her husband, Frank, had died in July 1952, so she lived alone. The house, at one time, before great-grandfather Vear Bean lived there, had been the Waterspout Mountain House, a hotel catering to tourists and *city folk* visiting from various New England cities. In the 1950s, it had living quarters and a modern kitchen on the first floor with all bedrooms on the second floor. A step down from the new kitchen was a second larger kitchen that had been used to cook guests' meals for the Waterspout Mountain House. That kitchen wasn't used or even heated in the winter anymore. Farther beyond that, and still part of the main building, was a storage area and two-car garage. Also on the property were an active chicken coup and a very old barn. The barn had been constructed with hand hewn beams and pegs to hold everything together. There wasn't a nail in the whole big structure! There were a number of animal stalls inside the barn and a hayloft above the stalls where hay had once been stored to feed the animals in the winter.

Outside the main house was a coal chute leading to a bin and coal furnace in the basement. Fresh water flowing down from a spring a couple hundred yards up Waterspout Mountain from the house provided good water for the kitchen and bathroom. Nana's kitchen stove was wood fired, and she could cook or bake anything with that old relic! The house was not wired for electricity as it was two miles from the main road where the electrical source would have been. I remember Nana saying, "Central Maine Power wants $2,000 to run a line in here, and we're not paying that!" That amount would be over $19,000 in today's dollars. Consequently, lighting in the evening was provided by a number of Aladdin kerosene mantle lamps that Nana had around the house. I did homework by the light of an Aladdin lamp. They were a little noisy but actually put out pretty good light.

The house and barn were at the top of Chandler Hill. Vear Bean had raised animals on the property at one time, and there were three large hayfields at different levels cascading down Chandler Hill from the house. The fields were defined by stone walls. The stones had originally been in the fields, another product of the glacier, but removed from the fields over the years to facilitate harvesting of the hay. The lower field had a brook meandering through it. The brook was lined with alder bushes, but it contained many tasty brook trout! I remember fishing that brook many times over the years. Back up on top of the hill, directly across the road from the main house was an apple orchard. The trees hadn't been pruned for years, but they still yielded various types of delicious apples. Nana would make apple jelly from the crab apples that grew on a couple of the trees. Growing on the stone walls surrounding the apple orchard were wild raspberry and blackberry bushes that I'd pick in the fall and enjoy with fresh cream from Blake's Dairy out on the main road.

Early in the summer of 1955, I sold my "rock and roll" Plymouth coupe and bought a 1946 Ford convertible. I immediately started customizing it. I *shaved* the hood and trunk in the style of custom cars in those times—basically removing the hood and trunk ornaments and installing remote mechanical opening mechanisms. I bought special headlight rims from a mail-order house and added Fiberglas filling on the fenders immediately over the headlight rims in sort of an overhanging *eyebrow* shape. Next came fender skirts, and I had the body painted a deep blue. The car already had a white top that was in good shape. The engine was the typical Ford V-8, and the manual transmission was shifted by moving a steering column shift lever through the classic *H-pattern*.

I was looking forward to the start of school and my junior year at Gould! I'd signed up for football again and a number of interesting classes in various subjects. Nana worked at Hanover Dowel off Railroad St. in town, so I'd ride the four miles to Bethel each morning with her. And as her shift ended earlier than my afterschool football practice, she'd wait in her car until I was finished. Then we'd go back to Chandler Hill for the night.

My teacher for English III, and as it turned out for English IV also, was David D. Thomson, or just DDT. He became my all-time most favorite teacher! He was interesting, made our class time whizz by, and we learned a lot. He was a stickler for detail and had a number of little sayings or cribs. One that I recall him saying *many* times was "The witches said *we* are weird" as a reminder to use the exception to the rule "*i* before *e*" for the word *weird*. I volunteered to work on the staff of the *Gould Academy Herald*, our school newspaper. I'll never forget one edition came out with a large-font front-page headline that contained the glaring word WIERD in it. Fortunately, I didn't write that headline, but DDT went wild! I'd never even seen him so upset.

Dad was friends with Rod McMillan, who owned a Texaco service station on Main St. in Bethel. Rod also owned a fleet of school buses and had a contract with the Town of Bethel to provide bus services for elementary children. I was sixteen years old, which was old enough to obtain a school bus driver's license in Maine! Before school started at Gould, Rod had given me a job driving one of his buses. Rod and I had taken what was to be *my bus* and drove it to Rumford, Maine, where I took the state's written and driving bus tests. I passed and became a proud school bus driver at sixteen!

My route took a twenty-mile circular path starting in Locke Mills on East Bethel Rd. to a right on Intervale Rd. for about two miles, where there was a grammar school. We would turn around and come back to the junction of East Bethel Rd. and continue picking up children on Intervale Rd. all the way to Rt. 26 then back to Bethel. That was the morning route. In the afternoon, I'd reverse the direction for dropping children off at their homes. I was paid $1.25 per trip for a weekly salary of $12.50. My friend Art Mills had a bus route that took him to Locke Mills empty where he'd turn around and pick up children living on Rt. 26 all the way back to town. It probably sounds irresponsible, but Art and I would stop side by side on East Bethel flats (in the area where Nana had her original house when Mother and I would come up from Miami to visit) and have a drag race. Both buses were empty, and there was almost no traffic on the road that time of day, so no children were being placed in danger. Art had an older school bus and usually lost!

Several memories from driving the school bus stick in my memory. The kids at times would be challenging to handle. When they'd get rowdy, start talking loudly, or leave their seats, I'd quietly pull over to the side of the road in a safe place and just sit there watching in the bus's interior rearview mirror. At some point, the kids would realize we weren't moving and say, "Hey, why are we just sitting here?"

My reply would always be "I'm in no hurry and have plenty of time. Whenever you sit down and be quiet, I'll get you home."

It worked every time, and they'd be quiet for some (usually short) period. There was one really disruptive and disrespectful boy who challenged me constantly. One afternoon, while taking my students home, he was particularly a pain. I warned him several times, and when we were about a half mile from his home, I stopped the bus, opened the door, and told him to get off and walk home. He thought I was kidding at first, but I reminded him he had been warned. He quietly got off the bus, and I continued on with the rest of the children. You could have heard a pin drop. Today I'd likely be fired for such an action, but there was hardly any traffic on that country road, and the risks overall were much different than today. His parents never complained, and Johnny was much more respectful for the rest of the year.

On the other side of being a tough disciplinarian, I would drive the bus in the evening a couple of times a school year so the children could go to the movies. Rod McMillan had no problem providing the bus and gas every now and then. The kids would have to pay for their own movie ticket, popcorn, etc., but I'd volunteer my time. Prior to movie day, we'd all decide on an appropriate movie the children wanted to see, they'd get permission from their parents, and

I'd make the rounds and pick up whoever wanted to go. Keeping a head count and making sure every child got back on the bus after the movie was a serious concern to me, but necessary. I think they all enjoyed and appreciated the special treat from their school bus driver. I drove that same bus and the same route during my junior and senior years at Gould.

The start of my junior year at Gould also brought some new boarding students into our class. One of them was a really down-to-earth guy from Bangor, Maine, named Bill Ripley. He always had a smile on his face and was immediately liked by both *dorm students* and *townies*. Bill was in many of my classes, and we rapidly became good friends. Rip and I also played varsity football together. Bill was his own person, reliable and honest but loved to sometimes do things out of the ordinary. Boarding students weren't allowed to have cars on campus, but I had my trusty 1946 Ford convertible! Several nice fall and spring afternoons found us skipping school to ride somewhere in my car. I remember one trip was to Rumford, Maine. We didn't do anything special. We looked in several stores, including a record shop. There was a record playing in the shop called "Don't be Cruel" by a young artist from Memphis named Elvis. On another occasion on a Saturday evening, Bill and I went out to Abner's on Songo Pond. Abner's was *way off-limits* for boarding students, but I think the thrill of it was somehow enticing to Bill. We talked about the ultimate escape to his home in Bangor in my convertible, but somehow we never did get it scheduled.

Prior to that time, Dad had been transferred to a GNP logging operation on the east side of Moosehead Lake named Lobster Lake. One spring break from Gould, we had planned for me to go visit Dad and Mother. I made arrangements to ride to Bangor with Bill Ripley's parents, who were picking him up from school then returning home. I stayed overnight with the Ripleys and the next morning climbed aboard the big Mack tote truck that Dad had arranged to pick me up for the run from Bangor to Lobster Lake.

As I recall, the Lobster Lake logging camp was very similar to the ones directly north of Moosehead Lake that I described earlier where Mother and Dad had lived. My parents had a movable cozy cabin built on wooden skids, and there were other movable cabins for the woodsmen in close proximity to each other, plus Dad's office and the *wongan* or company store. One thing that I remember as a bit unique at this camp was a small log building built over a stream that was used as a cooler for food by the camp chef. Apparently, the cold water of the stream would keep certain stores cool so they could be kept longer before use. There was a sturdy door, and the small windows were laced with heavy wire to keep out unwanted visitors. One night during this visit, we heard a loud noise coming from the direction of the stream and log cooler building. Nights in the deep Maine woods are normally as quiet as they are dark. Dad said, "Come on, Den. Let's go check this out." He grabbed a powerful lantern light, and we headed off in the direction of the sound. The stream-cooled log hut was down a hill from the main camp. As we approached, Dad directed the powerful light beam down the hill toward the stream, and I swear there was a black bear walking on his hind legs, carrying some packages of salted cod fish in this front paws! He was apparently hungry and had broken the front door open! I believe to this day that I saw it, but sometimes I also wonder if bears can really balance on two hind legs.

One year, when it was time for me to renew my Maine driver's license, I did something I probably shouldn't have done. At that time, there wasn't a solid plastic driver's license that the state would issue as is the case today. The driver's license application was a two-part paper form that the applicant would fill out. The top part would be kept as a state record, and the lower part would be returned to the driver as his or her driver's license with an *official* ink stamp on it showing authenticity. On the top part of the application, I clearly entered my date of birth as 2-1-1939. On the lower part, I squeezed the top of the 9 of 1939 to make it look more like 1937, making me eighteen years old and eligible to buy beer. I was actually a bit surprised when my license came back from the Augusta, Maine, DMV exactly as I'd filled it out without question.

Maine regulated the sale of hard liquor only through state-controlled stores, but beer and wine were sold privately after obtaining a beer and wine license. Absolutely *no* beer or wine was sold in grocery stores. There was a beer and wine store not too far out on Vernon St. in Bethel. We didn't abuse it, probably mainly controlled by a lack of cash, but occasionally my friends Howard Gunther, Art Mills, and I would want to do something daring and drink a beer. I remember Haffenreffer Malt Liquor and Budweiser were my favorites. The store owner would always glance at me with *the look* and ask to see my ID. I'd show it to him and make the purchase. I didn't really know him but years later surmised what was probably going on that I didn't realize at the time. Bethel had a population of maybe 2,100 at the time, and everyone knew each other. There's a good chance the owner knew Dad (Ed Robertson) and told him about my purchases. My friends and I were cool about it and never got into any trouble having an occasional beer, so my suspicion is that's why Dad never said anything to me. He was a fantastic man, very understanding and kind. I really was fortunate and loved him!

I'd always found members of the opposite sex interesting and fun to be around, and Gould had its share of good candidates, both boarding students and *townies*! One year at Gould, I met and dated one of two twins, boarding students from Nantucket, Massachusetts. They were really *identical* twins. Almost no one could tell them apart as their features were almost *exactly* the same! After a while, I could distinguish one sister from the other, however. There wasn't that much to do around school for dating places to go. I'd have to check her out of Gehring Hall, and she was required to be back in by a specific time. We usually went to the Bethel Theater or a school function of some sort.

I also dated Roberta Heath, Barbara Leach, Sandra Olson, and Ann Carter during my three years at Gould. These young women were all local, being either from Bethel, or in the case of Barbara Leach, from Locke Mills. It was all innocent fun, again going to Bethel Theater movies, the local soda shop on Main St., or attending Gould mixers and *sock hops*. I think I was even invited to a couple Gould Sadie Hawkins dances. Only a few classmates were *going steady*; it was more like everyone just going out and having fun. I did date a couple of special girls in my last two years at Gould—Sandra Olson and Ann Carter. They were good friends with each other and both fun people to be with individually. I had asked Ann Carter to go steady a couple of times, but she was conflicted whether she wanted to go out with me or a local guy who didn't attend Gould named Buddy Conner. I was also friends with Buddy, a nice-looking guy who drove a 1952 Ford, usually *very* fast! After going back and forth several times, Ann finally made up her mind early in my senior year and consented to *going steady*. I gave her my big Gould letter *G* that I'd earned in football, and she sewed it on her white V-neck button-up sweater which was typical in those days. Next, Ann hung the class ring I had given her from a chain around her neck. We were committed to not dating anyone else. Even though it was initially an off-and-on relationship, I always considered Ann Carter my *high school sweetheart.*

Ann Carter lived with her mother and brother Teddy in a house on Broad Street in Bethel, Maine. The home was originally a guest residence called The Elms, which was owned by William Bingham II. Mr. Bingham was a multimillionaire originally from Cincinnati, Ohio. During their lifetimes, the Binghams had taken an interest in Gould Academy and donated heavily to the school. It was their financial support that allowed Gould to build Bingham Hall (or the girl's gym). The Elms had a big conservatory where chamber music used to be played during their lifetimes. It was a large house by most Bethel standards. When Ann's mother was younger, she had been in charge of running the house while the Binghams were alive. After their deaths, they left the house to her to live in for as long as she lived.

Living on Chandler Hill and traveling into Bethel, Nana for work and me for school, was a challenge in the winter! It wasn't unusual to get four to five feet of snow from one storm. The town knew we were up there relatively isolated and alone, so the town snowplow would always give us a priority and start plowing Chandler Hill Rd. early in the morning. Nana had an old 1937 Chevy that had a front shock absorber design that also served as the front spring. The car's shocks were old and worn, and neither one had any fluid left in it. It was like riding with the front tires directly attached to the frame—rough! Going through the snow ruts was crazy. I'm not sure how she controlled the car at times. Even worse was when the spring season came and the gravel road turned into two to four inches of mud for two miles!

With the coming of the spring season, the sap in the maple trees started running. There were many maple trees in the vicinity of Nana's Chandler Hill home. I'd take a manual auger and drill a half-inch hole in the truck of some maple trees then pound a metal tap into the tree. The next step would be to hang a galvanized pail on the tap so sap could run into it. I'd do this for ten to twelve trees or as many buckets as Nana had at the time. Nana also had a wooden *yoke* that would fit over my shoulders. Each end of the yoke had a short piece of rope hanging from it and each rope terminated with a metal hook. I'd go to the trees after the pails were full of sap, hang the heavy pails from the yoke's hooks, and carry the two pails into the old kitchen where Nana had a nice wood fire going in the stove. There was a large flat-bottomed pan on the stovetop to dump the clear maple sap into so it could be reduced into maple syrup. Several trips with the yoke from the trees would fill up the pan. Once the sap started to concentrate due to evaporation of the water, you'd have to be careful not to let it evaporate too long or you'd end up with maple sugar instead of maple syrup!

The summer before my senior year started at Gould, Dad changed jobs, and he and my mother bought a house in Bethel on Chapman St. He was now the manager of the Hanover Dowel Mill on Railroad St where Nana worked. This was great news for me, as I could now live at home with Dad, Mother, and my brothers during my senior year at Gould. No more boarding out!

I played varsity football in my last year at Gould, lettered again, and continued my school bus route for extra spending cash. After football season, I tried out for the Gould varsity basketball team, my favorite sport! It was a real letdown when I didn't make the team. I really was that average a player, and seniors couldn't play JV ball, so it was the bitter end of my basketball career.

While living with Dad and Mother during my senior year, our family continued making trips to Providence, Rhode Island, to visit Uncle Dick (Richard Kirk) and Uncle Bob (Robert Kirk). Uncle

Dick lived there with his girlfriend, Stella, and Uncle Bob, who had taken a job as an electrician, had moved there with his second wife, Minter. We were always traveling somewhere by car in those days!

Mr. Thompson, my favorite Gould English teacher, was also the Gould drama coach. It was his influence that got me interested in acting, and I appeared in numerous one-act plays during those two years, plus the Senior Play. It was during the casting of the Senior Play that I learned at an early age the true reality of influence and politics in many areas. Again, I was a *townie*, and Gould catered to the *dorm students*, the school's real bread and butter financially. There was definitely a caste system of sorting students—not verbalized but ever present. The Senior Play in 1957 was *Onions in the Stew*, and of course directed by DDT. I really thought I had a good chance of landing one of the leading roles but ended up with *two* character parts, each character of the play changed into a twin brother by the director! In thinking about it later, I realized the parents of the leading role characters were all heavy contributors to Gould financially, and the *townies'* parents were not. I believe Mr. Thompson, in giving me two-character parts, was trying to compensate for what he had to do politically. I was a bit disappointed, but it was a good lesson to learn for later in life.

In the fall of 1956, during my senior year at Gould, my father (Larry Holt) had contacted Mother, saying he and his wife, Evelyn, were coming to Maine, and he wanted to see me if that was okay with her. We ultimately did meet one fall afternoon at Martha's Restaurant in town, and I got to know him a bit more after being estranged for so many years.

My birthday came in February 1957, and I turned eighteen. One of the Gould Academy "farewell to seniors" class traditions was a class picnic sponsored by the school and typically held when the Maine weather started to get warmer in the spring. It was intended to be a special event for each class. Ours was held in a small park just south of South Paris, Maine, and off Rt. 26. The park bordered a lake and was quite pleasant. The relatively small number of student participants in our year, both boarding students and *townies*, traveled down to the event in the Gould bus or faculty cars. I had prepared for the momentous occasion by purchasing a small bottle (maybe a half pint or pint) of Seagram's 7 Crown whiskey from the Bethel State Store. After all, I was "twenty-one" and old enough to buy alcohol! Not really sure how it evolved, but I ended up having lunch and enjoying conversing with Talisman Burns, a dorm student from Burlington, Massachusetts. The descriptive comment under her yearbook picture was "I can resist anything but temptation." Tali was actually a relatively outwardly quite person, but I always liked her and enjoyed talking with her in the classes we took together! I had placed the Seagram's 7 and some cans of ginger ale in a gym bag for the trip. Tali, other classmates, and I participating in the picnic were all enjoying our special outing. At some point, Tali and I retreated to an isolated spot by the lake, where I broke out the liquor and ginger ale. It was fun. We were having a good time as seniors, and the afternoon quickly passed. When it was time to return to Gould, Tali and I learned we were weren't riding back to Gould on the school bus as planned but in Headmaster Elwood "Moose" Ireland's car! OMG. We were both in trouble! While neither of us was *boracho*, we probably smelled of alcohol. We quickly claimed the back seat of Moose's car and made the trip back to Gould as stealthily as possible. To this day, I'm not sure if Headmaster Ireland detected anything or simply ignored it as a couple of his seniors having fun. (Fast-forward to January 1975, the class of 1957 lost our first class member, my good friend Talisman K. Burns. I'll always have fond memories of knowing her during her two years at Gould.)

My classmates and I graduated from Gould Academy that June. Sixty-four other classmates and I were in the graduating class that year. It was an outstanding experience for me. It taught me real-life lessons that I wouldn't fully appreciate until years later and provided an excellent foundation for me scholastically and socially. The teachers that molded me and the classmates that I had friendships with are something one cherishes and doesn't quickly forget. My silly saying that was put in everyone's yearbook by their class picture was "A smile for every boy and two for every girl." Roberta Bean and I were "class wolverine and wolf." Not sure what that says about how my peers looked at me, but I didn't take it as anything but positive. (Fast-forward to 2020, and twenty-four of these sixty-four other wonderful men and women have passed on. They all enjoyed good lives, had children and grandchildren, accomplished successful careers, and left good memories for their families.)

All my Gould boarding classmates and many local friends had been accepted to good colleges throughout New England and elsewhere. I really didn't have a particular field I wanted to enter, and if I did, my parents couldn't afford the high costs of college. I also didn't want the heavy personal burden of a student loan either, so I didn't apply to any colleges.

During the summer of 1957, I got a job working for the Town of Bethel driving a dump truck. It was an International brand truck and had a large four cubic foot bed. The town was gravelling one of its roads, and I made many trips from a local gravel pit to the road upgrading site. Art Mills and a couple of other friends worked for the town on the same project. It was a job that wasn't taking me anywhere but was a good temporary source of an income. I was able to save some money.

Teddy Carter was not only the brother of my girlfriend but also a friend. He was two years older than I was, having graduated from Gould in 1955. Teddy was anxious for a change in venue from Bethel, Maine. He knew I'd originally come from Miami and had had recent contact with my father who lived there. He tried to persuade me that we should travel to Miami after the summer and get out of Maine. I guess it worked, and during September of 1957, I discussed the plan with mother. She was always supportive of my wishes, and Teddy and I subsequently packed our things into his 1953 Plymouth and headed south!

Gould Academy graduation, 1957 (three Gould grads!)

Gould Academy football coaches, 1956
On the line: Paul Kailey, Joe
Roderick, and Bob Scott

Teddy Carter and Dennis,
off to Miami!

CHAPTER NINE

DENNIS RETURNS TO MIAMI

As I recall, the two-day drive to Miami from Bethel, Maine, was rather uneventful. Father and Evelyn lived in the back half of a duplex at 133 SW Thirteenth Street just off Brickell Avenue. It was a one-bedroom home. I'd discussed our desire to relocate to Miami in advance, so Father rented a motel room for Teddy and I just down Thirteenth Street from his home. Father had also spoken with a friend of his in the hotel business, Lou Lippi, and secured jobs for both of us at the Hollywood Beach Hotel (HBH) right on Hollywood Beach, Florida. The problem was, HBH was a seasonal hotel and didn't open until the end of October.

Teddy said, "Okay, what are we going to do in the meantime? We need to pay for our motel room and food and not deplete the cash we brought down with us." There was a Food Fair grocery store within walking distance just a bit west on Thirteenth Street, so Teddy and I got a job bagging groceries! Hey, it was a temporary job and got us by until the HBH opened! Food Fair wasn't a bad place to work, and it did tide us over until the end of October when the hotel opened.

One of the other bag boys at Food Fair was a genuinely cool African American guy our age, and Teddy and I quickly became friends with him. One has to remember, in the 1950s, America was by far not an integrated nation. Miami was more of a mixing pot of people, more like the north than the Deep South, but still not integrated. One day, our new friend invited us to spend an evening with him at his club in Liberty City. Probably being a little naive, Teddy and I accepted. We met him there, and I immediately understood how African Americans could feel when they were in an all-white setting! *Everyone* else in that club was black. There wasn't another white face in the club except ours. While everyone looked at us, wondering why two white boys were there, I really never felt threatened as I believe to this day that they all respected we had been invited by our friend, and if it was cool with him, it was cool with them too. We had a great time! The next day, I told Father where we'd been the previous night, and he went ballistic. No matter how much I tried to explain, he kept admonishing me to *never* do that again. My father was very prejudiced against African Americans and Jews.

As the end of October drew near, Teddy and I left our jobs at Food Fair and reported to Lou Lippi to help start opening Hollywood Beach Hotel for the season. Lou was the superintendent of service. Assisting him was Joe Ignatovich (or simply Joe I) and "Mother" Johnson, who were both bell captains. There were probably twelve or fourteen total bellmen on the staff at the beginning of the season. At HBH, the bell staff was not only responsible for check-ins, check-outs, and messages but also room service beverage. Serving liquor required that the bellmen be twenty-one years old. I wasn't yet twenty-one, so I was assigned to the *jets*! The hotel had three manual elevators or *jets* that required operators. When I say *manual*, I mean you didn't simply push a button to get to your floor. Inside the elevator was a round wheel with a rotating knob attached to the top of it. The outer doors were manually operated from the inside with a lever, and an inner door that stayed with the car was a collapsible metal *cage* that would slide horizontally to open or close. It was necessary for the operator to be able to see through the inner door to level the car at each floor. In order to move the car, the elevator operator would rotate the wheel one way to go up and the other way to go down. A brake would automatically be applied when the control wheel was in the neutral position. It took a little while for me to be able to get the elevator's floor lined up with the floor I was stopping at. These all-manual operations required some practice!

Both a bellman's and jet operator's salary at HBH was one dollar a day plus room and board! The single guys lived in the bell dorm, which was part of the hotel. We had a maid named Ziggy who would clean up our rooms and we were expected to tip her. Ziggy was as much of a mother hen as a maid in many respects. After all, we were really just kids. If any of the guys became sloppy and left things lying around, Ziggy would chew the guilty party out! There were three places in the hotel for the staff to eat. There was the main dining room for the executives, side hall for middle management, and the *zoo* for the rest of us peons—bellmen, maids, room service workers, waiters, maintenance personnel, etc.

The beginning of the season at Hollywood Beach Hotel started with conventions. The hotel had five hundred rooms on seven floors so large corporations, insurance companies, and brand-name firms like Johnson & Johnson could be accommodated easily. One of the better conventions for us was the American Bankers Association. They partied a lot at group functions and in their rooms, requiring many trips for room service beverage for the bellmen, and they tipped well! The thing about this particular group that always impressed me was even though there was a lot of alcohol consumed, they always had hors d'oeuvres available and seldom seemed to get drunk, unlike many of the other convention groups the hotel hosted.

The bellmen and Jet operators all had uniforms. The jacket resembled the Phillip Morris page boys, but without a cap. The jacket overall was a washable white canvas with blue trim for sleeve ends and blue Roman collar and front. There were also two rows of decorative brass buttons in the front. Trousers were blue and of a heavy polyester material with dual gold stripes running outside each leg, quite warm when you were running around during busy check-in days.

Teddy Carter was twenty-one and doing well financially as a bellman while my opportunity for tips was not very good operating one of the jets. The main lobby was on the second floor of the hotel. Bellmen basically worked seven days a week with an occasional day off in between conventions. There were two bell shifts that alternated daily. One day would be a split shift (8:00 a.m. to noon then again 6:00 p.m. to late), and the next day it was only a short shift from noon to 6:00 p.m. The bell captain's desk was just to the left of the check-in desk and cashier. The floor of the main lobby was terrazzo and had support columns surrounding a large carpeted area in the center of the big high-ceilinged lobby. Bellmen would *post up* one to a column around the room. When it was time for a check-in/check-out, Joe I or *Mother* would call, "Next front," and the person at the number one column to the bell captain's left would respond. This would cause rotation of the other bellmen standing at other columns around the lobby in a counterclockwise direction toward the bell desk. I can tell you, in later years, I found out that terrazzo was *hard*, and it took a toll on one's feet and legs if you had to stand on it for a while!

Directly in front of the bell desk was a column where the *last boy* posted up. The bell captain used this position to make deliveries to rooms, page guests throughout the main floor and convention areas, and similar minor tasks. Guests could call the bell captain and ask him to *page* someone on the main floor and, if found, give the guest the message. The *last boy* would take the page slip from the bell captain and start walking through the main lobby through the main dining room or other spaces where people had congregated while loudly calling out the name. Getting a *hit* usually resulted in a twenty-five- or fifty-cent tip, or the *last boy* could *strike out* and return to his post empty-handed. During our convention seasons, smart-mouthed, half-sober guests would like to joke around and have Mike Hunt paged or another fictitious name that sounded like a vulgar word or words when spoken. You could always see a group of conventioneers laughing like crazy as you passed by, calling out that name. After a while and knowing the rouse, I'd simply walk around, not say anything, and return to the bell desk with D/A for "didn't answer" written on the page slip!

When there was little activity going on, there was a cocktail lounge next to the bell captain's desk that was only open for happy hour on some evenings. That was a place where the bellmen and elevator operators could take a break and sit in a comfortable chair when things were slow, and there were plenty of those hours. The other extreme was when the hotel would have a thousand convention-eers checking out in the morning and another thousand checking in in the afternoon! When a day like I just described occurred, it was all hands on deck! As a *jet* operator, I'd be very busy taking guests between the lower level where the front door was and the lobby level for them to check-in and finally, of course, to the floor their room was on. On busy check-in days, the bellmen would ride up in my elevator carrying the guests' luggage and get the guests settled into their room. In order to get back to the bell desk to take another *front*, waiting for an elevator cost tip money, so they'd hit one of the fire escape stairwells on the north or south end of the hotel. Each floor of the hotel had two sets of stairs and a landing to go up or down within the fire escape wells. In order to save steps and time, most bellmen would jump to the middle of each staircase, onto the landing, then pivot around the landing and make one more leap to the middle of the second staircase on that floor. This was repeated until they got back to the second floor for another front.

It was a totally new scene for me, but I was enjoying being back in the state where I was born. Life was good. There was an interesting pool of waitresses at the hotel to date, although my funds were meager, to say the least. Directly behind the hotel was a great beach. I learned there were actually two separate reefs not too far out from the shore. I became interested in skin diving. I bought a mask, snorkel, and swim fins from a dive shop just a short distance north on A1A and jumped right in! Several of my other HBH employee friends were skin divers, and when we swam out, we always made sure we honored the *buddy system*. That's the safety precaution where if you're paired up with a buddy and encounter a shark, you have a fifty-fifty chance of not being attacked by the shark! Those seemed like good odds to me. Both reefs were teeming with beautiful tropical fish like Angel, Trigger, Parrot, Sergeant Major, Porcupine, Puffer, etc. Occasionally we'd see a Moray eel hiding in the coral or a barracuda swimming curiously around below us. I initially purchased a spearfishing gun and snagged some trophies, but as I had no place to cook the edible ones, I soon lost interest in spearfishing and purchased an underwater camera. Those fish were really a beautiful sight to see when I took a deep breath and dove down ten to twelve feet closer to the reef itself. It was an inexpensive camera, and the resulting pictures weren't of good quality, but it was fun.

Frequently, when I had a day or two off, I'd borrow Teddy's car and go visit my father and Evelyn in Miami. It was my opportunity to get to know my father better, and it was a good break from the often busy grind at HBH. As they only had a one-bedroom home, I'd sleep on the living room couch when I'd visit. Usually during my visits, Father would take us out to a nearby restaurant. His favorite dish was Veal Françoise. Evelyn was always proper and wore her white gloves to the restaurant. She and her sister Ann had originally come into this country with their mother from Windsor, Ontario, and settled in Detroit, Michigan. Their mother had taught them English manners, which included wearing white gloves when out in public.

Sometime during my first year at HBH, Ann Carter made a trip south to see me and visit her brother. I remember taking her to the Miami Seaquarium and other what I thought were interesting places around Miami and Hollywood that she might enjoy seeing. Ann had truly been my high school sweetheart for most of my senior year. We spent a week or so together, but somehow the old spark had gone for both of us, and when Ann returned home to Maine, things were just not the same between us.

Sometime around the end of November, Hollywood Beach Hotel entered into its social season. That was the period when the hotel stopped booking conventions and catered to families from northern cities like New York, Boston, and Chicago. Many came down to get out of the cold during school breaks or holidays. It was family vacation time. HBH's social guests were *totally* different from conventioneers! For starters, there was not the drunken convention scene but a calmer family vacation environment. They typically came with many children and *tons of luggage*, so much so that two bellmen were needed (and sometimes a luggage cart) to get everything up to the rooms in one trip.

At one point during 1959 at HBH, one of the bellmen, who was a local and graduated from Hollywood High, was talking up an upcoming rock and roll concert on February 3 at the Ft. Lauderdale War Memorial Auditorium called Big Golden Record Stars. The headliners were Buddy Holly, Jerry Lee Lewis, Rickey Valens, the Royal Teens (Who Wears Short Shorts?), the Crickets, and the Everly Brothers. Most of us bought tickets, and it was my first rock and roll concert. I had no idea these artists would go on to achieve such fame as they were all getting started at the time. It was amazing!

Prior to that, in the middle of January, the convention season resumed again, and it was one convention after the other until the hotel closed for the season, typically in April or May. The weather was beginning to get hot in Florida, and more pleasant weather in the north started people thinking about family vacations nearer to their homes versus Florida. Teddy and I helped close the hotel. I said so long to Father and Evelyn, and we headed back to Bethel, Maine.

CHAPTER TEN

THE UNIVERSITY OF MAINE

My mother had been encouraging me through letters and an occasional phone call to apply to the University of Maine for the fall 1958 semester. Earlier, after moving to Bethel, Mother had taken a job at the Bethel Inn as the dining room hostess and I believe had gotten to know Edmond Vachon, the Associate Head Master of Gould Academy as a result of her position there. He also knew me from my time at Gould. I'm not sure, but he must have sponsored some donor or other luncheons at the Bethel Inn and had had favorable contact with my mother. At any rate, she talked with Mr. Vachon and secured a partial Gould-funded college scholarship for me for the fall and spring semesters! My parents were still not in a position to help me financially beyond the scholarship, but I had some money in a savings account from working that could be used to make up the difference for a short period.

To make a long story short, I applied and was accepted to the University of Maine, Orono, campus for the fall of 1958. Dad and Mother drove me to Orono, Maine, where I was directed to check into Hart Hall, a new freshman dorm. The dormitory was known as Hart Hotel on campus, as it was quite a bit newer than other dormitories and up-to-date. I had a roommate that was a nice guy, but very intelligent and sort of a nerd. I later learned his IQ was north of 150! One of the first things the university did was put me through a battery of placement tests. The tests indicated I should enter an engineering curriculum, and that charted the course of my classes that semester and beyond. I gulped at the cost of my engineering books for the semester and bought an analog slide rule that I proudly wore in a case dangling from my belt. You could tell the Maine engineering students. They all had nerdy slide rules hanging from their belts! My friend GM Whitten from Rockwood, Maine, and who had been a year behind me at Gould, was now also a freshman at U of M like me!

The University of Maine was a land grant college, which meant it was mandatory for male students to take Army ROTC for the first two years. That was fine with me, and as I recall, those classes were only once or twice a week. I was issued an Army ROTC uniform, and I do remember being required to shine my brass emblems and belt buckle until they sparkled. My other classes were mostly interesting, and I settled into a new and very different routine quite quickly.

I had dated a cute waitress named Jenny off and on at Hollywood Beach Hotel the previous season. We kept in contact, and I learned Jenny had enrolled at the University of Connecticut at the same time I'd started attending the University of Maine. It was pure coincidence, but in speaking with a young assistant professor who monitored our chemistry lab, I learned that he was driving to Storrs, Connecticut, in a few weekends to see his fiancé and watch the UConn Huskies vs. Maine Black Bears football game. I made arrangements to ride to Storrs with him and coordinated it with Jenny also. As I recall, it was a beautiful sunny fall weekend in Connecticut. I stayed at Jenny's place a couple nights. Unfortunately, UMaine lost, but it was an enjoyable weekend all the same. I then rode back to Orono with my lab monitor and resumed classes on Monday.

We had a break over the Thanksgiving holiday, so I invited GM Whitten to join my family for Thanksgiving. GM knew both of my parents from Rockwood and gladly said "Yes." Neither of us had a car, and no one from my family could come pick us up, so we started hitchhiking the 175 miles from Orono to Bethel, Maine. GM and I decided it might help with the ride situation if drivers recognized we were college students! We both had sweatshirts with large letters spelling out *University of Maine* on the front. Route 2 runs very near the UMaine campus and goes through Bethel, so we had a direct route to follow. On the one hand, it was kind of funny, but I was a little shocked when two *different* cars passed us by. Both the drivers of each car and his female passenger were flipping us the bird as they drove by! As I mentioned, this didn't just happen once; it happened two times! Guess locals in that part of Maine didn't like college kids. We did make it to Bethel that day and enjoyed a very pleasant Thanksgiving with my family. I believe Dad or someone was able to drive us back to school, so we thankfully only had to hitchhike one way.

At the end of the semester break, I returned to UMaine and Hart Hotel to continue my education. Financially, I used the second half of my Gould Academy scholarship and most of the rest of my personal savings. The fraternities were in *rush mode* for freshmen during that semester, and I was somewhat interested. Teddy Carter had a two-year degree in agriculture from Maine and was a member of the Sigma Nu fraternity while there. I had actually spent a long weekend visiting Teddy and staying in a spare bed in the frat house while I was attending Gould Academy. Sigma Nu was known as a wild drinking fraternity on campus and famous for their parties, not necessarily the favorite frat house of the university president or his staff! Teddy had apparently recommended me to the fraternity, so I was rushed. Dad had been a member of Alpha Tau Omega when he was at UMaine, an engineering curriculum-oriented frat house, so I was also rushed by ATO. These were two *totally* different fraternities! Sigma Nu was more like Animal House, and ATO was made up of a more serious and focused group of men. (Apparently, things didn't change much over the years as in April of 2012, UMaine suspended Sigma Nu for five years "after repeated violations of the student conduct code.")

My second semester at UMaine was different for me than the first one. I continued my mandatory ROTC classes, learning the sixteen-count manual of arms rifle positions and drill and ceremony marching commands. Little did I know that these routine drills would be useful for me several years later! Overall, I was having a hard time focusing on studying, and the looming burden of where the funding would be coming from for my sophomore year was troubling me a lot. My grade average was fair, probably more like President George W Bush's than President Clinton's, but not at a level that was satisfactory to me. Late in the second semester, I dropped out of the University of Maine and never returned. I went back to Bethel, stayed with Dad and Mother at their 1 Chapman St. home for a short time, and then made my way back to Miami. The Hollywood Beach Hotel was still open, so I worked there until it closed for the season. During that brief time, I bought a 1957 Chevrolet Bel Air convertible. It was baby blue with a white convertible top. It had a 287 cubic inch V-8 engine and automatic transmission. Not really powerful for the day, but more of a current car than I'd ever owned. I added matching fender skirts and two black cone-shaped bumper guards to the front bumper to customize it a bit!

CHAPTER ELEVEN

LIFE WORKING IN MASSACHUSETTS AND FLORIDA AFTER THE UNIVERSITY OF MAINE

As the summer was approaching, I asked Father, "Do you know of any summer job opportunities that are available?" He did have another longtime friend in the hotel business, Mac McManus, who was going to be superintendent of service at a summer resort known as the Mayflower Hotel in Plymouth, Massachusetts. The hotel was actually a bit south of Plymouth on Boston's South Shore on Manomet Beach. I was hired as a bellman and drove to Plymouth in my 1957 Chevy convertible. The trip north was kind of interesting. I left Hollywood, Florida, about 8:00 p.m. one evening as it was a bit cooler than driving in the daytime that time of year. I-95 had not been conceived yet, and the Florida Turnpike didn't start until Ft. Pierce farther north. There were two options going north—Route 1, which went through *many* towns and their stoplights in the towns along Florida's east coast, *or* Route 441 that curved inland a bit and went through less populated areas of the state. I chose Route 441. After driving for a while, I headed east near Ft. Pierce and continued up the Florida Turnpike. I drove all night but got tired around North Carolina, so I pulled into a remote corner of a fast-food restaurant and grabbed an hour or two nap. When I woke up, I grabbed a bite to eat and continued on my way. Many hours later, when I arrived in Plymouth, Massachusetts, late in the afternoon of the second day, I had been traveling for twenty-two hours! I was shaking all over and totally worn out. I must have slept for a while catching up.

The Mayflower Hotel was wooden, quite old, but clean and well maintained. There were living accommodations for the hotel staff where I quickly settled in. Most of the other bellmen were from the Boston area and had *weird accents*. I guess not really weird, but much different than I'd been used to! The doorman, Gene O'Neill, was from Cambridge, Massachusetts, and we soon became good friends.

It was an interesting summer, yet not too different from any bellmen's job in South Florida. One difference was that one day, I checked-in Rocky Marciano, the world heavyweight champion boxer at the time, who lived in nearby Brockton, Massachusetts. He had come to the hotel for several days to relax. With him were three of his *bodyguards*, who took care of his tipping. I think I received a couple quarters as a tip for checking him and contingent into their rooms. The quarters somehow slipped out of my hand on the way out of the room, projected themselves up into the air, and landed with a loud clank on the wooden floor outside Rocky's room. The quarters bounced around on the floor for what seemed like forever. I was unhappy but not polite. *This cheap guy is the heavyweight champion of the world?* I thought to myself.

I tried New England snorkeling that summer, but the conditions weren't very conducive compared with South Florida. The water was colder, and there were thick kelp forests growing from the bottom to about a foot from the surface. Snorkeling for me didn't last very long off Manomet Beach.

One very nice thing about the South Shore was there were many new things to see. Plymouth Rock, where the Pilgrims first landed in 1620, was nearby, and in general Plymouth was a quaint little New England slice of history. Not too far down the South Shore was the Sagamore Bridge that led to Cape Cod. Gene O'Neill knew the whole area well and recommended many places to go after work. One of my favorites was Storyville Jazz Club in Harwich, Massachusetts, at the *elbow* of Cape Cod. There was a Storyville Jazz Club in Boston, but this was a summer only club. On different occasions, we saw the Dave Brubeck Quartet and Sarah Vaughn perform. They were awesome!

One thing I remember about my 1957 Chevy convertible was it was a *Florida car* and wasn't equipped with a heater! Some of the nights on the South Shore in the summer could be quite cool, and a heater/windshield defroster would have been nice to have.

During the course of that summer, I met and dated a local girl named Jane P. Her parents were of Portuguese descent and owned Ernie's Pizza, a restaurant in North Plymouth. Jane was cute, perky, and genuinely a fun person to be with. I really liked her a lot. When we weren't going somewhere around town, we'd hang out at her house. Her parents were usually working at the restaurant, and while her grandmother lived with them in the house, she was generally in her room.

The Mayflower Hotel was owned and managed by Irving Sinberg. He had a daughter named Bea who lived in a separate cottage down the hill from the main hotel. Bea was divorced and had a twelve-year-old son. She was always calling for room service after normal working hours and wanted the bellman to hang out with her after we delivered her order. She seemed lonely and somehow took a liking to me. Bea was a pleasant person to talk with, but as she weighed somewhere around 275 pounds, she had trouble talking and breathing at the same time. As an asthmatic, she'd occasionally have to pause and pull on her inhaler to be able to continue the conversation! Bea did have a new Cadillac convertible and would let me use it whenever I wanted to, usually to go on an errand for her in town.

When the summer of 1959 was over and the Mayflower was closing, I was ready to return to South Florida and the Hollywood Beach Hotel. I helped close the Mayflower, but when it was time for my final paycheck, Irving Sinberg was nowhere to be found! Other seasonal employees were having the same issue. Irving was in hiding and deliberately trying to avoid paying his employees their final paychecks. I don't vividly recall the details, but I contacted Bea, and she told me where I could find her father. I confronted him and asked for my final pay, which he told his accountant to issue. I still didn't know at the time if the check was good (and it was), but some of my fellow workers that year didn't fare as well and got stiffed for their last pay period. I was learning the hard lessons of life!

Returning to HBH that year was going back to a familiar setting for me! Lou Lippi, Joe I, and Mother Johnson were still in charge, along with a new crew of bellmen including Ricky from Indiana; Jimmy Lawless, a guy with a heavy accent from Cork Ireland; Joe Santoro from Providence, Rhode Island; Freddy Lippi (Lou's son); and others. Even though I wouldn't be twenty-one until February of the following year, I started the season at HBH as a bellman. Three other bellmen and I rented a *snake ranch* in West Hollywood beyond the Hollywood downtown area and a distance west on Hollywood Blvd. The rents were less expensive there, and let's face it, we didn't make a lot of money as bellmen. However, no more *bell dorm* for us! The furnished single-family home had two bedrooms each with two twin beds. My roommate was a nice guy named Mike from Vermont. He was an avid golfer and would occasionally convince me to play a round of golf with him. I hadn't even seen a golf game since caddying at Mount Kineo Hotel, but I enjoyed getting out, and South Florida's weather that time of year was quite nice.

For the earlier part of this season, I'd get phone calls from Jane P, whom I'd gone out with that summer, at all hours of the evening. She'd enrolled at Boston University for the year and had apparently gotten into the partying scene, because each time she called, it was obvious she'd been drinking a lot!

The HBH opened with the usual convention season. I started assisting the sound engineer, Clarence, with the sound and audio support for our convention groups in my spare time. I really enjoyed setting up the meeting rooms with speakers, mikes, and projectors. I was right in my technical element! My job during the meeting was changing slides on the projectors. Back then, remote operation of a projector by pressing a button on a remote didn't exist. I'd press a button on the projector itself and advance the slide based upon a visual signal from the presenter or by following a written script. It brought in extra money and was a little more challenging than simply *hopping bells*!

Because of my extra job supporting HBH's conventions, I got to know the hotel's convention VP, Georgia Hunter, quite well. Her office was on the second floor, right off the lobby and behind the *jets*. I think Georgia came to respect me for what I did to support her operations, and she was a pleasant woman to work with. Coincidentally, she had an executive assistant named Jean that I ended up dating off and on for a large part of the season.

The *social season* came around the end of November as usual. This was a good time financially for the bellman as those guests tipped *much* better than conventioneers. However, with the better tips also came the complaining Jewish wives. Don't get me wrong, I'm not anti-Semitic. Jewish wives are just very vocal about what they want, and the husbands almost never argued with them! It didn't happen all the time, but on busy holiday, check-in days, the guests would check-in, I'd push the luggage rack overflowing with bags up to the room, and the wife would say, "Oh no, this isn't going to work. I don't like this view" (or similar). Then after the wife complained on the house phone to the desk clerk downstairs, I'd have to patiently wait (while other fronts were checking in guests and lining their pockets with bills) and eventually go to the front desk, get several keys to new rooms, and go back up to show the new room choices. Grrrrr!

Along with the fussy mothers, young Jewish girls would join their parents for the holidays at HBH. Typically, these young ladies would initially check out the hotel pool and spend some time on Hollywood Beach, then get kind of bored with the new scene. For some reason, there seemed to be more female than male older teenagers that checked in, so the girls (out of desperation?) started looking at the hotel staff for entertainment. In the case of the bellmen, they'd come down to the lobby and talk with us in the closed cocktail lounge where we would be taking breaks. It was all very innocent, but I did meet one or two of the older girls just outside the hotel and took them to Dania Beach just north of Hollywood to swim and hang out on the beach on one of my afternoons off. I think this was the year that I assumed the pseudonym of *Danny Rabinowitz*. Somehow it stuck with the other bellmen, and from then on I was *Rabinowitz* or just *Witz*.

I learned another lesson during my second year at HBH. Whenever Mother was bell captain, she had a tendency to palm tips that we thought should have gone to the bellmen. For example, a guest would come up and ask Mother to have something delivered to a room or rooms and give her some change. As *last boy* and being directly in front of the bell desk, we could see the transaction and often the amount. Mother would usually wait awhile and then give the task to someone, minus part of the tip. We all observed this and would talk about it among ourselves. Some of us felt we were being cheated. I wouldn't have minded if Mother had been up-front about it and said she was keeping part of it as *her* tip. We all objected to the sneakiness of it and decided we would ask Lou Lippi for a bell staff meeting, which he agreed to. We met in the lobby card room, including the two bell captains.

When Lou asked, "Okay, now why did you guys call this meeting?" There was *dead* silence. No one said a word. After an embarrassing period of silence, I spoke up and relayed our grievance. Lou listened then said, "If you don't like the way this operation is being run, you can always leave!" So much for unity and sticking together! I never did that again without making sure I had a group's backing.

There were plenty of things to do in South Florida when off duty. Besides the beach, snorkeling, and bars, there was dog racing at Hollywood Park, Miami Jai Lai (BTW, I never in many times at Jai Ali cashed a winning ticket), and horse racing. During *the season*, the three racetracks in the Miami area would alternate dates. Tropical Park in South Miami would open first, and then when it would close, Hialeah would open, and finally it was Gulfstream's turn. Gulfstream was in Hallandale, very near HBH, and Jimmy Lawless, Danny Grusso, or other bellmen and I would go, probably every other week or so. I'd buy a *Daily Racing Form* newspaper and study past performances of horses in each race before betting. Some races I didn't bet at all. I never won a ton of money, but I found it very exciting and a great way to spend an afternoon. We'd occasionally go to Hialeah when it was open, but mainly Gulfstream as Hialeah was a longer drive.

Social season was followed by the second convention season, and the house was again nicely booked for the remainder of the year. The bellmen that I mentioned earlier were a good bunch of guys and all unique in their own way. Jimmy Lawless usually had a smile on his face and was always antagonizing someone. Ricky from Indiana had a very different, almost stiff way of walking. One day, Jimmy (in front of a group of us, of course) said, "Ricky, you walk like you have square balls!" From then on, Ricky was known as *Square Balls*, not Ricky. Joe Santoro was a self-confident Italian stud from Providence, Rhode Island. One could actually call him cocky. Very early in the season, he became known as *Joe Hollywood*. He loved it! Freddy Lippi didn't hang out with the rest of the bellmen when off duty; he spent most of his free time hanging around with Murph the Surf, a local personality alleged to be associated with the South Florida mafia. Danny Grusso, one of our bell captains, was no doubt the most stable person of the group. He was married and had a child. Danny would quite frequently invite several of us over to his house where his Irish wife would serve one of the best Italian meals I've ever eaten—spaghetti, tomato *gravy*, sausage, and small short ribs! Danny was a genuinely class act! Life was different than living in New England, and I was enjoying it immensely!

After we closed the Hollywood Beach Hotel for the 1959–1960 season, I decided not to go back north for the summer but stay in South Florida. Father was superintendent of service at the Biscayne Terrace Hotel on Biscayne Boulevard in Miami at the time and gave me a job as a bellman. Not being a resort hotel, per se, it was a different atmosphere for me, but I was okay with it. I worked there for maybe a month or so when this *high roller* couple checked in. The husband was a gregarious fast talker, and they both charged heavily to the room. The couple was there for probably a week, so their bill had built up to a healthy sum. A house, mandatory procedure for bellmen checking out a guest, was to submit a slip with the guests' name and room number on it to the hotel cashier for clearance. This was supposed to be before taking the guests' luggage to the front door for check out. However, on busy days, what routinely happened to speed up the process was for the bellman to submit the slip to the cashier, go to the room for the guest's luggage, and then go back to the cashier for clearance that the bill had been paid on our way to the front door. Well, Slick Willy and his wife (purposely) picked an unusually busy day to check out. Unfortunately, I got the *front*, submitted my slip to the cashier, and went up to the room to get their vast amount of stuff. Everyone was suspicious that this couple were stiffs, and I should have been more cautious, but long story short, I took their things to the front door and went back to the cashier for clearance. They *had not* paid their bill, so I quickly went back to the front door to stop their exit, but mysteriously they had expedited the car loading process and were long gone from the hotel grounds. It was clearly my error, and I was really embarrassed, especially because of Father's position in the hotel's service department. That afternoon, my father walked over to me, and for the second time in my career, I was told "You're fired!"

CHAPTER TWELVE

LIVING IN SOUTH FLORIDA YEAR-ROUND

It was the summer of 1960, and I had just turned twenty-one in February. I planned to return to the Hollywood Beach Hotel in the fall, so I was looking for a place to live on Hollywood Beach. I answered an ad from a person who was looking for a roommate to share expenses with. I responded to the ad and met Pete, who was a waiter at the Diplomat Hotel on South Ocean Drive, Hollywood, Florida, just about a mile south of the Hollywood Beach Hotel. Pete's apartment was on Polk St., north of and within walking distance south on Surf Road to HBH. The unit itself was in a cluster of connected, one-story apartments. Each had two bedrooms, living area, one bath, and a kitchen. It was small but comfortable. I signed a contract and moved in.

I think Father knew everyone in the hotel business in South Florida, and through one of his connections, Joe Joyce, I got a bellman's job at the Aztec Hotel, a relatively new hotel on Collins Avenue at 159th St. in an area known as Sunny Isles. It had a great location directly on the Atlantic Ocean with a nice beach and, of course, a large pool. It had a little over two hundred rooms and sadly, like many early hotels in Miami and Miami Beach, has since been demolished. The Aztec was relatively busy during the summer, considering the warm weather in South Florida, but we did have a number of families vacationing as school was out and additionally groups of two to three single women as well. I always wondered why we seldom saw groups of single men, but we speculated it was because the guys had to work in the summer between school years, and many of the young women didn't. At any rate, when these young women checked in, they didn't want anything to do with any of the hotel staff from bellmen, dining room waiters, pool lifeguards, etc. However, after a few days, their mood seemed to change. They'd get bored and decided they probably could lower themselves to at least talk with us. I always felt that realization was ironic as it seemed to be a universal trait of the majority of young women who came to the beach to party, drink, and have fun. Then when there were few, if any, guests of the opposite sex, their feelings changed.

Financially, things at the Aztec weren't that lucrative for me, so I decided to privately sell my beloved '57 Chevy convertible and purchased a 1954 Ford Crown Victoria, two-door coupe. It was an awesome *ride*, but not equal to my 1957 *baby blue* Chevy convertible.

One night, I couldn't sleep. I tossed and turned and finally got up about 3:00 a.m. As I had the next day off, I thought, *Why not drive to Key West? You've never been there, and it's only a little more than three hours south.* I got dressed, loaded up my Crown Vick, and headed down Route 1 south! The drive through Miami and Homestead wasn't exceptional, but by the time the sun was coming up, I was in the Keys. There are many bridges and *keys* (or islands) along the way, Key Largo, Travernier, Islamorada, and so forth. The water was gorgeous shades of light blues, dark blues, and green shades, but mixed with the pure white of the sands was a sight I'd never seen! I drove over Seven Mile Bridge, which was a bit hairy. A new wider bridge spans those seven miles now, but back then it was a narrow one lane-bridge in each direction. Cars coming from the other direction weren't a problem, but big trucks crossed the bridge, too, which didn't leave much of the roadway on my side. It was a little nerve-racking! It was still early when I reached Key West, and the small town was still waking up. I was able to find a restaurant on the water open and had breakfast. After breakfast, I drove around Key West a bit, passed by the bars that had not opened yet on famous Duval St, and finally drove to the very end of Route 1 and its southernmost terminus just to say I'd been there! I had a nice drive back to Hollywood Beach and my apartment, where I finally was able to get some sleep.

The Aztec was reasonably busy until the end of August arrived, but unfortunately, so did Hurricane Donna! It was still off the Atlantic coast when the US Weather Service issued the warning. It was a dangerous category 4 storm. The married employees helped board up and secure the hotel initially, but then they had to go home to take care of their homes and families. The general manager, Irv Schwartz, a few other single employees, and I stayed around to be there while riding out the bad storm and assist as necessary. I checked into one of the guest rooms. The hurricane was scheduled to hit us early evening, so Irv asked me to open up the hotel bar, the Tequila Cocktail Lounge, where he offered free drinks to the remaining guests that were *hunkering down* with us for the storm! I got to know one of our guests, Janet Dargavidge, from West Chester, Pennsylvania, while I was tending bar. She was an enjoyable person to talk with, and we hit it off immediately. While the storm was raging outside, people at my bar were oblivious to all that and having a fun *Hurricane Party*! Free drinks may have contributed to the gaiety, do you think?

Fortunately, the hurricane didn't do any major damage to the hotel, and the guests and remaining staff survived as well. I believe Donna had been downgraded to a category 3 or less storm by the time she reached the Aztec. Several days later, when the water on Hollywood Beach dropped a bit, I borrowed Irv Schwartz's 1960 Cadillac convertible and drove home to check things out. The water in the streets still hadn't receded enough, and I couldn't get to Polk St., so I went back to the Aztec for another night to hang out with Janet, who hadn't ended her vacation in Miami Beach yet. When I returned home the following day, I found our unit hadn't flooded as it was on a raised parcel of land (actually sand), but a neighbor who had stayed through the hurricane told me, "The storm surge had come up to almost the bottom of the front door."

I had a friend, Art, who worked at an ocean-front hotel several blocks south of the Aztec. According to Art, big black limousines would periodically pull up to the front door of the hotel some mornings and let off clandestine looking people. Later that day, the parade of limousines would return to pick up their passengers. Apparently, the mafia was quite active in the Miami Beach area, and these were meetings of heads of the various families and their capos!

The remainder of the summer at the Aztec went by without any significant events that come to mind, and I returned to the Hollywood Beach Hotel to help with the opening in October. Many of the same bell staff returned—Lou Lippi, bell captains Joe I and Danny Grusso (Mother had retired, and Danny was promoted), Joe Hollywood, Square Balls, etc. Plus we had some new faces. We opened with several insurance company conventions, Johnson & Johnson, and my favorite group, the American Bankers Association. I continued with my part-time job assisting the sound engineer.

Janet Dargavidge, whom I'd met at the Aztec, kept in touch with me by mail and an occasional phone call as I was starting the season at HBH. Then one evening, she called me. Janet had obviously been drinking and told me she was coming back to Florida. She wanted to see me and wanted me to pick her up at the airport the next morning! Janet actually did get on a flight from Philadelphia, and I met her at the airport. It was sort of an unusual event for me. She stayed for several days and then flew home. Janet and I stayed in touch for some time after that then lost touch with each other.

It was during the fall period after HBH had opened that five of the other bellmen and I drove to Ft. Lauderdale and chartered a fishing boat for a half day of deep-sea fishing. After we embarked on the boat and started out to sea, it took us almost an hour to get out to the Gulf Stream where we began fishing. It was a beautiful forty-foot fishing boat, probably a Hatteras, with two twenty-foot outriggers that extended outward from the port and starboard sides, midships with two attached trailing lines, and mullet as live bait. Two additional lines were trailing from the stern of the vessel, one on each side. If you've never been deep sea fishing, this is a common configuration for trolling with ocean rigs. We caught a number of beautiful dolphin (the fish, not the mammal) which we released. The captain had beer aboard as part of the charter, and we were all having a great time. It was a beautiful day! To organize things a bit, the six of us would rotate and were assigned to one of the four lines trailing the boat. The other two *off duty* fishermen would drink beer and just enjoy the day on the Gulf Stream. My *on rotation* was assigned to one of the outriggers. Suddenly, my line broke free from the clip holding it fast to its outrigger tip, and my reel started whirring as the line played out! The mate grabbed my rod and pulled hard to set the hook, then gave the rod back to me after I sat in one of the swiveling aft-facing chairs and strapped myself in. I had a big one on the line!

Getting this fish close to the boat was one of the most thrilling experiences of my life to date! The mate had pulled the other three lines into the boat to avoid any tangling, so mine was the only line in the water. I'd pull the tip of the rod upward, and then lower the tip rapidly while at the same time quickly turning the reel handle to take up the slack line. This repeated *multiple* times until I pulled the fish close to the boat. It was a beautiful sailfish! While these were relatively abundant in Florida's Gulf Stream, catching one wasn't that common. The mate was ready to bring the beauty into the boat when suddenly, it must have seen the boat and dove downward and away from the boat. The star drag setting was exceeded, and the reel started screaming as the fish was paying out the line at an incredible rate! I was already exhausted. My arms were limp, and I would have to repeat this process again if I wanted to land this baby. Long story short, I did repeat the process. The sailfish made some beautiful leaps out of the Gulf Stream, shaking his head and trying to dislodge the hook and falling back into the water with a splash. It was almost as if the sailfish was *dancing on the water*. It took me the better part of fifty minutes to get the sailfish close enough to the boat to land it. I remember remarking at the time that this experience was better than xxx (you fill in the blank). I recall the captain of the charter boat lamenting, "Why couldn't this have happened when high rollers were chartering my boat?" Guess he felt like he might have gotten a better gratuity if it hadn't been a bunch of fun-loving bellmen chartering his boat.

Marine conservation policies among fishermen at the time required that unless the angler was going to mount the fish, it had to be released. This was a six-foot, six-inch beauty, and I just couldn't release it. I agreed to the taxidermy of the catch, and Al Pflueger's shop in Miami did an excellent job mounting and preserving the sailfish! It has traveled all around Maine, Connecticut, Virginia, and now is with us in Georgia, where it has a proud place in my office!

During this period, my father had taken a position as manager of the new Miami Playboy Club at Seventy-Seventh Street and Biscayne Blvd. He worked at the Playboy club for over a year, and I was impressed that he'd met Hugh Hefner during his tenure there. However, I thought he worked a terrible shift, which was from 6:00 p.m. to 6:00 a.m.! He'd often tell me one of his most important functions was inspecting the Playboy Bunnies before they went on the floor for the evening. The Bunny costumes were very skimpy for the times, and apparently some of the bunnies would stuff the upper bra sections of their costumes with tissue paper until parts of their breasts would be exposed that were against even Hef's policies! Father would have to make them remove the tissue paper before they went to work (at least he said)! He would invite me to the club on occasion and introduce me to some of the Bunnies. Other times, when I was visiting him when he was off duty, he'd call one of the Bunnies, allegedly on club business, and pass the phone to me when he was done. They were all good-looking young women, but ambitious, clearly out of my budget range, and candidly, I felt out of my league! Father was an optimist and never gave up.

Getting back to the Hollywood Beach Hotel, there *was* one, significant new employee at HBH that year. Georgia Hunter had a new executive assistant! When I asked Georgia about her, she said, "Oh, that's Diane Beattie. She's a recent Katherine Gibbs School graduate from New York City!" As I'd dated Georgia's assistant Jean the year before, it seemed natural to me that I should do the same this year! I'd see Diane around the hotel talking with convention heads, coordinating events, etc., and occasionally I'd see her in the main dining room having lunch. I was very interested!

One day, when I didn't see her in Georgia's office, I asked Georgia, "Where's Diane?"

Georgia told me, "She's down at the front door waiting to meet Father Callahan to escort him upstairs."

Naturally, I just *had* to go down to the front door to check this out. I approached Diane and said, "I understand you're waiting for Father Callahan."

Diane replied. "Yes, I am, and what's it to you?"

My quick response was, "You don't have to do that. I'll turn my collar around and take your confession." Guess I didn't make a very good first impression. She thought I was a real jerk!

I did ask Diane out, and she consented after a while. I learned later that Georgia Hunter had warned Diane, "Watch out for the bellmen. They're bad news. The one possible exception is Dennis Robertson, but still be careful." Diane and I would occasionally go out to some of the local hangouts for a drink after work. There was the Bamboo Bar on Johnson St. and Hollywood Beach that was within walking distance and sort of a cool beach-type bar. I also took Diane to a lounge on Dania Beach that I liked. I'd been introduced to this lounge by Ray, a waiter who worked at HBH, and I liked the place a lot myself. It was somehow much classier than most beach bars. There was a multilevel keyboard organ on an elevated platform directly behind the bartender. The organ player, Dave, was amazing and played the best music! Diane particularly liked the way Dave played the new instrumental hit "Telstar" on his electric organ!

The word had apparently gotten around the hotel that there was no *hanky-panky* with Georgia Hunter's new executive assistant as Jimmy Lawless would usually ask me in his heavy Irish accent, "Ar u goin' out wit the virg' ta-nite?" Diane and I went to Gulfstream Park for the afternoon several times when it was open. I would buy the *Daily Racing Form* newspaper and tout or research each horse's past performances thoroughly before each race. Then we'd walk down to the paddock and watch the horses going around before the race went off. I'd have selected my choice or choices for that race, but I wanted to see how the horse looked—peppy, lethargic, tired, etc.

Diane would see a jockey's silks and say, "Oh, look at that one. I like number 7. The jockey's colors look so bright. I think he's going to win." When we went back upstairs, placed our bets, and watched the race, guess whose horse would win most of the time? (Not mine! My horse would still be running.) Diane was a lot of fun to be with and very enjoyable to be around.

I always felt Diane was special, so one evening, I invited her to join me and made reservations to see Frank Sinatra at the

Fontainebleau Hotel on Miami Beach. Because my income as a bell-man was limited, I asked Diane if we could go on a Dutch treat basis (each person shares the cost fifty-fifty). She agreed. On the night of the performance, we drove to Forty-Fourth Street and Collins Avenue to the Fontainebleau where I surrendered my Crown Victoria to the doorman for valet parking. I gave the maître d' at the entrance to the Liv Nightclub a generous tip that I hoped would get us nearer to the stage. Happily, we were taken to a reasonably close table for two to watch Sinatra's performance. I'd ordered a split of Canadian Club and mixers for us to share. Old Blue Eyes was outstanding as usual! I must have consumed most of the CC and ginger because when it came time for Diane to pay her share of the tab, she was looking for change of a bill to cover her half. I told her, "The smallest bills I have are tens." She said, "Okay," and I handed her two ten-dollar bills. Diane gave me her twenty-dollar bill, and I paid the tab, satisfied we were all square. I think it wasn't until the next day when I looked at the meager amount of folding money remaining in my money clip that I realized I was *short*. Then it hit me what really had happened the night before!

Diane's grandmother, Marie Berry, owned a home on Roosevelt St. in Hollywood just west of Young Circle. One afternoon, Diane and I drove out to her grandmother's home to meet Grandma and Diane's mother, Dolores Johnson. It was a typical Florida house of those days, stucco exterior finished in a light turquoise color. Diane's mom had lived in Ridgefield Park, New Jersey, for many years where Diane grew up and went to school. However, there had been problems between her husband, Jim. As a result, Diane's mother had temporarily moved in with Grandma Berry in Florida.

Back at Hollywood Beach, Diane had a second-floor room in Ocean House, a block or so north of the HBH itself. This was an HBH residence where single, executive, and middle management staff were housed—quite a bit nicer than *the bell dorm*! Just another block up North Boardwalk was the Surf Bar. It wasn't very big, but it was a favorite, local hangout for HBH employees. I didn't really know of their friendship before, but Diane had a view and was within earshot of any loud noises on North Boardwalk from her room. She would sometimes observe Georgia Hunter and my boss, Lou Lippi, weaving back and forth toward the hotel after closing the Surf Bar!

The social season came, and with it the hotel's policy of providing free orange juice to the guests after check-in. The bellman or bellmen that did the check-in were responsible to go to the service closet on that floor where there was a cooler of fresh orange juice, pour a number of water glasses full of OJ equal to the number of guests in that party, then take it back to the room. One bellman from Providence, Rhode Island, who will remain unnamed, would let a small amount of urine slip into the glasses of the guests who had given him a poor tip for the check-in. That wasn't bad enough, but he'd wait in the room until one of the guests took a drink of the OJ. If it looked like the guest(s) weren't going to drink the OJ until later, he'd say, "Try the orange juice and let me know if it's okay." He wouldn't leave the room until he could watch at least one of them drink it. The remainder of the social season passed with the same advances by the female offspring of the guests toward HBH staff employees, only with a different cast of characters!

I'm not sure I really knew what *true love* was at the time, but I really liked Diane Beattie *a lot*. I very much enjoyed being in her company, but she consistently resisted moves by me to go to bed with her. I assumed morals instilled by her mother, Dolores, and reinforced by her Catholic upbringing and her personal feelings told her one should save intimate relations for marriage were what prevented her from abandoning her values. It turned out to be a bad rationalization on my part, but as someone once said, "There are a lot of pebbles on the beach." Diane and I started going out less frequently, and before the season ended, I was dating other girls. I started dating the HBH nurse and one of the hotel waitresses. I was in a learning phase of life.

The Hollywood Beach Hotel closed its second half convention season in the spring of 1961, and the staff all had a little downtime. Lou Lippi was going to be superintendent of service at a summer hotel in Groton, Connecticut, called the Griswold, but its season wasn't going to start for several weeks. Lou had asked me to be his bell captain that summer, and I accepted! Several bellmen, including Jimmy

Lawless, Square Balls, and others of the HBH crew, were going to the Griswold with us. I gave up my apartment on Hollywood Beach with Pete and temporarily moved into the home of Jimmy Lawless's aunt with him in Hollywood. It was a warm spring and starting to get relatively hot in Florida for that time of year. The house of Jimmy's aunt had no air-conditioning, and I remember taking two showers a day if I did any outdoor activities just to keep cool.

Shortly before the Griswold was scheduled to open, Jimmy and I drove north to North Wildwood, New Jersey, where his aunt owned a bar called *O'Brian's* on the South Jersey Shore. His aunt spent the colder winter months in Hollywood, Florida, and her summers on the Jersey shore. Jimmy and I spent a couple days with his aunt before heading north to Groton to open up the Griswold Hotel. Chubby Checker's "The Twist" was very popular that year. One night, when we were in the bar at O'Brian's, Jimmy played several songs on the jukebox. I had asked one of the local girls to dance, and when Chubby Checker's "The Twist" came on, the two of us immediately starting *twisting*! That Jersey girl was a good dancer and I could *twist* a bit too. The next thing I heard was smart-ass Jimmy announcing from a microphone in his Irish accent, "And on the dance floor is Dennis Robertson! He's a twist instructor from Hollywood, Florida. Give him a round of applause." God love the Irish. I still think about Jimmy, his Irish wit, and the many good times we had together when we were young!

CHAPTER THIRTEEN

THE 1961–1962 SEASONS AT THE GRISWOLD AND HOLLYWOOD BEACH HOTEL

The Griswold was yet another somewhat different experience for me. The hotel was directly on the Thames River across from New London, Connecticut, and was a bit downstream from USN Submarine Base Groton. The Griswold's summer guests were primarily from Boston and New York City, some older retirees getting out of their cities for a week or more during the summer, and very few younger people. With Lou Lippi's guidance, we formed into two shifts and got organized. As bell captain, I worked primarily days, overlapping both shifts. The *front door* was a concession that had been paid for by a person or group of people. This was fairly common in those days, and these individuals were truly independent contractors that didn't answer to Lou Lippi or me. It actually worked out well, and there was a seamless transition of guests between them and my bellmen.

The Griswold was on the eastern bank of the Thames River shortly before the river dumped into the Long Island Sound. There was fairly constant traffic of US Navy submarines going to or from the sub base. They all passed directly in front of the hotel and by our front door! Many of us had interest in this *stealthy* branch of our Navy and would record the hull number of the subs we saw on the inside of the doorman's *key box*. This was a normally locked wooden box that the doormen would keep the guest's keys in while their car was valet parked. Over the summer, we gathered a number of US submarine hull numbers and identified them through encyclopedia lookups. Sometimes a sub would be going out to Long Island Sound without a number displayed on its sail. I later learned that boat was going on a tactical mission and didn't want its identity known.

For after-work entertainment in the Groton/New London area, there was a limited number of things to do. There was a local bar right behind the Griswold called Black Maggie's that some of us hung out at on occasion. There were bars in downtown Groton near General Dynamics Electric Boat Division shipyard, but they were mainly patronized by workers at EB and not any younger people. As there was a contingent of Italians on the bell staff, they found the Italian American Club in Warwick, Rhode Island, about forty-five minutes from the Griswold! The members there were great. Our Italian bellmen fit in perfectly, and one night after a few drinks, I was admitted as an honorary member of the Warwick Italian American Club. I was honored!

We typically had a large number of older, mainly widowed, female guests from one of the five NYC boroughs staying with us. Lou Lippi wanted to offer a transportation service from the Griswold to *The City*, as they called it. The hotel had a ten-person van, and I became the driver! Usually about once a week, I'd drive some of the guests back to The City, generally into Manhattan, the Bronx, or Brooklyn. There was no GPS in those days, so once I arrived near the borough the guest lived in, the guest would direct me to their home and I'd have to remember how to backtrack out or get lost! It was interesting in the sense that I'd never seen these parts of our country and was taken in by the differences from areas I'd been familiar with in the past.

That summer went by quickly, working and hanging out at Black Maggie's and other places. Square Balls and I did have one confrontation. I really don't exactly recall the specific issue, but on a *very* busy check-in day, he did something I felt wasn't right. He argued with me, and I relieved him of the watch and told him to leave. Lou Lippi wasn't extremely happy with me, but when I relayed the details, Lou understood and supported me. The whole bell team had to work faster to check-in the guests as smoothly as possible, but I never had any more issues with Square Balls.

When my first season at the Griswold ended, I returned to Bethel, Maine, to visit with my mother and Dad before driving back to Florida to again open up the Hollywood Beach Hotel for conventions. My brothers Ned and Dave were growing by then. Ned was eleven, and Dave was ten years old. It was good hanging out with them and getting to know them a bit better as I wasn't around them that much anymore.

At the end of September, three of the HBH bellmen who lived in the New England area drove up and met me in Bethel, Maine, to do some fishing. We drove up toward Moosehead Lake and hit some of the good fishing spots along the way. It was there that someone came up with the idea that we should drive to Quebec City, Canada, which we did end up doing. As soon as we crossed the St. Lawrence River from Lévis and into Quebec City, we started looking for a bar where we could talk with some Frenchwomen. I believe the first place we stopped at was a bistro. We ordered a drink and soon noticed there were absolutely no women in the establishment! Come to find out, this was one of the places in Canada where men gathered to get away from their wives who could not enter to bother them! We had a hard time communicating with the French waiter but learned we needed to go to a cabaret where women were allowed in. As I recall, we spent two days in Quebec City taking in the sights and then returned to Bethel, where they returned home and I got ready to return south.

Before returning to Hollywood, I made arrangements to rent another furnished *snake ranch* for the 1961–1962 season with three other bellmen, this time in Hollywood proper and closer to HBH. The house was just north on Route 1, then east on Cleveland St. It was another typical Florida house, constructed of cinder blocks with a stucco covered outside to prevent termites and other Florida bugs from destroying it. It had two bedrooms, living room, kitchen, and two baths. I remember one of my roommates bought a new 1962 Corvette that year as soon as they came out. It was an awesome machine with a 4-speed stick on the floor and a very powerful V8 engine. It was the fastest accelerating car I'd ever driven, and the rear end would *fish tail* when the accelerator was floored from a standing stop! It was a real chick magnet back then.

Many of the old crew had returned: Lou Lippi, Joe I, Danny Grusso, Jimmy Lawless, Square Balls, Joe Hollywood, and again some new faces. After the usual routine of opening the hotel for the season, we started the usual *split shift* that Lou Lippi had implemented many seasons ago. On our *long days*, we'd work 8:00 a.m. to noon then be off until 6:00 p.m. when we'd work until 9:00 p.m. or later, depending upon how busy the bellmen were that particular evening. Our *short days* consisted of noon to 6:00 p.m.

I started the season as a bellman, but early during the first half of the convention season, Lou's night bell captain had a family emergency back home and out of state and had to leave. Lou asked me to be his night bell captain, and I accepted the offer. The bellmen were still on the *split shift* routine.

During convention seasons, the 6:00 p.m. to *late* shift every day would be busy with room service beverage as our conventioneers drank and partied *a lot*! There were no ice machines on each floor like you'd find today, so deliveries of large buckets of ice would be a popular item, plus, of course, individual drinks from the service bar downstairs. This activity would keep the *late shift* quite busy, more so with some groups than with others. The night bell captain would gradually let bellmen go home until he thought he could handle the workload himself. Of course, he'd make more tips taking the service calls himself, but there was a fine line between judging spurts of activity and exactly when calls had slowed down enough to not need another bellman to help with the load.

There was a night telephone switchboard operator named Myrt on duty during the same hours as mine, and she quickly taught me *the ropes*. It didn't take me long to realize she was a valuable ally, and we became friends that depended upon each other. Myrt's switchboard was old-fashioned even in 1961! There was a maze of plug-tipped cords that retracted into the horizontal surface of the switchboard. Vertically, in front of the operator, was a board of receptacle holes, one for each room in the hotel plus outside lines. Myrt had her headset on and would answer a call then pull the correct retractable cord and plug from the base of the switchboard and plug it into the correct hole in front of her. There were usually many cords criss-crossed over the surface of the vertical piece of switchboard. How anyone could operate and keep track of that maze beats me!

Myrt knew everything that was going on throughout that hotel! There were no cameras everywhere like in hotels now, but she some-how had a virtual three-dimensional view of all goings-on. I think part of her knowledge came from listening in on calls she felt were suspicious. There were desks near the elevators on each floor. During the day, these desks were manned, but not at night. When I was run-ning *fronts* by myself, and after I'd dismissed the last bellman for the night, Myrt would take any service calls for me. If I was running ice or beverages to a room and Myrt had a new order for me, she'd know where I was and ring the phone on the service desk for that floor. This would save time for me, and we could service the guests faster as well.

When things slowed down, usually around 3:00 a.m. or so during convention season, there was a couch on a raised part of the floor in a back corner of the lobby. I'd turn out the lights in that area and let Myrt know where I was so I could take a snooze. If there was a call during my nap time, Myrt would ring the house phone by my head, and I'd spring into action!

The third person on the midwatch with Myrt and me was a night security officer. Frank was a retired NYPD cop and quite seri-ous about his job. There were often a single or sometimes a team of two hookers working the hotel during convention season. You could spot them immediately as they came into the hotel. Frank loved it! He'd typically let them go up to the room and watch for them to come down after being paid by the *John* before he'd shake them down. He'd say, "Either pay me or I'll call the Hollywood police and you can go to jail." Frank illegally lined his pockets, but in a way it was a deterrent as the word got around on the hooker network that there was a night security officer at HBH that shook you down.

I had a locker in a service closet on the third floor of the hotel where I eventually built up a supply of popular liquor types. Besides ice, I was able to offer drinks by the glass after the main and service bars closed for the night. This was a cash only service for the conventioneers. Occasionally, a group of convention people that were still partying after main bar closing wanted a bottle of liquor. Liquor stores in Florida are open twenty-four seven, so I'd relay the order to Frank and he'd have a cab go buy the bottle at the closest liquor store. There wasn't a way to issue a hotel charge slip, so these were cash only transactions too. The net to the guest would be the cost of the bottle, plus the cab fare and a slight *markup* that Frank and I would split. This didn't happen often, but our afterhours price was usually about equal to or less than the guest would have paid for a bottle of liquor in their room during the day.

A morning ritual for me was to go into the baker's section of the HBH kitchen and get some sticky buns to take up to Myrt. She had been at the HBH for a long time, and the stairway to her switchboard was very near the kitchen. As Myrt was a chatty person, she'd usually stop and kibitz with some of the kitchen personnel before leaving for the morning. The kitchen staff all knew these sticky buns were for Myrt!

My *social life* was still going well this season. There was a house across from our *snake ranch* on Cleveland St. that was rented by three girls. As they were neighbors, we single guys were interested and got to know them. I eventually invited one of the girls on several dates. While talking on one of the dates, and after she got to know me a little better, I was shocked by something she told me! Apparently, her father, after drinking, and on more than one occasion, raped her! I had never heard of anything as disgusting as that. I really didn't want to know the details but wondered where her mother was while all that was happing. I really felt bad for her. I think she may have been mentally scarred for life from those incidents. Very sad!

I also dated one of the HBH waitresses named Terri that year. She was fun to be with, and we hit it off well. Terri grew up in Naples, Florida. We drove across Alligator Alley a couple of times to her home where I met her parents. Jimmy Lawless called her Fat Terri and would ask me in his Irish accent, whenever he wanted to give me a hard time, "Ar u takin' out Fat Terri ta-nite?" Terri had a big chest but really wasn't fat or very heavy in my view.

Sometime during the season, I was lured into a presentation about a new land development project in Naples, Florida, by Gulf American Land Corporation. They had successfully developed Cape Coral, which incorporated a massive canal system going throughout the community. Cape Coral became a residential expansion area across the Caloosahatchee River from Fort Myers, Florida, and was home to many residences. The presentation was about GAL Corporation's new project called Golden Gate Estates. It could easily become an expansion area for the city of Naples, Florida. The line went out, and I grabbed the hook! I made an investment in a two-and-a-half-acre piece of Golden Gate Estates. The acreage consisted of eight lots that could be resold for future profit. Four of them bordered a canal that would eventually lead to the Bay of Naples then out to the Gulf of Mexico. What a deal! Of course, the whole property had to be developed and the canals dug. The timeframe was projected to be several years in the future. I put a small amount down, and the remainder was to be satisfied with a loan of forty-four dollars a month. Fast-forward three years into the future. There had been many other companies selling (scamming) Florida land during that time, most not as reputable as GAC Corp, and the market got saturated with too much land for sale and not enough buyers. Gulf American Land Corporation went bankrupt, and the canals were never dug nor the development envisioned completed. I was stuck with a $44 per month note and annual taxes to Collier County on the property!

The end of the season was nearing, the last convention had checked out, and it was time to close HBH and head north. There was a dining room waitress that I was friends with from Maine named Joanie. She was divorced and had a three-year-old son. I actually felt bad for Joanie and offered her and her son a ride to Maine with me. I was going to see my mother and Dad before starting another summer at the Griswold in Groton, Connecticut, so why not?

We closed the Hollywood Beach Hotel, and Joanie and her son traveled to Bethel, Maine, with me. I had given my mother a heads-up that I had two people that would be spending the night, so she made arrangements in the Chapman St. house for our visitors.

I was shocked when my mother started treating Joanie as a future daughter-in-law! I told her, "Mother, I'm just giving Joanie a ride home from Florida. There's nothing serious here." The next day, I drove Joanie to her parent's home in Lewiston, Maine, and returned to Bethel. OMG, I think my mother was trying to get me married and have grandchildren she could dote over.

I enjoyed the rest of my time with Dad, my mother, Ned, and Dave in Bethel. Then I drove to Groton to open the Griswold for another season. My same crew was there from last summer. I was the bell captain, and I was looking forward to the start of a great new summer. The season opened as usual, and then early in the year, two women from New York City came up for vacation. One of them was Sylvia Sali from Jackson Heights in Queens. Sylvia and I seemed to hit it off, and I remember spending a lot of time with her for the rest of her visit. When her week at the Griswold with her friend was over, Sylvia returned to Jackson Heights. I kept in touch with her.

Then one day, I received an urgent phone call from my mother. She said, "Den, I have a letter from the Selective Service that starts with 'Congratulations.'" I'd been drafted by the Army! I'd lived in Maine when I was of the age required to register for the draft and obtain a Social Security number at the Oxford County seat in South Paris, Maine, so the letter went to my address in Bethel. It was April 1962, and to my knowledge, there were no wars or conflicts anywhere in the world. My thought process was I didn't want to sleep in a tent and eat rations out of a can! As I've related previously, my father was a Navy man, as was my grandfather Kirk, so I immediately drove over to New London, Connecticut, to speak with a Navy recruiter. Apparently, the Navy recruiter was happy to see me and learn of my situation as he put his arm around my shoulder and said, "Come on, son, I'll fix this for you!" I enlisted for an obligation of three years, the minimum Navy enlistment at the time, left the Griswold, and drove back to Bethel to await orders.

CHAPTER FOURTEEN

THE START OF MY US NAVY CAREER

When the official orders came in, and because I'd enlisted in New London, Connecticut, I was ordered to report to Grand Central Station in New York City on 29 May 1962, to be sworn in. Wow, that seemed final!

Because the travel time to New York City from Maine wasn't short and my *show time* at Grand Central Station was in the morning, I called Sylvia Sali and made arrangements to stay at her house in Jackson Heights the night before my orders required me to report for duty. I said so long to Mother and Dad, left my trusty Ford Crown Vic with them, and they took me to Portland, where I boarded a plane to LGA. From LaGuardia Airport, I caught a New York City subway to a station near Sylvia's home and spent my last night (for a while) as a *civilian*.

The next morning, while Sylvia was walking me to the subway, we agreed to keep in touch with each other by mail. I caught the next subway train that took me to Grand Central Station. When I arrived, there was a large group of guys mainly from New York City boroughs who were enlisting at the same time. Many of them had coiffed hair swept back into pompadours or DAs (the first word is *duck's*) and parted in the back. They all seemed very proud of their *'dos*! At the appropriate time, we all raised our right hands and repeated the oath: "I [name] do solemnly swear I will support and defend the Constitution of the United States against all enemies, foreign and domestic, that I will bear true faith and allegiance to the same, that I take this obligation freely, without any mental reservation or purpose of evasion, and that I will faithfully discharge the duties of the position upon which I am about to enter. *So help me God.*" I took that oath *very* seriously throughout my Navy career and am still proud of upholding it now. Presidents, cabinet members, and members of Congress take this same oath. Too bad some politicians today don't seem to honor the oath they took.

By this time, it was midafternoon, and we all boarded a government-chartered train for an overnight trip to Chicago. The majority of the recruits were young, claimed a coach seat, and played cards or craps most of the night. I was twenty-three and found an unoccupied compartment, which is a semiprivate room with a pull-down bed, and slept in peace the rest of the night! Upon arriving in Chicago, a bus took us all to the Great Lakes Recruit Training Center north on Lake Michigan to start our Navy careers.

I won't go through all the boring details, but the Navy basically took the *civilian* out of us, brought us down to the basic individual, and then lifted us back up to be obedient members of the US Navy. One part of this process that I did find very amusing was our mandatory trip to the barber shop early during the training cycle. I loved it when the Navy barbers would ask the NYC boys with their cherished DAs, "How do you want it cut today?" The next step was the Navy barber took his clippers and did a *buzz cut* on everyone—their beautifully coiffed pompadour's hair falling to the floor. We all ended up with *baldies*! One of the first steps for recruits is to get Navy uniforms. I was issued a seabag full of clothing, black shoes and boots, two stencils cut out with my name and service number (683-77-99), and a bottle of white and one of black stencil ink. No matter how hard I objected, I was issued white and dress blue uniforms that were one size bigger than I wore. I was admonished, "You're going to wear size large in the Navy!"

The company commander of the company I was assigned to was DL Simmons, SF1. He was a first-class E-6 with a ship fitter rating. His job at Great Lakes was to "push boots," as they said then. There were about eighty-eight recruits in his company. Very early in the training, DL interviewed a handful of us. He was looking for leaders to get the company organized. Most of the recruits were seventeen or eighteen years of age. I believe, because I was twenty-three and had ROTC training experience in the sixteen-count manual of arms and marching orders, he chose me to be the Recruit Petty Office Chief or simply *RPOC*. I was issued a ceremonial sword and belt and wore it for the remainder of my training. Two others in the company were chosen as squad leaders. The company of recruits was now divided into two squads of roughly forty-four recruits each. At first, DL stayed with us twenty-four seven, sleeping in a private room in the barracks. Our double bunk beds were lined up on each side of the rectangular room like you may have seen in movies. We'd march *everywhere*: to chow three times a day, to classes, exercises, etc. It was my job to get everyone in formation outside the barracks and shout out the necessary marching commands to move the company wherever we were going. The squad leaders were responsible for counting cadence aloud to keep their squad in step: "left, right, left, right." I'm sure we looked like a ragtag group with not everyone in step at first, but things did come together, and we soon looked like a sharp Navy recruit company wherever we went.

Sylvia Sali kept her part of the bargain, and I'd receive two or three letters a week from her. I'd write back whenever I had the time. At Hollywood Beach Hotel, we had a habit of calling someone we were going out with frequently "the bride." A couple of times, I probably casually mentioned something about getting mail from "the bride" regarding Sylvia. I never meant it to go that far, but after a while, everyone in the company thought I was married and it had gone on too long to correct it.

Our company commander was a strict disciplinarian. Whenever the majority of the company wasn't doing something he thought we should be doing, he'd have everyone, except me, get down and do push-ups. I always felt guilty that I wasn't doing push-ups too, but that was his leadership style, and no one ever complained to me. It was fairly common for one of the recruits to not complete a week's section of the training and get pushed back a week into the company behind us. Swimming was a common requirement that some of the recruits didn't pass the first time. Conversely, we'd pick up recruits from the company ahead of us if they didn't pass a section of their training. When we got a new recruit into our company from that process, DL would find a reason, and the next thing I knew, the new recruit was being banged against one of the barrack's walls! Even the big kids were subject to this "I demand respect" type of discipline.

Probably two to three weeks into boot camp, DL started leaving us alone after the evening meal and went home to stay with his family. I was in charge, assisted by my two patrol leaders! My orders from the company commander were to get the barracks cleaned up for morning inspection, march the company to the chow hall, and meet him there. It later became the first part of this, but after breakfast, march the company to xyz event and meet him there. I was being given more and more responsibility.

There were other trainers, usually E-6s or E-7 chiefs that rode around in jeeps, checking on all the companies when their company commanders were not with them. I remember on one occasion, we'd just returned from firefighting training. Everyone had to take a shower, clean up the barracks, and fallout in formation prior to me marching them to evening chow. I had a Master-at-Arms who was in charge of supervising barracks cleanups. We had a tight schedule to get to the chow hall. Firefighting is dirty, and you'd get grit on your boots and clothing. Just as I was about to get the company going, and after my Master-at-Arms and his crew had finished cleaning up the head, along came two of the roaming leaders in their jeep. They told us to halt, and they were going to inspect the barracks before we could go to chow. When they finished the inspection, one of them said, "Who's in charge here?"

I spoke up, saying, "I am, sir."

The next words out of his mouth were "There's grit on the floor of the head. You've failed inspection. Get down and give me fifty, son." I immediately did as told and executed fifty push-ups! Again, no one ever said anything, but I had to believe there were some in the company that were pleased I'd finally had to do push-ups, and this time they could just watch.

The eight weeks passed fairly quickly, and during the last week, we all got on-base liberty for several hours late one afternoon. A small group of us who were of legal drinking age went over to the EM

(Enlisted Men's) Club on base and had our first beer in seven weeks. Just before graduation, DL had called everyone together for a secret ballot vote for the company Honor Man. He told us the criteria for selection should be the person they individually thought had done the most for the company.

Graduation day came, and all the companies formed on the grinder of Recruit Training Command Great Lakes for a parade past the reviewing stand of RTC officers. As we were approaching the reviewing stand, I gave the order, "Company, eyes right." We all looked ninety degrees to our right, and at the same time I lifted my saber up to a forty-five-degree angle and brought the hilt to my chin. We held that position until clear of the reviewing stand before I gave the order, "Company, readdddyy front."

After the parade, all the graduating companies formed up and lined up with their company members four deep in front of the reviewing stand. The Commander of RTC Great Lakes gave a congratulatory speech, and at one point each company's Honor Man was asked to come forward to receive his award. I was actually quite surprised, but my name was called. I was the only RPOC that was given that honor that day, and I was truly grateful to the company! Upon graduation from boot camp, everyone's monthly pay went from seventy-eight dollars to eighty-nine dollars, and we were promoted to E-2, in my case to seaman apprentice.

Before I left Recruit Training Command, I told DL that I'd like to have a beer with him someday soon, but we never did. He was an okay guy and helped me get through a fairly rough boot camp experience. One of my memories from boot camp was when one of the sailors would come to me and ask a question like "How do I do this or that?" I was going through this experience for the first time just like they were and often didn't know the answer! I'd do my best to get the answer for them regardless. My one regret: I should have been more sensitive to giving smoke breaks. I wasn't a smoker myself and should have found time for more frequent smoke breaks for the people who were addicted. The result was some of the guys apparently became desperate and were caught smoking in unauthorized areas outside the barracks and got demerits.

While still in boot camp, we were all given aptitude placement tests. Apparently, my engineering background at UMaine ranked my abilities toward electronics, so I was temporarily given the rating of FT for Fire Control Technician and given orders to report to the next Basic Electronics A-School class—at *Great Lakes*! I wasn't leaving the Chicago area, so no travel or leave time. It was the first part of August when I reported to A-School, which was still on the Naval Training Center in an area near boot camp, but closer to Lake Michigan. I was assigned to an old *A-type* barracks building that was constructed during WWII!

As our class didn't start for a couple of weeks, some days I'd catch a Chicago and North-Western train from the N. Chicago station to downtown Chi-Town for some *liberty*. Never having been to Chicago before, I did a little sightseeing, and then not having a lot of extra cash, I stopped into the USO where I was treated very well. There were snacks and things for servicemen and women to do for amusement. It was a great home away from home.

A-school was going very well for me, and I was learning a lot of interesting things, like vacuum tube circuits, transistor theory, capacitors, resistors, etc. There were *no* integrated circuits or *chips* invented yet. The thing that was getting challenging was the Chicago/Great Lakes weather! The old barracks was like a sieve. The wind blew off Lake Michigan and penetrated the old windows of the barracks. We'd find fine snow on the floor near the windows in the morning! Fortunately, there was an electrical plug at the head of my lower bunk. I asked Mom to send me an under sheet electric blanket, which was a huge relief after it arrived! The chow hall was across a big grinder or parade field from the barracks. When the wind was blowing the snow around, which was most of the time, I'd pull my warm pea coat over my head, button the top button, and look out of the space just below it and navigate my way across the grinder to the chow hall. I'd only eat once a day as it wasn't worth it to me fighting that trip more than once a day. I'd lived in Maine growing up and experienced -40-degree temperatures, but never such constant wind! There was a *geedunk* closer to the barracks where we'd buy a coffee and maybe a donut in the morning. Fortunately, the building housing the classrooms was closer too.

When the Chicago weather outside wasn't raging too hard, some of my classmates and I would hang out at the EM club on the base. I remember a quart bottle of Budweiser was only fifty cents! They usually had a band playing on weekends or at least DJ music for dancing. Local women were allowed into the club, which made it more interesting. I met a teacher named Mary there one evening. She was fun to be with, and I met her off and on after that at the club. Occasionally, Mary, a friend of hers, and one of my classmates and I would leave the base and go out in her car to a place Mary knew. She was a conservative mid-westerner but fun company.

A-School continued, and I was faced with choices for the next phase of my US Navy career. I was finishing at the top of my A-School class and had choices. What rating of electronic job choices should I chose? I requested FTM, which was Fire Control Technician Missile, and got it approved! Do I want to volunteer to be on one of the submarines I saw going by the Griswold Hotel in Groton, Connecticut, or did I want to request surface ships? I chose submarines and put in my request chit. "Approved!"

I did finish in first place in that Basic Electronics A-School class and took a couple of weeks' leave in Bethel, Maine, to wind down and visit Mom, Dad, and my two brothers. While on leave, I received orders to report to Sub School New London, Connecticut, NLT 25 March 1963, for training. I was going to attempt to join the select force of US Navy submariners (pronounced "sub-marine-ers"). This elite group makes up only about 2 percent of all US Navy personnel.

CHAPTER FIFTEEN

BECOMING A SUBMARINER

Sub school was probably one of the most challenging experiences of my life to date. When our class was first formed, our lead instructor told us, "Look to your left, then look to your right. One of those men will be washed out and gone by the time you graduate." The training was quite thorough. We learned the basics of underwater propulsion systems (all related to diesel boats), air, hydraulic, and electrical systems. For physical challenges, we all had to pass a *pressure test*. They put us in a 30' long x 8' diameter hyperbaric chamber with two rows of seats on each side and an air lock at one end, then increased the pressure gradually to fifty PSI. It was like being inside a tire that was being blown up! Probably, fortunately for me, two sailors needed to have the pressure built up more slowly as they couldn't equalize through their eustachian tubes and eventually had to be evacuated via the air lock. I was having trouble, but these pauses gave my ears a chance to equalize. It still hurt like hell, and when the test was done, I could shake my head and hear sloshing in one ear. We were interviewed by a doctor on the way out. He asked me if I had any abnormal symptoms, and I told him about the noise when I moved my head from side to side. He said I probably broke some blood vessels in my inner ear, but I passed the test!

The next challenge was ascending from the fifty-foot level of a tall hundred-foot escape tower on the base. This exercise was practicing escape routines from a sunken submarine. About eight to ten of us climbed up a spiral staircase outside the tower and entered a small chamber attached to the side at the fifty-foot level with our instructor. There was a closed inner door that would provide access to the inside of the tower. Each trainee wore an air-filled Mae West-type vest that had two pressure release valves on it to keep the vest from exploding during the ascent. The next step was to close the outer door, flood the chamber to about chin level, and pressurize the inside of the chamber equal to the outside tank water pressure. (At fifty feet, the pressure would be twenty-two PSI on both sides.) I remember there was a very short sailor beside me that had to grab my shoulder as the chamber was being filled because the water was rising above his nose! I didn't realize it at the time, but my experience snorkeling and scuba diving in South Florida had helped prepare me for this event. Conversely, I could tell by the fearful look in their eyes that some of my fellow sailors weren't quite so confident. Lastly, the inner door to the tank was opened, and we were instructed one by one to step out on a small platform just outside, let the vest pull us up, and exhale bubbles all the way so we wouldn't get an air embolism. If one held their breath on the way up, pressure of the air in the escape chamber was greater than surface air pressure, and your lungs could rupture. The divers inside the tower were doctors and ensured the trainees weren't going to do something harmful to themselves. If a trainee wasn't exhaling, they'd be pulled into one of the small chambers along the ascent route by one of the doctor/divers.

When it became my turn for the ascent, I confidently took a deep breath, stepped through the small hatch into the escape chamber, and pushed off the small ledge. I was on my way up! Wrong. I hadn't followed orders, and someone inside the tower grabbed my legs and held me for a moment. Oh crap! As I was ascending, I was looking up and could see the water color changing. I thought, *When will I get to the surface?* It seemed like an eternity! There were divers all along the ascent path. Just as I thought I was running out of breath, I popped out of the water and could breathe air again! That ascent successfully completed, one more was required to pass this part of the training, so I did. And I did!

One of the final required sections of sub school was a battery of physiological tests. Some of the questions seemed weird, like "Why do you hate your mother?" and other questions that didn't make any sense to me, but apparently, I passed those tests too. One of the fun requirements was spending a day or *kiddy cruise* on an operational US Navy submarine. Our class was scheduled to go out on SS346, the USS *Corporal*, a Guppy III boat, on 10 April 1963. I was really looking forward to that day and had written to my mother about it.

The *Corporal* had been built during WWII, so it was around twenty years old. I remember having lunch in the crew's mess while on board. Right above where I was eating was one of the main vent operating assemblies. These vents were operated hydraulically from the control room. The only problem was there was a leak in this one and a slow dripping of hydraulic oil into my food!

Unbeknownst to us aboard the *Corporal*, the USS *Thresher* (SSN-593) had been lost that same day during deep-diving tests about 220 miles east of Boston, Massachusetts. The *Thresher* was the lead boat of her class of nuclear-powered attack submarines. She had come out of the Portsmouth (NH) Naval Shipyard that morning with 129 sailors and civilians aboard. All lost their lives that sad day. The official Navy report of the accident was that there had been major flooding in the engine room when they were down deep. Nuclear submarines were powered by a reactor and large steam-driven turbine. The nuclear reactor superheats water in a high-pressure primary loop. Heat from that loop is transferred to a secondary loop and nozzles aimed at the turbine blades. The nozzles produce steam, causing turbine rotation. The final phase of the secondary loop is converting steam back into liquid, then the loop cycle is repeated. A sixteen-inch intake hole in the hull and another sixteen-inch exit hole cycles seawater through that system to cool the steam into liquid again. This system is duplicated in the port and starboard loops. That results in four sixteen-inch hull valves and four more sixteen-inch backup valves protecting these huge hull openings. The Navy thinks the flooding started in the area of that system.

That flooding failure alone wouldn't necessarily have caused the *Thresher* to go to the bottom; however, there was apparently a second failure. The Captain would have ordered an emergency blow of the main ballast tanks to quickly achieve positive buoyancy. During an emergency blow, pressurized 3,000 PSI air from storage containers inside the ballast tanks is released by valves into the main ballast tanks to quickly force out the seawater. The emergency blow valves on the *Thresher* froze due to a poor valve design, and high-pressure air stopped flowing into the ballast tanks! The *Thresher* was doomed at this point. It must have been a helpless feeling for the Captain and crew to have executed all the correct emergency procedures, but still feel the boat sinking downward toward crush depth.

My mother heard about the *Thresher* loss and frantically called the New London sub base commander knowing I was aboard a submarine that day. I'm sure she never actually spoke to the base commander, but she was comforted to learn that the boat I was on safely returned to port!

I wasn't first in my sub school class, but I was one of the top five. Upon our graduation ceremony, I became Dennis Robertson, FTMSN (SU) for submariner unqualified. I'd advanced to E-3, FTMSN during A-School. (At that time, there were two FT ratings: FTM for Fire Control Technician Missile and FTG for Fire Control Technician Gun. I would be trained on missile systems.)

Note: reference the Appendix, item II, for a poem that I wrote during this period.

My next orders were to Dam Neck, Virginia, for *C-School*. I was to report NLT 7 June 1963. Guided Missile School in Dam Neck, Virginia, curriculum for me was a ten-month-long intensive study of the MK 84 fire control (more accurately, "missile firing") system and the Polaris missile itself. I'd originally signed up for a three-year *hitch* in the Navy, but to qualify for this extended C-School, the Navy required a six-year commitment. I had developed a new and exciting technical interest in electronics while in the Navy, so I committed myself for the required six years! On December 10, 1963, while at Dam Neck, I was discharged from the Navy, the remainder of my three-year obligation was forgiven, and I signed a new contract for six years.

The Guided Missile School campus itself was quite nice! It was on the Atlantic Ocean with new classroom buildings, a beach, and EM and officer clubs that were directly on the beach. Not a bad place to have to spend ten months! I didn't have a car here, but I really didn't need one either. The resort town of Virginia Beach was about seven miles north of Dam Neck, and there was a Navy bus that ran regularly between the two locations. This was a *great* duty station!

My ten months in Dam Neck were a *very* enjoyable time in my Navy career! Our classes were challenging, but by the same token, I gained not only an in-depth knowledge of new concepts of both analog and digital electronics but also current space and missile technology. I was in my element and loving it! Classroom technical challenges mixed with good shipmates and beach environments like the EM Club and nearby Virginia Beach rounded out my world. Life was good!

My shipmates/classmates were also enjoyable to be with. Tom Solywoda from Red Hook, New York, and I quickly became friends. Soly had sort of a self-confident, challenging attitude that I understood but didn't always agree with. A couple of our other classmates had a band that included two fellow sailors playing guitars and one of their girlfriends who sang, plus a manager that was booking the band gigs at local VB (Virginia Beach) clubs on the beach. I acted as an assistant manager for the band. We did okay, and it was fun booking the gigs and watching our fellow sailors entertain beach bar patrons.

This was the period when many folk groups were just getting started. One of our classmates in the barracks had a stereo record player in his locker. He'd frequently pull it out and play new $33\frac{1}{3}$ rpm albums by upcoming groups. One of my favorites was Peter, Paul and Mary. They were just starting to get recognition in 1963 and had released an album that included "Puff, the Magic Dragon." They had also performed "If I Had a Hammer" and "Blowin' in the Wind" at the 1963 March on Washington. Suddenly, our band learned that Peter, Paul and Mary were coming to a bar on the beach here in VB! We *had* to go see them, and when the night of their appearance came, we were there!

After their performance, we all approached them and introduced ourselves. I was mesmerized meeting such stars that I admired so much! I thought the young Mary Travis was beautiful. We did ask PP&M one professional question (as it had happened to our band frequently): "What do you do when the crowd starts talking louder and some people obviously can't hear your music? Do you raise the volume?"

I think it was Peter Yaro who replied, "No, we just start playing lower and lower until the crowd notices what's happening and starts listening again." I'll never forget that advice from a legendary group whose music I still admire today!

The summer was going by rapidly. The Navy subject matter was still very interesting, which made it easier for me to enjoy these classes. My classmates and I generally spent leisure time on base at the EM Club at a beach table, but whenever we could afford it, we went into VB. I remember one or two nights when my friends and I were having so much fun in Virginia Beach that we missed the last bus to the base. As resourceful submarine sailors, we found a comfortable spot under the boardwalk and slept there for the night.

While at Dam Neck, I was eligible to take the advancement exam for E-4, which I passed and was advanced to PO Third Class. The only *rub* was there were no Navy advancement tests for ballistic missile Fire Control Technicians like myself, so we had to take the E-4 advancement exam for surface or FTG sailors. I had obtained a manual for the E-4 FTG requirements and learned surface fire control systems that I'd never even seen in order to pass the exam!

An event that most of us who experienced it will never forget is the assignation of John F. Kennedy in Dallas, Texas. It was November 22, 1963, and I was in class at Dam Neck when someone came into the room and told us to turn on the classroom TV. We all watched in horror as the news unfolded! Having turned twenty-one in February, the November 1960 presidential election was the first one that I was eligible to vote in. I'd voted for JFK as I felt he was going to breathe some fresh young air into the presidency. Now it had suddenly ended before he had a chance to accomplish many of his goals.

During my time at Dam Neck, Virginia, my social life had almost come to a complete *stop* as far as dating was concerned. This gave me ample time to reflect upon and evaluate my past life. I came to the conclusion that Diane Beattie was the one person who was not only fun to be with, but she shared many common interests with me, and perhaps more importantly, she had the honesty and morals of the person I'd want to spend the rest of my life with. I decided to write a letter to Diane. I knew her home was in Ridgefield Park, New Jersey, and I thought her address was 525 Teaneck Road, so I wrote the letter and mailed it. I later learned her correct address was 517 Teaneck Road! Fortunately, her neighbor who lived next door at 525 Gaye Ten Eyck delivered the letter to Diane!

When the year 1964 arrived, I was still attending C-School at Dam Neck. Classes were going well, but it was winter in Southern Virginia, and my classmates and I were not hanging out in Virginia Beach or sitting outside the EM club anymore. At the end of March 1964, I graduated first in my C-School class and received orders to report to USS *James Madison*, SSBN627 NLT 22 April 1964. The Madison was in Newport News Ship Building and Dry Dock's yard being overhauled. The *Thresher* tragedy had caused the Navy to redesign the main ballast tank blow valves, and all the submarines of that type with the original valves were having the new design installed in a program called Sub Safe.

I took two week's leave before reporting aboard SSBN627. We had been writing back and forth while I was finishing C-School, and I had made arrangements to meet Diane at her home in Ridgefield Park, New Jersey, during my leave and on my way to Bethel, Maine, to pick up my car. I caught a flight to LaGuardia in New York City and rented a car for the trip to New Jersey. As I was traveling under orders, I was in full dress blue uniform, complete with my white *Dixie Cup* hat. When Diane met me at her front door, she had a little kitten on her shoulder. She invited me in, and while she went into the kitchen to get us a soda, I sat in the living room. While Diane was in the kitchen getting our drinks, Grandma Berry came into the kitchen and asked Diane, "Who's that sailor boy sitting in the living room?"

Diane replied, "That's Dennis Robertson from Hollywood."

To which Grandma replied, "Oh, go on with ya!"

I visited with Diane and Grandma Berry (Diane's parents weren't home) and then headed back to LaGuardia to catch a plane to Portland where Dad would be waiting to pick me up. Diane followed me back to the airport in her parents' car, and we continued talking until time for me to board. I was probably initially a bit nervous as I approached her home, but it was great seeing and talking with her again!

My visit to Mother, Dad, and my brothers was only several days, then I got into my car and drove to Newport News and the USS *James Madison* where I dropped off my seabag on the Madison's barge in the shipyard, parked my car, and boarded a plane to Miami for a visit with Father and Evelyn before reporting for duty aboard my first submarine. I had a nice visit at 133 SW 13th Street. We went to dinner several times, and I again enjoyed the city where I was born!

While in Miami, I received a change of orders telegram from the Navy. Instead of reporting to the Madison, I was ordered to report to USS *James Monroe*, SSBN622. The *Monroe* was also in Newport News Ship Building and Dry Dock Company's yards for PSA (Post Shakedown Availability). She had just completed firing two missiles down the Atlantic missile range and sound trials off Andros Island in the Bahamas. PSA is the Navy's last chance to get minor things corrected and updates performed by the ship's builder before it entered the fleet.

The reason for the change of orders was the Navy had carefully planned new FBM submarine construction coming into the fleet and crew training completion so they would coincide appropriately. With the *Thresher* disaster and resulting Sub Safe rollout delays, the submarine crews were entering the fleet before the physical individual submarines were ready to deploy.

As 22 April 1964, approached, I left Miami, said goodbye to Father and Evelyn, and flew to Newport News, Virginia. My first stop once reaching Newport News Ship Building and Dry Dock Company was to the Madison's barge to retrieve my seabag and take it over to the *Monroe's* barge and report for duty. We were all issued hard hats and security badges that were required to be worn anytime we were in the shipyard.

On the way to the USS *James Monroe's* barge, I remember walking under the bow of the aircraft carrier USS *America* (CV-66) that was under construction at Newport News SB&DD Co. during that time. It was afloat with the most forward part of the bow at the waterline at least a hundred feet away from the pier. As one would walk under it, the top of the bow at the flight deck level must have extended at least another 250 feet farther forward in the other direction and a minimum of five stories over my head. The ship was enormous!

The Navy had spent one month short of two years preparing me for this job. No wonder they required a six-year commitment before starting the training! While at Dam Neck very early in the training cycle, I was required to fill out a Statement of Personal History. The FTM rating I was trained for required a Top-Secret clearance, and this document was gathering information to start that process. It took nine months to complete, but I had my TS before going into the fleet. I later learned that agents of the DNI (Department of Naval Intelligence) had gone to *many* places where I lived in the past, including Bethel, Maine, and questioned neighbors about me in the process of completing my background check.

CHAPTER SIXTEEN

MY FIRST BOAT

The USS *James Monroe* was a Lafayette class (SSBN616) FBM submarine. She was 425 feet long, had a hull diameter of thirty-three-feet, and drew about thirty-two feet of water! The boat displaced almost 8,250 tons of seawater when submerged. Inside there were seven compartments separated by watertight doors, from fore to aft: torpedo room, operations compartment, missile compartment, auxiliary machinery room number 1 (AMR1), AMR2, reactor compartment, and engine room. The operations and missile compartments had three full deck levels. Others except the single level torpedo and engine rooms had two levels. It was a *big* boat! She was powered by a Westinghouse S5W reactor that drove a single, thirty-three-foot screw to move the boat through the water in excess of twenty knots. The *Monroe* had four forward torpedo tubes for defense and carried a 16 Polaris A2 ballistic missile payload for offense.

All FBM submarines have two crews, Blue and Gold, when operational. Each crew has the boat for about three months on a rotating basis. In the yards, both crews were together, and because shipyard workers or *yard birds* were working on the boat during three shifts a day, we slept on floating barges near the boat in the shipyard. Each barge had a ship's office and berthing for the whole crew.

In a short time, I met my Gold crew FTM shipmates. There was Chief Lowe, Larry Fetter, "Cowboy" Preston, "Soupy" Campbell, Ed Strosnyder, and several others. It was a totally new experience for me, but I had no trouble integrating with the fire control gang! The Gold crew skipper was CDR. Warren Cobean, LT. Kavanagh was the

Weapons Officer, and LT. MacGregor was our AWeps. These last two officers were responsible for our team of FTMs, MT missile technicians, and Torpedomen. The total USS *James Monroe* crew consisted of 14 officers and 130 enlisted sailors.

During PSA, I saw the *Monroe* in a floating dry dock, and I realized just how huge these FBM submarines really are! The dry dock is flooded and lowered into the water so the sub can be directed into the dry dock until resting on a set of blocks. Next, water is pumped out of the huge tanks inside the dry dock's walls. This causes the dry dock to gain positive buoyancy and float upward, which exposes the whole outside of the sub's hull. The *Monroe* was then cleaned and given a fresh coat of marine paint. Seeing an FBM sub's exposed hull like that for the first time is an amazing sight. Only about one-seventh of the sub is visible when on the surface. The other six-sevenths are below the waterline.

Newport News, Virginia, was an interesting town, very industrial, and with a generally poor population. Newport News Ship Building and Dry Dock Company was the largest employer in the city. There wasn't much very exciting to do near the shipyard. The restaurants were all fast junk food types, and there was an assortment of tattoo parlors nearby as one would expect to find near any Navy base or area where there were military personnel. (BTW, I never had the urge to get a tattoo!) I found a Chinese laundry near the shipyard that did a great job on my dungarees and pressed two vertical creases in my chambray work shirts in just the right places, and all at a reasonable price.

At the end of May 1964, I had completed two years in the Navy, and my base pay went up from $125 per month to $175 per month. Plus by then, I was receiving hazardous duty pay of $100 per month and a proficiency pay, level 3, of another $75 per month. The Navy offered three levels of *pro pay*: P1, P2, and P3. These were designed to encourage sailors to enter the ratings that the Navy was having trouble filling. At $75 per month, P3 was the highest paying level.

USS *James Monroe*—SSBN622

SSBN622 launching, Newport News, VA

SSBN622 in dry dock

USS *James Monroe* commissioning, Newport News, VA

A2 missile firing during DASO, Cape Kennedy

USS *James Monroe* on initial sea trials, off Virginia Coast

SSBN622 swim call, Andros Island, Bahamas

About four or five weeks after I reported aboard, USS *James Monroe's* PSA was completed. She left Newport News, Virginia, and traveled south to Naval Weapons Station, Charleston, South Carolina, to load 16 Polaris A2 missiles prior to departing on her first patrol with the Blue crew in command. The single sailors of our Gold crew were transferred to a barracks on the Charleston, South Carolina, Submarine Base, SSBN622's new home port.

During this time, I was in constant communication with Diane back in New Jersey. Diane was working in New York City on Forty-eighth Street and Fifth Avenue at the advertising agency of Ogilvy, Benson & Mather. I was *very* seriously in love for the first time in my life and asked her to marry me. When Diane finally accepted, I purchased a diamond ring shaped like *a football* at GEX. (I later learned it was called a marquis setting.) As I was remote, I *romantically* sent the ring in the mail! During my first visit to her home in Ridgefield Park, Diane told me she was currently engaged to Steve Massie, someone she'd known from her grandmother's summer cottage in Breezy Point, New York, since she was young. I'd actually seen Steve and Diane in a drugstore on Hollywood Beach after we stopped going out in 1962. Apparently, when Diane broke off the engagement, it was quite traumatic for Steve.

When I told my mother and father about the engagement, my mother was ecstatic, and my father said, "I'm surprised you'd buy a pair of shoes without trying them on first, Chum?" He always called me either Chum or Dum-Dum. Nothing like positive parental support!

Our Gold crew had a couple of relatively leisurely months interrupted only by some refresher training classes at the Charleston sub base while the Blue crew had the boat on its first patrol. I was in contact with Diane, and we set a wedding date of October 31, 1964 (Halloween) for when I returned from patrol. Diane and her parents started the wedding planning process!

Our Gold crew was scheduled to relieve the Blue crew in Rota, Spain, when the *Monroe* returned from patrol. When the day came, we boarded two MATS (Military Air Transport Service) KC135s operated by the Air Force at Air Force Base Charleston and took off for Spain. The KC135 was a military version of the commercial Boeing 707 aircraft. The big difference is the optional seats are mounted facing aft for safety, and there are no frills or insulation inside the skin of the aircraft. The Air Force personnel had given us all a small pillow as we boarded. I didn't realize it at the time, but that pillow came in handy during ascent to cruising altitude and upon descent for landing as condensation formed on the aircraft's inner skin and dripped down on the sailors seated below! We used the pillow as a shield to deflect the dripping water. KC135s didn't have the range to make it to Rota, even following a *great circle* route, so we had to stop in Gander, Newfoundland, to refuel.

We landed in Rota, Spain, the next morning and were transferred by bus to sub tender AS-19, USS *Proteus*, moored at a pier on the base. The typical scenario is for the relieving crew to be berthed on the tender for three days during a change of command process. During the period, both crews met in their assigned spaces aboard the boat and discussed specific items that need to be repaired and *turn over items*—what went well on the patrol and what needed to be fixed before returning to sea. After the formal change of command ceremony on deck, both Blue and Gold Captains exchanged responsibilities and the other crew (Blue in this case) got on two KC135s for their return to the USA and their families.

The Gold crew moved from the *Proteus* and onto the *Monroe*, and we all began our preparations to take this awesome vessel on its second deterrent patrol. It was a challenging undertaking, but we were up to it! Our skipper, CDR Warren Cobean, was a seasoned submarine officer and respected by his crew. Our XO for this patrol was LCDR Richard Lumsden. The boat was in *port and starboard* duty sections during our time beside the tender. This meant one half of the crew had the duty for twenty-four hours, and the other half had it for the next twenty-four hours on a rotational basis. As the Navy was sensitive to local Spaniard's feelings of having a nuclear submarine docked nearby in their country, no uniforms were allowed while on liberty, only civilian clothes. Of course, with our short haircuts and American accents, it was quite obvious who we were!

The town of Rota, Spain, had become a typical Navy *watering hole* after the US Navy moved in (and spoiled it?) some years ago, with bars springing up, the availability of *putas*, and just about anything else a sailor wanted while on liberty. I can't say I didn't go into Rota and have a drink with my shipmates, because I did. There was more to this area of Spain that I came to love, however. Rota is in the region of Spain known as Andalusía. Andalusía is steeped in history. At one point in time, the Moors invaded that area of Spain and remained for eight hundred years until finally being expelled by the Spanish. During that time, many buildings were built that had a Muslim influence. The Alhambra in Granada is a good example. There is a rich tradition of Spanish gentlemen and ladies riding on fine Andalusían horses and many Spanish sherry bodegas. There also exists in this region an abundance of pride that emanates from the Andalusían's heritage. These are proud people.

I quickly learned that the *Proteus* had a recreation staff of sailors whose job it was to arrange local tours, for example, to a sherry bodega in Jerez de la Fonterra or a nearby Spanish historic attraction, for anyone who was interested. This group would even book trips to bullfights and the like. During our time before going on patrol, the Gold FTMs took advantage of these services and saw a lot of Andalusía!

Besides the different Spanish culture, I always felt the air smelled curiously different in Rota. Just outside the base, one could walk out near a jetty protecting the harbor, and you could see colorful fishing boats and grizzled old fishermen tending their nets. It was unlike anything I'd ever seen stateside! Rota is on the Atlantic Ocean side of Spain and adjacent to the Bay of Cadiz. The town of El Puerto de Santa Maria, Spain, on the Bay of Cadiz was another liberty spot and was only a cab ride from the Navy base. I remember a restaurant and bar called El Cangrejo Rojo (the Red Crab) in El Puerto de Santa Maria. There were a lot of German tourists in Spain, and I recall a couple of us talking about computer technology with a German citizen on holiday who worked for IBM in Germany. Puerto and Cadiz were a cut above Rota, probably because they were away from the US Navy base a bit.

One very different thing from life in the US that I observed while in Spain was the Guardia Civil (Civil Guard) who were *everywhere*. Francisco Franco was the dictator of Spain during this period, and he ruled with an iron fist. Two uniformed Guardia *policemen* typically rode around on a single Vespa-type motor scooter, each with an automatic rifle over their shoulder and brimmed patent leather hats with the back turned up. On more than one occasion, I saw them jump off their scooter and start beating someone on the street. We had no idea what that person had done, but we didn't want to be the attention of those Guardia Civil thugs!

While the new charm of Spain was intriguing for me, our crew had a mission to accomplish, and that was to ready the USS *James Monroe* for its second patrol. The missile fire control system had been turned over in good shape by the Blue crew. We typically had a couple of SPALTS (Special Project Alterations) to the various subsystems we maintained to install, but otherwise all our systems were *go* for another deterrent patrol.

About two-thirds of the way through the upkeep period, the boat would get underway for *sea trials*, basically a shakedown trial run prior to patrol. This would involve *angles and dangles* to make sure all interior items were secured and wouldn't break loose during patrol. Once we got out into the Atlantic Ocean where it was deep enough, we'd go to *test depth*, checking out all the ship's systems under stress. I have to admit, this was a stressful drill for some of us. The Captain would take the boat down a hundred feet at a time and the OOD (Officer of the Deck) at the Conn would announce over the 1MC, "Check for leaks" after each increment of a hundred feet. The exact depth is still classified, but I can tell you if you stretched a line (rope) tautly between both sides of the operations or missile compartments on the inside of the hull before the deep dive, it would have a huge sag in the middle of the line at test depth! Overheads buckled and decks that normally had at least an inch between their outer edges and the pressure hull would meet each other. The pressure of the seawater at that depth literally compressed the hardest type of steel, HY80, available at the time.

Several days after sea trials were successfully completed and we were tied up beside the tender, the COB (Chief of the Boat) announced over the 1MC, "All hands lay topside to load stores." This operation literally involved every able sailor on the boat! Officers supervised, and the rest of us formed a chain, passing everything we'd possibly need for the next sixty to seventy-two days from the tender to our belowdecks storage areas. It was a massive operation taking three to four hours by all hands, but it was going to be our vital food supply while submerged.

We made some final preparations for a day or two, then cast off our lines from the *Proteus* and got underway. USS *James Monroe* headed out into the Atlantic Ocean until we reached a depth in which we could safely dive and *pulled the plug*. Inside the boat, we heard the Claxton sound, "Auh ooga, auh ooga" and then "dive, dive" over the 1MC from the OOD! The mighty boat and its crew were off on a sixty to seventy-two-day deterrent mission during the Cold War with the USSR to help keep our country safe from nuclear attack.

CHAPTER SEVENTEEN

LIFE ON AN FBM DETERRENT PATROL

From Rota, there were several patrol areas where the USS *James Monroe* would have orders from SUBRON 16 to operate. Most of the enlisted crew weren't told where our patrol path would take us. It was on a *need-to-know* basis only. (Per *Jane's Fighting Ships*, the pattern for FBM patrols was set by the range of the Polaris missile itself, which initially was restricted to the Norwegian Sea because of the A2 missile's short 1,500 nautical mile range.)

Because of the *Thresher* incident and subsequent Sub Safe alterations and delays of deployment for all new subs, the USS *James Monroe* had an abundance of men aboard. As the junior FTM, I would not be standing watches in Missile Control Center (MCC) but rather, my duty station for my first patrol would be *diving and driving* in the Control Room!

The Control Room was in the upper level of the operations compartment toward the after end of the compartment. There was a raised platform where all the ship's periscopes terminated within the boat and where the OOD (Officer of the Deck) had the "deck and the conn," Physically, the Control Room was directly below the external *sail* of the submarine. The ballast control panel (or BCP) and the diving station were in front of the OOD's raised platform so he could observe everything going on with control of his submarine. In the control room on the quartermaster's table (BQN), a chart indicated the boat's position and course. Latitudes and longitudes were clearly marked, and the Captain, Navigator, and OOD knew where we were headed.

The diving station consisted of two planesmen sitting behind aircraft shaped steering *yokes* and a Diving Officer. The three functions of the rudder for steering, the sail planes for depth control, and the stern planes for up or down angles of the boat could be electrically switched between either of the two yokes. Typically, one planesman controlled the depth and angle of the boat and the other the heading. In front of this station were gauges that indicated position of the various control surfaces, like rudder, sail planes, compass heading bearings, and a depth gauge. I was one of the planesmen for the first part of the patrol. Controlling an 8,250-ton submarine when submerged sounds like a tremendous responsibility, but it was actually a junior enlisted position. I'd had no previous experience, but I picked it up very quickly!

We traveled submerged for a number of days before reaching our patrol area. The crew was now in three section duty: on for six hours then off for twelve hours while the other two sections had the watch. We had daily movies in the crew's mess for entertainment, and of course, sleep was a necessity. As we had no contact with the world above us, a twenty-four-hour day was foreign to us. On this duty cycle, we were effectively living an eighteen-hour day cycle.

As a *non-qual*, I was expected to work on getting to know *all* of the boat's electric, hydraulic, and air systems (including the nuclear reactor), hull openings, shut off valves, and be able to answer questions by other ratings. In submarines, probably more than most branches of the military, each crew member depends upon the other. For example, if flooding occurred in a compartment a sailor didn't usually stand a watch in, that person needed to know where to shut off a hull valve, secure a system, or otherwise respond to the emergency. *Non-quals* who didn't keep up an acceptable pace of getting systems signed off were subject to restrictions on the boat, like no evening movie.

We all had *qual cards* that had to be signed off by a person knowledgeable about the system in his area of responsibility. I worked on qualification in submarines whenever I was off duty. I was anxious to earn my coveted *dolphins!* In my spare time, I'd go to MCC and hang out with my FTB brothers. (Somewhere along the way, Fire

Control Technicians on FBM submarines classification was changed from *M* for missile to *B* for ballistic missile.)

The chow on a submarine is outstanding, perhaps to partially compensate for the stressful conditions we lived with each day! The Navy has a daily allowance per person aboard its surface ships, but the daily allowance for submariners was more than for surface ships. There was a freezer and a walk-in chill refrigerator aboard. Fresh vegetables and the like stored in the chill fridge would run out in three to four weeks, but great while they lasted! Breakfasts were just about anything you'd want, from scrambled eggs to omelets, but dinners were what I looked forward to. *J5* or steak was my favorite. Lunches were basic, but because of sailors being on duty twenty-four seven, our cooks would have a *mid-rats* snack-type meal for those getting off the midnight watch.

FBM submarines basically only need to know two things to accurately be able to launch their missiles if the USA was ever attacked by an adversary: the enemy target's position on earth and the exact position of the FBM sub itself. The first element of the firing equation is fixed. Knowing our *exact* earth's position was a bit more complex. In the navigation room directly behind the Conn in upper level ops, there were four SINS (Ship's Inertial Navigation System) pods. They were a complex system of stable platforms and gyros. As gyros would drift after a certain number of hours, the *posit output* would become less accurate. There were several methods to correct this, each of which required that the boat come to periscope depth. The Captain could raise the Type II periscope and *shoot stars* (it was basically a sextant) or raise the satellite mast and await a Transit Satellite to rise and set. This was actually an orbiting satellite that would be uploaded with updated position data from a transmitting antenna somewhere in the Midwest, and as it passed over our position, it would make the position data available via the boat's satellite periscope to our NavETs (or navigation ETs) aboard. Armed with either or both of these updated position fixes, the NavETs would enter this data into the SINS devices to reset them. Accurate ship's latitude and longitude data was constantly being transmitted to our fire control computers!

Sometimes when we'd go to periscope depth to get one or both of these position fixes, we'd encounter State 7 seas (forty-foot waves)! While this may seem like a fairly routine procedure, the weather very quickly confirmed to me where we were patrolling! Picture trying to keep a 425-foot long, 8,250-ton submarine precisely at seventy-two feet periscope depth with forty-foot waves all around you! The one thing an FBM on patrol *never* wanted to do was to *broach* or let the conning tower stick out of the water, which could give our position away to Ivan! While the planesmen were doing their best under the circumstances, you'd hear the Captain or OOD ordering, "Get me up! Get me up!" as the tip of the periscope dipped below the water!

I continued diving and driving and working to get my qual card signed off for the first part of the patrol and was then relieved of my planesman duties and started standing watches in MCC. By now, all the fresh produce in the chill refrigerator had been consumed, and we started getting more frozen food to eat. It was still better than aboard a surface vessel, but without the variety.

A couple of weeks before the end of our seventy-two-day patrol, you could see people starting to get touchy. For me, personally, people's mannerisms that wouldn't normally bother me *did*, and these were mostly little things that living in such close quarters for so long exacerbated. The other issue was boredom. Our Chief of the Boat, or COB, was Ezra Boone, who was a great COB, but he never stopped talking! We'd nicknamed him *Loudmouth Lime* after a favorite *bug juice* flavor of the day. The COB had qualified as Diving Officer and had the watch in the control room one period. About ten or twelve of us were off duty in the crew's lounge, and someone came up with a plan! Like all modern submarines, the *Monroe* had a forward and an after trim tank. The purpose of which is to trim the boat fore and aft when submerged. If the bow was a bit heavy, seawater in the forward trim tank would be pumped aft to the rear trim tank in the engine room to *balance the boat*. Otherwise, the planesmen would have to keep a slight up pressure on the stern planes to keep the boat level as it moved through the water, and that wasn't very efficient.

So now that you have that submarine knowledge, let me explain our group's next moves. We'd all go forward as far as possible into the torpedo room. We could hear the trim tank valve open and water being pumped out of the forward trim tank sending it aft. When the pumping stopped and the valve closed, we'd all walk aft into the engine room and within earshot of the after trim tank valve and pump. Same drill: valve opens, water pumped out and forward, pumping stops, and valve closes. Now it's time to repeat as we all went forward into the torpedo room again. I'm not sure how many times we repeated that maneuver, but we were very bored, so it could have been many! When we got tired of the *game*, we all went up to the dive station in the control room and started laughing at the COB. He immediately knew why he was having *trim issues* and vowed to get even with us!

As our seventy-two-day patrol was coming to an end, the Navigator plotted a course south and back toward Rota. At the appropriate time when we were close enough, the boat began its surfacing check list. The normal procedure when surfacing, is to go to periscope depth, raise the #1 scope, and check for surface traffic while manually rotating the scope 360 degrees from the Conn. Low and behold, there was a *fishing boat* in the area as if it had been waiting for us.

Assured we weren't going to surface under another vessel, the OOD sounded the Claxton three times. "Auh Ooga, Auh Ooga, Auh Ooga," and then over the 1MC announced, "Surface, surface, surface." High pressure air at 3,000 PSI was released normally into the main ballast tanks. The *Monroe* gained positive buoyancy and continued up to the surface. The good boat and crew had been totally submerged for over two months, and we hadn't surfaced or gone ashore to a liberty port during that whole time as the surface Navy does!

We continued to the surface, and the OOD, Captain, and two lookouts climbed up to the auxiliary conning station in the forward top section of the sail. It was confirmed then that the vessel was not merely a *fishing boat* but a Russian trawler with more antennas sticking up from its deck than a porcupine!

The trawler caught up with us from behind and was making crisscross paths across our wake. I assume trying to get radiation samples or whatever from our wake. Just short of us entering the marker buoys that would lead us into the Navy Base, the trawler veered to starboard and disappeared over the horizon. I heard later that this didn't happen all the time, but it did occasionally.

When the USS *James Monroe* tied up next to sub tender USS *Holland* (who had relieved USS Proteus while we were on patrol), she had completed her second Polaris deterrent patrol! It was October 1964. After a while, I came topside just to see land again, and I remember how almost foul that first breath of *fresh* air smelled! We'd been living in a perfectly controlled, pure air environment, and the smell of that *fresh* air just seemed strange. The returning crew was not allowed to go ashore on liberty after returning from that patrol cycle. Guess the Navy understood the enlisted sailor libido and decided against it!

After a three-day turnover and change of command ceremony topside with the Blue crew, we boarded two MATS KC135 transport jets and took the long flight home to Charleston AF Base's airfield. As I recall, we again stopped in Gander, Newfoundland, to refuel on the way home.

Diane and I had set a wedding date of October 31, and her father had made all the wedding arrangements for that date. I thought everything was all set. I was very much looking forward to seeing her again! My first call after arriving at the sub base in Charleston was to Ridgefield Park, New Jersey, and Diane! To my great surprise (and disappointment), when I spoke with her, she told me she had cold feet and had told her parents to cancel the wedding plans. OMG, what a horrible turn of events! I was an E-4 and not making a lot of money, but I'd put a financial plan together while I was at sea and thought, with some savings, I would be able to support us initially after marriage. Being discouraged, I sort of gave up, and after a trip to Ft. Sumter Chevrolet in Charleston, I bought a 1964 Chevy Corvair Monza. The Corvair was Chevy's equivalent to a Volkswagen. It had a rear 4-cylinder, air cooled engine and a 4-speed stick manual transmission. It got great mileage and cornered well due to its low center of gravity and rear engine that added weight to the rear wheels.

I continued to talk with Diane by phone and suggested that I drive up to talk with her, which she finally agreed to. It was *off crew time* for the *Monroe* Gold crew, and we all had thirty days that were call-in muster only and pretty much the crew's time to refresh from the long patrol duty. I drove the new Corvair to Diane's home, and we talked for hours. At one point, Diane told me she'd like to meet my mother and Dad, and we drove to Bethel, Maine, to visit with them. I'm sure Diane was a bit nervous as she'd never met either of my Maine parents. The visit went well, and during the course of our time in Maine, Diane again decided she wanted to marry me! She called her father, Daddy Jim, and he scrambled to again put a wedding together, this time in one week!

Visiting future parents-in-law, Bethel, Maine

Dennis and Diane with Corvair

USS *James Monroe*—SSBN622

Angles and dangles
during sea trials

Larry Fetter at ITOP
Console during WSRT

Slot car track, crew's mess, on patrol

Robbie, by DGBC, on patrol

LPO Lowe in MCC on
patrol (notice tape player)

MCC watch standers at
firing console on patrol

USS *James Monroe*—SSBN622

Cowboy and Robbie
on liberty in Spain

Cowboy and Larry Fetter
on liberty in Cadiz

SSBN622 tied up beside USS
Holland in Rota, Spain

USS *James Monroe*, underway

Gold crew awaiting bus to
go home, Rota, Spain

Off-crew party at Fetter's
home on James Island, SC

CHAPTER EIGHTEEN

THE MARRIAGE OF DIANE BEATTIE AND DENNIS ROBERTSON

I was ecstatic, and I think Diane felt more comfortable with the marriage after having seen me again and meeting my mother and Dad. As I mentioned, Diane's father, Jim, now only had a week to put the wedding together. The date of November 7, 1964, was set.

We drove back to Diane's home on Teaneck Road in Ridgefield Park, New Jersey, and serious plans for our wedding continued! Before I went on patrol, we had to furnish the necessary documents to allow St. Francis Catholic Church in Ridgefield Park to verify that we were both eligible to get married in the Catholic church. This wasn't a problem for Diane as she was a member of the parish, but for me it required my baptismal certificate from Sts. Peter and Paul in Miami, and I had to pass a refresher course in Catholicism as I hadn't been a practicing Catholic after leaving Miami. Fortunately, those details had been resolved before I left on USS *James Monroe*'s first Gold patrol.

Our wedding was going to take place on Saturday, November 7, 1964, at 3:00 p.m. As neither my Mother and Dad from Maine nor Father and Evelyn from Miami were going to be able to make it, the groom's representation at the wedding was going to be quite small! I also was scrambling around for a best man. Diane suggested her sister Cherilyn's boyfriend at the time, Jimmy Luciano, and he agreed. Apparently, some of Diane's aunts and uncles thought it was a *shotgun wedding* because of the hasty arrangements. Little did they know it was *very* far from a situation where Diane was pregnant!

The night before the big day arrived, I spent the night next door at the TenEycks so I wouldn't see *The Bride* until she appeared in the church before walking down the aisle with Daddy Jim. Diane's maid of honor was her sister Cherilyn and several other friends, including Nancy O'Reilly and Gay TenEyck, were her bridesmaids. Some family members of Diane's were kind enough to occupy the groom's side of the church so it wouldn't look quite so lopsided! The wedding itself was amazing for me! I had a little apprehension when Jimmy and I were waiting at the altar with Father Dougherty. "Here comes the bride" started to play, and Diane didn't appear at the back of the church to walk with her father down the aisle. It was probably only thirty seconds or more, but it seemed like many minutes to me! I thought, *Did she change her mind again?*

It was a great traditional Catholic wedding. Diane looked amazing in her white wedding dress! We were blessed, took the vows, and exchanged rings before walking down the aisle together for the first time. As we exited the church, there was rice being thrown and congratulations from all present.

Daddy Jim had arranged the wedding reception in Manhattan at Manero's Steak House, so Diane and I rode into The City with her sister, Cherilyn, and Jimmy. At the reception, besides having a great time sitting next to my new *bride*, we danced, cut the cake, and I got to meet Diane's uncles and aunts for the first time: Uncle Ken and Aunt Mary Louise, Uncle Joe and Aunt Madeline, Uncle Bill and Anna, and Uncle John and Aunt Gerry. Of course, Diane's Mom, Dolores, and Daddy Jim, and Jamie, Diane's younger sister, were there, plus Grandma Berry whom I knew, but nonetheless it was a bit intimidating being with so many relatives I'd simply never met. I would have been more relaxed, perhaps, if any of my four parents were there supporting me.

Although Jim and Dolores Johnson had raised Diane since she was a baby, they were not her birth parents. Jim was actually Diane's first cousin. Diane's natural mother, Veronica McPartland Beattie, died of appendicitis in July 1941 when Diane was ten months old. (Penicillin had not been discovered then. If it had been available at the time, perhaps it would have saved Veronica's life.) Diane's natural father, William Beattie Sr., was a VP of Standard Oil of California and worked in Manhattan. He offered to pay his oldest daughter, Marilyn, to take care of baby Diane, but she refused. Veronica's sister, Aunt Mae, had a son, Jim Johnson, who was newly married to Dolores Berry Johnson. Diane's birth mother, Veronica, really liked Jim and Dolores and had asked them to take Diane if no other family member could if anything happened to her. Fortunately, Jim and Dolores honored their commitment, and that's how Diane came to live with the Johnson family. Unfortunately, Diane had two sisters and three brothers that she never really got to know: Marilyn, Dorothy, Billy, Edward, and Donald in birth order.

Immediately after the wedding reception, Diane and I got into the Corvair and drove south as far as Jessup, Maryland, where we found a motel to spend our wedding night. After bringing in our luggage and getting settled in, Diane went into the bathroom to change into a sheer nightgown she'd received as a wedding gift. Diane was in there so long that I thought she'd never come out, but she finally did!

The next morning, we got back into the car and drove to Charleston, South Carolina. We found a place to live temporarily at the Hub Motel on Azalea Drive, Charleston Heights, South Carolina. It was a studio apartment and *very* basic! I was going into the sub base to work on a daily basis. The Gold crew would be deploying for our second patrol in about a month. During this time, the Gold FTMs and their wives would get together for parties at someone's house quite often. Larry Fetter and his wife, Diane no. 1, and Diane no. 2 and I became good friends. (Diane no. 1 and no. 2 because Diane Fetter was the first Diane of the FT gang's wives.) The Fetters lived in a house on James Island, and often the parties were at their home. Diane had been introduced to smoking during summers at her grandmother's cottage in Breezy Point, New York. I think partially because I was not a smoker, she was really trying hard to quit. Diane would do very well until everyone was smoking around her, and then ask someone, "Can I bum a cigarette?"

Our *new homeport* of Charleston, South Carolina, turned out to be a *culture shock* for Diane! She had never seen *white drinking fountains* and *colored drinking fountains* and *white bathrooms* and *colored bathrooms* in the New York/New Jersey area where she had grown up. Actually, living primarily in New England the latter part of my life, I hadn't either. This was like a foreign land to Diane! I'm sure she silently thought, *What have I gotten myself into?*

Married life in the Navy was different than living in the *civilian* world for both Diane and I. Besides my base pay, hazardous duty (submarine) pay and P3, now that I was married and not eating on base, the Navy paid for *commuted rations* or ComRats. This was equal to what feeding me on base would have cost the government. We shopped for food in the commissary on the sub base where prices for food were less expensive than on the outside and also had privileges at the Navy Exchange. The Navy Exchange sold items similar to what you'd find in a small department store, but also with discounted prices. I could also purchase uniform items at the Navy Exchange, dress white or dress blue items, work dungarees, white *Dixie Cup* hats, etc.

One wise thing I had done previously in Charleston was to open a savings account at the Navy Federal Credit Union on the base and to start a modest allotment from my salary each payday. The interest rate was 10 percent! This NFCU office became very convenient for our financial transactions, so we opened up joint checking and saving accounts in addition to the account that was receiving the allotment coming out of each of my paychecks.

The time to deploy eventually came the first part of December 1964, and the Gold crew was taken from the sub base by bus to the Charleston AF Base to board our two KC135s for the trip to Rota, Spain. The plane I was assigned to took off on time. However, Larry Fetter and his half of the crew's plane had developed engine problems, so that half of the crew was sent home and didn't leave until the next morning. Diane no. 2 stayed at the Fetters the night I left for Rota. The next day, Diane no. 2 drove our trusty Corvair to New Jersey to visit with Daddy Jim and Dolores while I was at sea. Diane no. 1 returned to the Fetter's home in Pontiac, Michigan, while Larry was gone that patrol cycle.

Dave, Den, Mom, and Diane—
Chandler Hill home

Dad and his smokin' buddy

Di and Ned skating at
Locke Mills, Cabin

Three Bros, Chapman St.
House, Bethel, ME

CHAPTER NINETEEN

THE REMAINDER OF MY PATROLS ON THE USS *JAMES MONROE*

The remaining three Gold deterrent patrols on the USS *James Monroe* went well. While on patrol, many of my shipmates were ardent slot car builders/drivers. Probably in the yards, someone had constructed a fairly large quad track slot car layout on plywood whose two halves could be separated for storage. It would be set up in the rear of the crew's mess while underway on patrol for slot car race nights. During off-crew, our slot car enthusiasts would build the fastest cars possible to challenge their shipmates on the next run. This was a *big* event! Even the skipper and officers had their own cars and would enthusiastically get into it! I didn't realize it at the time, but this was a great morale builder and had a valuable *bonding* effect on the whole ship's company. I didn't have a slot car, but Larry Fetter and Soupy Campbell, with his *409 Chevy* slot car, represented the fire control gang very well! We also had casino and poker nights where actual money was used.

Another favorite pastime of the *weapons gang* was listening to music in Missile Control Center (MCC) while on patrol. We had a reel to reel tape recorder that was used to record WSRT's or Weapon System Readiness Tests. A WSRT is an exercise randomly ordered by the Pentagon to all FBMs on patrol to simulating launching all 16 Polaris missiles. (We were told an admiral in the Pentagon rolled a set of dice to determine the frequency as WSRTs occurred every two to twelve days.) The tape recorders were officially installed to record voice conversations on the circuit used by the Weapons Department during the WSRTs. At the end of patrol, the tapes were all packaged up and taken back stateside for a Navy contractor named Vitro to analyze. We had other ideas for using the tape recorder while deployed, and Weapons Department sailors would record music they liked while on-off crew and brought their tapes with them to listen to for entertainment while deployed. I'll never forget the *Monroe*'s Navigator, LCDR Bosquet (or Biscuit) Wev, who would come down to MCC when he was off watch and request a specific tape. He'd sit on our workbench on the port side of MCC with the tape recorder above and behind his head, close his eyes, and get lost in the moment. We never knew exactly where he was in his mind, but he was probably at home with his family and very far from the challenges of being on patrol for a couple of months. Biscuit Wev was a great officer and one of the better ones I ever went to sea with. I respected him very much.

One event that happened infrequently on patrol, but it did happen, would typically unfold like this: an SSBN has an array of passive sonar sensors in a *U shape* around the bow of the sub. The sonarmen monitor these receivers constantly to determine what's in near proximity of the boat, sometimes a whale! Because the huge thirty-three-foot multiblade screw driving the boat at the rear creates a sound *blind spot*, the OOD every so often executes a maneuver called *clearing the baffles*. The boat comes to port or starboard ten or fifteen degrees, allowing the sonarmen to *see* if there's anything behind us. Occasionally, there was! In one specific incident that I remember, there was a Russian Alpha or November class fast attack submarine following us. It would follow us for a day or more, and finally the Russian Skipper would get tired of playing *cat and mouse* and peel off in the direction of the Russian sub base at Murmansk to return to the sub's homeport.

The *Monroe* Gold crew was on a cycle that scheduled us on patrol and away from home during Christmas! Not to be deprived of expressing our holiday spirit, the crew would put up a self-decorated artificial tree in the crew's mess, and we had a smaller one in MCC. I finished getting my qual card signed off about halfway through the patrol, and CDR Cobean pinned my *dolphins* on my poopy suit in a brief ceremony in his stateroom with the XO. I was officially a submariner!

During a patrol, we were very much isolated from the outside world and our families; however, each crew member was allowed to receive four *family grams* from loved ones. Each was limited to no more than fifteen words in length. The FBMs trailed a wire while on patrol that was intended to primarily receive *launch orders* from Very Low Frequency (VLF) transmitters stateside. As a morale booster, the Navy allowed limited communication, *one way*, from family members back home. It was generally something we'd very much look forward to while on patrol. Some of us would write letters to our wives or family before going on patrol with dates designating when we wanted the letters to be put in the mail. The off-crew yeomen would manage the sending of these letters, just as our yeomen would do when the Blue crew had the boat.

I adapted to patrol life again, but as I've mentioned previously, toward the end of a sixty to seventy-two-day patrol, completely submerged all the time, minor characteristics of people would start to annoy me. At the end of the second Gold patrol, we pulled back into Rota and tied up alongside the USS *Holland*. During the changeover period, several of us took liberty and went into Rota. It was customary for a newly qualified submariner to *drink* his dolphins! I think it was Larry Fetter who ordered a terrible mixture of one shot each of vodka, rum, whiskey, and crème de menthe from that Rota bar. My coveted dolphins were dropped into the vile mixture, and it was my job to gulp all that mixture down (without letting it come up) and recover the dolphins with my teeth at the bottom of the glass! I was quietly proud. Only about 2 percent of all Navy service members are submariners, and I felt fortunate to have made it into that select group!

Back in Charleston, Diane no. 1 and Diane no. 2 had been searching for a rental home for Diane no. 2 and I. One good possibility was at 26 Ferrara Dr. in Charleston Heights, South Carolina. It was a two-bedroom single family home on a street with a small park in the center. It was also near the sub base and would be a short commute for me during off-crew. The landlords lived right next door! When my Diane went up to the owner's door to inquire about the rental, she spoke with Reba Kearse, who asked Diane some questions. Shortly, Diane heard Reba say, "Rubin, they're in *the Navy*!" Apparently, that was a big issue for some landlords, but not for Rubin, as the Kearses approved of our renting their property. The rent was ninety-five dollars a month, and the house was furnished!

One of our first trips when I returned stateside was to GEX, which was a government employee-focused membership warehouse store in Charleston, South Carolina. We purchased a small black-and-white TV and a nice stereo system with quality built-in speakers in the wooden walnut console. Those pieces nicely complemented the furnished decor of the house we rented and would provide a source of entertainment! One negative issue was that our budget wouldn't allow for a phone in the house, so Diane had to go out to the nearest pay phone when she wanted to talk with her mother.

In truth, Diane and I were still just getting to know each other better, and in the process there were infrequent periods of minor conflict. I really don't recall what specifically touched it off, but we had a *discussion*, and at the end, Diane said, "You're nothing but a *big zero*!" What can one say in response to that? I was silent. The Corvair needed a *bath*, so I pulled it into the backyard in the grass just behind our kitchen window to wash it. Our gravel driveway would get mud on the tires during the wash cycle if it was washed there. Not wanting to further extend the conflict, I took an old Navy issue T-shirt, and with a black Magic Marker, drew a large *0* on the back, put it on, and proceeded to wash the car. The next thing I knew, Diane came out of our back door laughing and gave me a big hug!

I kept in touch with Soly (Tom Solywoda) whenever we were both in port at the same time. Diane and I would invite him over to our house to have dinner or just to hang out. I'm not sure Diane was so keen on Soly, but she tolerated him for my sake.

As our Gold crew's time to relieve the Blue crew came near, during May of 1965, we learned we would be meeting it in Holy Loch, Scotland, and not Rota, Spain. The *Monroe* had been transferred to SUBRON 14. That was fine with me as some of my ancestors came from Scotland, and I'd never been there!

By now, the FBM crews were no longer being transported to our remote deployment locations by MATS KC135s but by commercial airliners under contract to the Navy. Imagine the difference between comfortable seats, insulated interiors that didn't drip condensate on you, and real live *stewardesses?* (The airlines must have selected the *tough-skinned* stewardesses, as sailors can be brutal!) By comparison, it was almost like flying first class! We flew into Prestwick, Scottland, this time and then traveled by bus to Dunoon, Scotland, where we caught a launch to the tender AS-31, USS *Hunley* anchored in Holy Loch. After settling in, we had chow on the tender and awaited the arrival of the Blue crew from patrol the next day.

After the change of command ceremony, we occupied the boat, and the Blue crew departed for Charleston, South Carolina, and their families. As we continued to ready the USS *Jimmy Monroe* for the Gold crew's third patrol, there was a new country, Scotland, for us to explore.

Dunoon was a relatively quiet town. There were several bars in town that all observed *Queen's Hours.* Bars were required to close between the hours of 1400 and 1700 by law. Another Scottish tradition that I observed while in Dunoon was that the barmaids didn't shave the hair under their arms (yuck)! When they would be serving drinks to my shipmates sitting on the inside of the booth while in short-sleeve dresses, the hair would be right in the face of the patrons sitting on the outside of the booth! I just wasn't used to that in the States.

We were also required to dress in *civilian clothes* for liberty in Scotland. Larry Fetter, Soupy, Cowboy, and I were usually together exploring Scotland. We went to Edinburgh on the Firth of Forth and toured Edinburgh Castle and Holyrood Palace where Mary, Queen of Scots had been held for some time. I was amazed to see an eight-hundred-year-old building on the Edinburgh Castle grounds. I remember thinking at the time, *Our country is not even two hundred years old yet, and this building has been around for four times that period of time!* Through the USS *Hunley's* recreation department, we booked tours and visited Loch Lomond and castles in the area of western Scotland. I'll never forget on one of these tours going into a restaurant with a fast-food type of counter for ordering and trying to order lunch. Not only didn't I recognize the items on the menu (what is haggis?), I also could hardly understand the ladies behind the counter. Their Scottish accents were *so* strong!

Glasgow was the closest city to Holy Loch, and bus service was available from Dunoon. We went there several times during the upkeep period, but it was never my favorite. It was more of an industrial town. Even though we were in civilian clothes, some of the younger locals would drive by in their cars and shout out the window, "Yank, go home!" We also had one incident after leaving the tender and heading out into the Firth of Clyde to get to sea, where some Green Peace protesters in rubber rafts came out to demonstrate against our nuclear presence in their country.

As the time for the third Gold patrol came, we basically had the same FTB gang for this patrol with the exception of Chief Lowe, who was replaced by a skinny E-6 FTB who had transferred in from another Boomer. We'd been assigned to the same patrol area where rough seas were the norm! When there are rough seas above the boat at periscope depth, it rolls from side to side *a lot* as these subs have no keel. However, even at four hundred feet, there's still a noticeable roll always present. The deeper the boat goes, the less the amount of rolling. I remember tucking my arms and feet under my mattress when trying to sleep so I wouldn't be tossed out of my rack! It really got rough at times.

After the usual two months plus on patrol, we proceeded up the Firth of Clyde to Holy Loch and tied up beside the tender. Another three-day change of command process with the Blue crew, then transportation to Prestwick and a plane ride home! I can tell you that after all those days submerged with a group of submarine sailors, the perfume of the stewardesses sure smelled good! It was July 1965.

Diane had a portable sewing machine and was a great seamstress. One thing I had done while in Dunoon prior to patrol was go to some shops that sold authentic Scottish tartan fabrics and made some purchases. I bought Robertson tartans, of course, and several other family types, like Clan MacGregor, that I brought home. When I returned to Charleston after patrol that run, Diane made a short skirt out of the Robertson tartan fabric that looked really great on her!

Diane no. 2 had stayed in Charleston while the Gold crew was on our third patrol. She had a job working in the office of a construction company. Diane no. 2 and Diane no. 1 became good friends and ended up staying together at our house or the Fetter's home most of the time Larry and I were away.

As usual, the first thirty days or so the Gold crew was home, we only did a phone-in muster once a week. My father was working at the Lucayan Beach Hotel on Grand Bahama Island at that time. Diane and I really never had a honeymoon, so Father and Evelyn invited us down for several days for a visit. We rented a car so we could see the island and stayed at Father's condo. Cars in the Bahamas drive on the left side of the road like in the United Kingdom. I remember going into roundabouts *the wrong way* and not being sure where to look for traffic. The other issue was signaling your intended direction before turning. I'd move the lever on the left side of the steering column up or down like we do in the USA, and to my surprise, the windshield wipers would come on! The functions of the two levers are just reversed when the steering wheel is on the right side of the vehicle. It must have been easy for the native Bahamians to be able to tell when a tourist was driving a car. Just look for the windshield wipers to come on when a car was turning!

While the Gold FTB gang had primarily hung out with other FTBs or MTs (missile techs) on our crew, there were some other Torpedoman's Mates (TMs) in the Weapons Division that tolerated us! Dwayne Swanson or Swanney was one of them. He was a big guy, originally from Montana. He was also married and had two small children. During off-crew periods, Swanney was always inviting us over to his home for one of his cookouts.

For swimming, Diane and I would often go to the Isle of Palms beach. It was sort of a family tradition. I have pictures of my Nana and Grandfather Kirk in their *swimming costumes* with long ruffled sleeves and knee-length pants at that beach when he was stationed in Charleston. I remember lying on the beach in February, and it was quite warm. There weren't many homes on the IOP then.

During our second two months of off-crew time in Charleston, we reported to the sub base on a daily basis, Monday to Friday. I had a training refresher class for a couple of weeks during the period. As November 1965 approached, we were getting ready to board our flights for another patrol, the Gold crew's fourth. After a commercial flight via a Great Circle Route and a stop in Gander, Newfoundland, to refuel, we arrived in Prestwick, Scottland. Finally, the usual trip to Holy Loch and boarding the USS *Hunley* to await the Blue crew for the change of command.

After moving aboard SSBN622 for the upkeep period, just getting into Dunoon for liberty was now a challenge! November in Scotland during inclement weather was uncomfortable when outside, and the wind and snow would blow almost horizontally across Holy Loch. We were in our warmest civilian clothes, but in an open LCM-type liberty launch, there wasn't much protection from the elements.

Dunoon's bars were still observing *Queen's Hours*, of course. Just before 1400 hrs local time, the barmaids would grab a tin bucket with some water in it and, with a pair of tongs, take the still burning individual pieces of coke out of the one stove in the room and place them in the bucket. After cleaning up, they would place the coke back in the stove so the coke would be dry for the evening hours that started at 1700. The Scots were definitely thrifty!

After the usual month beside the tender, getting the boat ready for patrol, sea trials, and loading of *stores* for two months, we departed Holy Loch for patrol. It was the end of November 1965.

LCDR Lumsden was going to be our XO again. He was a real Southern gentleman. I'm not sure how it all got started, but during the patrol, a back-and-forth developed regarding grits with the XO. He was always selling how great they were! To which one of our enlisted shipmates (Baker) replied, "I'd rather eat shit than grits!" This got back to the XO, and the next day's Plan of the Day (which the XO prepared daily) had a line item stating, "Everyone will be served a ration of grits during the breakfast meal, and LCDR Lumsden will be in the crew's mess to ensure everyone eats it." Sure enough, when breakfast time arrived, there was the XO in the chow hall observing the consumption of grits by the crew! It was really only a continuation of the rouse. The XO was really a good guy and an advocate of all crew members, especially with administrative issues.

A couple of us in the Weapons Gang decided to continue it a bit, however. We made a palm tree out of old newspaper, *potted* it in a used no. 10 can from the galley, and placed it immediately outside the XO's stateroom door with a sign that read "Please water me daily." Of course, this was a takeoff on Captain Queeg of the *Caine Mutiny* book/movie. Captain Queeg was the unstable skipper of the destroyer-minesweeper USS *Caine* who had a palm tree that he watered all the time. The XO went along with it, as the palm tree stayed outside his stateroom for weeks!

We had a very rare fire control system failure on that patrol. One of our missiles was down and not available to be fired. This went on for some hours, and two watches had had a crack at troubleshooting it before my watch came on duty. The failure had been narrowed down to an analog section of the MK 84 system and a bank of pluggable modules in a twenty inch by twelve inch section at the very bottom of one of the pullout doors of the system in MCC. We could see where the system was failing with an oscilloscope trace, but even exchanging all the modules in that section with those from a working missile's section didn't fix the problem.

After the missile was down for about sixteen hours, the Captain came down to the crew's lounge and sat reading a book immediately outside the door into MCC to emphasize the urgency of the matter! Our Weapons Officer that patrol was a *Mustang*, Lieutenant McCarthy. A *Mustang* officer is an enlisted person who goes through one of the Navy's upgrade programs and graduates as an ensign. These officers are capped when the reach an O-5 or Navy commander and can't advance farther.

(If you're not technically oriented, you might want to just skip to the next paragraph!) Anyway, at this point, it was LT. McCarthy and me uncomfortably on our knees between the rows of the MK 84 system in MCC trying to further identify the failure. We had troubleshot it down to a power issue. These plug-in modules consisted of discrete components of transistors, resistors, and capacitors (remember, there were no integrated circuits or *chips* in those days) on a circuit board which was mounted into sockets in the back panel. The power feeding that section was supposed to be +20VDC and -45VDC, but it had shifted to +30VDC and -35VDC, which made all the modules in that section stop functioning properly. The next step was to do something no one was taught in the ten months of MK 84 fire control system training at Dam Neck. We detached the whole section from its mounting and removed its back cover. It immediately became apparent that one of the bus bars that carried power to the individual modules was not tight on the pins of that section, and a corner was not making contact with the pins. This had shifted the power by 10VDC from ground! The next step was to check to see if we had that rare spare part in our supplies which were kept in the missile compartment. I was skeptical. Well, someone who had decided what spare parts would be carried on patrol by an SSBN had done an excellent job. We had a spare! The bus bar in the section for the missile that was down was replaced, and everything was restored to normal. Running tests for the previously down missile indicated it now passed all tests. We'd fixed a very unusual failure. I think that missile was down for over twenty-four hours. I know I immediately hit my rack for some overdue sleep, and the Captain abandoned his post outside MCC and returned to the Conn!

Prior to the start of Gold patrol four, I had put in a chit requesting a transfer to new construction or shore duty. I was ready to give up my sea legs for a while and spend more time with my wife. We were also trying to start a family and had been consulting Diane's gynecologist why we hadn't been successful to date. I was anxious to return home to see what if any US Navy orders awaited me! (I knew Diane would have some *orders* for me when I got home!)

After SSBN622's eight deterrent patrol and the Gold crew's fourth successful deterrent patrol, she surfaced off the western coast of Scotland, traveled up the Firth of Clyde to Holy Loch, and tied up beside the USS *Hunley*. For me, it was the last time that I'd be on patrol with sailors that had become more than shipmates but friends—Larry Fetter, Soupy Campbell, and Ed Strosnyder. The change of command took place, and soon after being relieved by the

Blue crew, we all flew home to Charleston by commercial aircraft. It was February 1966.

While on the *James Monroe*, I'd earned my *Blue Nose* award. There was an initiation ceremony aboard while underway on the way home from patrol for those of us who hadn't been initiated before. Fun, but silly stuff looking back on it today!

CHAPTER TWENTY

MY NEW DUTY STATION, USS *WILL ROGERS* SSBN659

Orders were waiting for me upon my return to CONUS (Continental United States), and I would be transferred to the USS *Will Rogers* (SSBN659) that was currently on the ways in Groton, Connecticut, at General Dynamics, Electric Boat Division's shipyard or just *EB*. The *Will Rogers* was a Benjamin Franklin (SSBN640) class boat and the last of the 41 for Freedom FBMs. I was ordered to report aboard NLT 22 March 1966. I had advanced to E-5, FTB2(SS) on the *Monroe* and was tentatively assigned to the SSBN659 Blue crew under Captain R. Y. "Yogi" Kaufman.

While we really didn't have much furniture to move, only a TV and a stereo console plus personal belongings, we didn't have much time to prepare for the move either. As soon as we drove to Groton, we started our search for an apartment. There was a new apartment complex called Boardsen Place that was south of Electric Boat *(EB)* on Shennecossett Road that seemed quite livable. Number 24 Boardsen Place, a one-bedroom apartment, was available for $110 per month, *but* it was unfurnished! Prices in New England were definitely more expensive. We liked the location, so we purchased a bedroom set and living room furniture at Sears to get started and moved in.

When I first reported to the USS *Will Rogers* barge in the shipyard at EB, there was only a skeleton crew onboard, and they were an amalgam of future Blue and Gold crew officers and enlisted personnel. SSBN659 had not been launched yet and was still on the way.

There were sections of the pressure hull missing in rectangular shapes near the keel with ramps leading up into the boat itself at a forty-degree-angle where *yard birds* moved in and out of the boat like ants. This was our egress into the boat as well. The MK 84 fire control system was just being installed and checked out by a Navy contractor named Vitro. The system was only available for testing on the mid-shift, so when we had duty, we worked the midnight to 0800-hour shift, observing the testing by Vitro. Diane had taken an administrative job at Pfizer Co. through a temp agency. On those days, when I had mid-shift duty aboard the boat and would be coming home, Diane would just be leaving for work!

Over the course of the summer, the crews of the newest and last Boomer, USS *Will Rogers*, started filling in. The FTB gang initially consisted of Dave Smith (Shitty Smitty with the Meatball Ass or just Meatball), Droop Marvel, Wingnut Sorensen, Jon Peckinpaugh, and yours truly, Robbie. Our LPO was Chief Dario Villegas (or El Jefe) from Brownsville, Texas. Dario had been a commissary man or cook when he'd first joined the Navy but went to Navy fire control school and converted. El Jefe, by his own admission, wasn't the most knowledgeable person in electronics, but he knew his technical limitations, was an excellent leader, and we all looked up to him! My friend TM2(SS) Dwayne Swanson or Swanney was also transferred to SSBN659.

Diane and I were really happy in the Groton/New London area! There was so much to do. We went to the beach nearby, just a bit south on Shennecossett Road. (Admiral Kimmel, Commander of the Pearl Harbor Navy Base on December 7, 1941, and his wife had a retirement home there.) The water never seemed to warm up in the summer, but the beach was nice. Not too far north in Rhode Island was Narragansett Beach, which was very popular. There were a lot of summer stock playhouses in Connecticut towns along the Long Island Sound, like Old Lyme, Niantic, etc. We also enjoyed visiting Mystic, Connecticut, and Mystic Seaport. We didn't have a large budget, but we made the most of what we had. I recall seeing *The Graduate* with Dustin Hoffman in the New London Theatre that year.

USS *Will Rogers* construction was going as planned. Then as her launch date approached, the rectangular construction access holes in her pressure hull were filled with steel inserts and welded securely in place. SSBN659 was launched on the afternoon of 21 July 1966. Muriel Humphrey, wife of our VP, was the sponsor. Her job was to crack a traditional bottle of champagne on the bow just before the boat started its trip down the ways. As SSBN659 slid down the ways, her proud plank owners lined up topside aft of the sail on the missile deck and, standing at attention, held a salute as horns blared loudly. I was one of those enlisted crew members and officers riding her down the ways and into the water for the first time! It was a thrill! As the *Will Rogers* nuclear propulsion system was not operational yet, two large weights dropped into the Thames River from her port and starboard sides once she was in the water to stop the boat from drifting to the New London side of the river. Tugs brought the boat back to EB and a dock to finish her construction.

The crew's responsibilities in the shipyard were mainly to familiarize ourselves with the new sub's systems, attend training classes on the sub base, and to monitor installation progress of the boat's systems that we would be responsible for once the *Rogers* was turned over to the Navy. Personally, I enjoyed the break in a patrol cycle of three months on and three months off. My current assignment to new construction duty allowed me to spend more time with my wife, Diane!

Summer in Groton turned into fall and then into winter. During the fall period, we decided to buy a new car. The Corvair had served us well, but its heating system circulated air around the engine to produce heat. Something must have been leaking in the system as exhaust smelling fumes would enter into the passenger compartment to the extent that both Di and I would have a headache after a trip. We went to Blue Ribbon Pontiac in Noank, Connecticut, and bought a new 1967 Pontiac Grand Prix! What a *boat*! It was *champagne gold* outside with a black vinyl top and black interior leather.

Connecticut winters on the Long Island Sound generally weren't too harsh, but we did get some snow. One of our favorite places to buy seafood was Costa's Lobster Pound in Groton. I fondly recall driving up to Costa's in the winter to buy several *cull*, one-pound *chicken* lobsters at $0.99 per pound! (A *cull lobster* is one with only one claw that can't be sold for full price.) Costa's store was right on the river, and there was a slight downgrade from Thames St. The Grand Prix would want to slide a bit going down the grade when there was snow on the ground and then spin a little, trying to get back up to Thames St., but we were young, carefree, and up to the challenge! Once getting back to our apartment at Boardsen Place, we'd get a big pot of water boiling and get ready to enjoy some fresh Maine lobster! I remember the smell from cooking the lobster would linger in the house for a while, but it was all worth the delicious taste!

When Christmas came that year, Di and I decided to select and cut down our own Christmas tree! Just a short distance down Thomas St., off Shennecossett Rd., was a tree farm. We found the *perfect tree*, cut it down, and dragged it home. Decorating it was a first as we'd never cut down our own fresh Christmas tree while living in Charleston. Life was good!

Submariners must requalify in the escape tower periodically. The time for me came while at EB. This time, the two ascents were made with a new escape device, the Steinke Hood, that covered your whole head, but instead of blowing constantly, we were required to keep repeating, "Ho, ho, ho" until reaching the surface.

Just across Thames St. from EB were several bars where the EB workers would congregate after their shifts to have a beer or two. It didn't matter if it was 0800 in the morning. Many *yard birds* could be found relaxing after their shifts and having a beer(s) for breakfast! Some of my *Will Rogers* shipmates and I would gather in one of those watering holes afternoon or evenings after our shift on the boat and join them. One big challenge for me was learning how to play shuffleboard. If you haven't played it, a shuffleboard table consists of a long piece of raised laminated hardwood twenty inches wide by twenty-two feet long. The surface is periodically swept clean then sprinkled with cornmeal to reduce traction. Each player has three quoits or pucks that are eased down the table skillfully on an alternate basis. There are marked areas at the end of the board signifying one, two, or three-point landing zones. Landing one of your quoits within one of those areas would score the indicated points. If your quoit lands hanging over the very end of the board in area three without falling off, you'd have a *hanger*, which was worth four points. By alternating shots, each player has a chance to knock off his opponent's *quoits* that represent a score. The winner of one match would be challenged by someone who had written their name on a board next to that shuffleboard table. The loser would buy the winner a beer, and it would repeat throughout the night.

The shipyard workers had many years of playing shuffleboard under their belts and loved challenging green new construction submarine crews who hadn't had a chance to develop their skills like the shipyard workers had. We were at a definite disadvantage! During the period of our time at EB, I did start to win once in a while, but probably never broke even financially on my *lessons* learning the game. It was fun and challenging, however!

Our Gold crew shipmate Jimmy "Droop" Marvel fell in love with one of the barmaids, Charlene, in one of these shipyard bars and was bedazzled by her. Before the *Will Rogers* left EB and joined the fleet, they were married.

Chief Villegas was a master at getting things done for our pre-commissioning FTB crew! I don't know where he learned these skills, but he could *comshaw* almost anything! *Comshaw* is a Navy slang term for obtaining something outside official channels or payment, usually by trading or bartering. We initially started out small, a gallon of milk or some coffee beans for two engraved brass mugs with a large initial engraved on them. Submarines in those days still had voice tubes between lower level AMR no. 2 and upper level AMR no. 2 to issue communications to other watch standers in that compartment. These three-inch brass tubes made a perfect mug when cut to a six-inch length, fitted with a bottom, a brass metal handle, and initials. I still proudly have mine today! I don't recall all the enhancements to MCC that El Jefe secured for us pre-commissioning, but MCC was a shining example of a space to be admired when we finally left the yards and SSBN659 was commissioned.

The commissioning ceremony took place at EB on 1 April 1967 (my father's birthday). My father couldn't make it up from

Miami, but my good partner, Diane, was there to support me like she always had been doing and continues to do to this day! While Yogi Kaufman tried to set the example and exhibit outstanding leadership to his crew, I just had apprehensions about going to sea with him as my *hard butt* skipper. I worked *the system* a bit and was reassigned to the Gold crew under CDR Wm Cowhill's command. He was all business but a practical commanding officer, and I could relate to his leadership style much better.

USS *Will Rogers*—SSBN659

Christening sponsor:
Mrs. Humphrey

SSBN 659 launching at EB

SSBN 659 launching at EB launching sequence

Dropping weights

Note: All photos marked with "1997 Yogi" were provided to the author by ADM R. Y. Kaufmann himself.

USS *Will Rogers*—SSBN659

CDR Wm Cowell, Gold crew skipper

USS *Will Rogers* at EB
pre-commissioning

In dry dock with crew!

Main ballast tank vents
opening for dive!

Weapons Department in MCC
for an NTPI (Robbie, Lt.
Graham, and Peckinpaugh)

USS *Will Rogers* underway
on sea trials

Note: All photos marked with "1997 Yogi" were provided to the author by ADM R. Y. Kaufmann himself.

CHAPTER TWENTY-ONE

USS *WILL ROGERS* GOES ON ITS POST-COMMISSIONING SHAKEDOWN EXERCISES

Shortly after commissioning, SSBN659 was scheduled to go through extensive sea trials in deep water off the New England coast. I remember Admiral Rickover coming aboard in Groton prior to this sequence of tests. Rickover was a person every nuclear officer respected yet feared. He had a reputation for asking tough questions and could make or break an officer's career. The Gold crew had the boat when Rickover first came aboard, and I remember the topside watch appropriately piping him aboard. As the "father of the nuclear Navy," it was Admiral Hyman Rickover's responsibility to observe our nuclear reactor's operation, including *scrams* and other emergency procedures, and officially accept SSBN659's nuclear propulsion system on behalf of the US Navy.

One of the challenging things relegated to the Gold crew was taking the USS *Will Rogers* down to test depth for the very first time! This would also do something called *setting the pressure hull*. The pressure hull always compresses significantly on a deep dive to test depth, but on a submarine's first time at test depth and after it surfaces, the pressure hull doesn't quite return to its full diameter. I'd been to test depth with the USS *James Monroe* many times, but she'd been that deep before! This was the first time the US Navy's newest FBM was to stress the welded seams of HY80 steel laid down during construction at EB. Had some of the yard bird welders had beers at a bar across from the shipyard before their shift, or had the EB X-ray team verifying the welds for each section of pressure hull seams done their jobs properly? Here's where we'd find out! After the *Will Rogers* was submerged and in deep water, the OOD ordered the diving station to "Make your depth [for example] four hundred feet." And over the 1MC, "all hands check for leaks." This would go on slowly and cautiously, a hundred feet at a time, until the boat reached test depth. After this successful first deep dive, we routinely returned to periscope depth and then surfaced! The sphincter muscles in my butt relaxed, and I could breathe again!

After conducting more mainly engineering propulsion system tests over a period of several weeks, we turned the boat over to the Blue crew, who would take her to Naval Weapons Station, Charleston, South Carolina, to load several special test and instrumentation A3 Polaris missiles. After loading *TI* missiles, the Blue crew took the boat to the Cape. Diane and I rode down to the Cape with the Peckinpaughs and were invited to stay with Jon and Donna at his aunt's home in Cocoa Beach, Florida.

At some point, CDR Cowhill and the Gold crew again assumed command of SSBN659 and conducted the next phase of the *Will Rogers'* preparation to enter the fleet which involved sound trials off Andros Island in the Bahamas. Thanks in a *large* part to Petty Officer Dave Smith, this turned out to be an extremely memorable period of my time aboard USS *Will Rogers*! The *Rogers* needed to undergo sound classification in the SOSUS area of Andros Island adjacent to the Tongue of the Ocean like all US Navy nuclear submarines have done. US Navy SONAR systems of the day were so sensitive that they could differentiate between submarine types of the world and even down to the specific sub itself. (I wonder what the capabilities are today?) The Navy wanted to establish USS *Will Rogers's* specific sound signature. The Gold crew again had the boat.

There wasn't much demand on most of the crew during this period. The boat would make passes back and forth across the huge SOSUS hydrophones submerged near the Tongue of the Ocean while SSBN659's sound signature was being established. So CDR Cowhill requested liberty for one-third of the crew for twenty-four hours at a time from the *Squad Dog* or Squadron Commander, which was granted! The other two sections left aboard were on *port and starboard duty*, which meant that each section had the watch for twelve hours then were off for twelve hours.

I'd never been to Nassau before, so I was looking forward to this liberty! I think Meatball and I were the FTBs on the second day to board the tender for the trip to Nassau on New Providence Island. The small tender returned to the *Rogers* with the first wave of liberty sailors, *poured* them off the shuttle boat (they looked terrible!), and as they painfully made their way belowdecks, we boarded the boat for our turn in Nassau. We saw the sights and visited tourist spots on the island. Of course, sampling some tropical drinks was an attraction! There was a teacher's convention going on at the Fort Montague Hotel, and many of the crew ended up there for a drink later in the day. It was really a lively place, and some of our single sailors booked rooms for the night! Rumor has it that several of these teachers had their way with a couple of our young Beaver Patrol sailors. I don't remember exactly, but I think Meatball and I each ended up finding a comfortable couch on the Fort Montague's front porch and catching a couple of hours of shut-eye. Prior to 0800, we were all back at the pier in Nassau and on the shuttle tender for our return to *Will Rogers*. After a short trip, we met our boat off Andros Island, and upon going aboard, we were relieved by the last liberty section to go ashore. Exhausted from liberty, we hit our racks until time to assume duty again twelve hours later!

These adventures would later give PO Dave Smith or Meatball the basis for a *gigantic* fabricated sea story that would be published in the *New York Times*!

One of the final shakedown phases for USS *Will Rogers* was to conduct DASO, or Demonstration and Shakedown Operations at Cape Kennedy. The main purpose of DASO was to confirm an FBM's ability to fire missiles down the Atlantic Missile Range. Previously, each FBM crew would fire a missile or two. However, at this point in the A3 program, the Navy had enough data, and *Will Rogers* would only fire *one* missile. The two Commanding Officers flipped a coin, and CDR Cowhill won! The Gold crew would have the privilege! I think Yogi wasn't very happy about that as he always wanted to be, or appear to be, number one.

Prior to DASO operations at the Cape, the Blue and Gold crews alternated command of the boat for short periods leading up to the Gold crew's launch of a Polaris A3 missile. Dave Meatball Smith was our FTB supply PO, and as such ordered spare parts for repair of the missile fire control system elements and, being a clever guy from Massachusetts, any other items he thought might be required to support our operations. *Well,* one of these *required items,* per Petty Officer Smith, was sunglasses for the *whole* crew! Meatball requisitioned 125 military sunglasses for the Gold crew and a NavET supply PO, twenty-five briefcases for his shipmates!

I'd have to ask Smitty which officer on the Gold crew signed off on that requisition. I understand the max requisition amount on the requisition chit was initially left blank, but when it reached Captain Kaufman that the Gold crew *all* had new, GI or Government-Issue sunglasses, officers included, the shite hit the fan, and you can guess what happened next! The sunglasses and briefcases were returned to Navy supply, and I'm sure CDR Cowhill got some heat from Yogi.

The day of the launch arrived on 31 July 1967. Up until now, it was mostly the Engineering Department that had been heavily involved in the shakedown testing. They play a critical part in the overall scheme of things as the engineers provide the power to get the boat to the patrol and launch areas. However, now it was time for the Weapons Department to shine. SSBN659 had been fitted with a tall mast welded to the very top of the sail. The tip of this antenna would be sticking above the water when the boat was at firing depth to transmit test and instrumentation signals to the blockhouse on the Cape that would be overseeing the launch.

Two stacks of temporary test and instrumentation electronics had been installed port side in MCC. These shipboard special electronics plus the package in the missile that replaced the warheads would monitor and record every aspect of the undersea launch and flight of the missile for future analysis after the launch.

There was a countdown clock in the Conn and one in MCC and, of course, a checklist of tasks that needed to be executed along the countdown period. As I recall, the countdown had started very early that morning at T-12 hours, and the launch was scheduled for mid to late afternoon. As the launch time approached at maybe T-3 hours, the boat was hovering at firing depth with a fifteen-degree list toward down range. This was to ensure that if something went wrong and the missile didn't ignite upon launch, it wouldn't fall back on the submerged missile deck but would miss the boat to one side. The FTB gang was already at Battle Stations Missile with some on sound-powered headphones on the Weapons Department's 10JC circuit. LT. Graham, our Weapons Officer, was sitting in front of the two firing panel consoles with the Weapons Officer's firing key out of its normally locked safe and in front of him. Chief Villegas was on the right at the main part of the console, and other FTBs were at their battle station positions within MCC and the missile compartment. Smitty and I were *rovers* and stayed in the immediate area of the main console. LT. George Ditmore, the Assistant Weapons officer, was stationed in the missile compartment at the LCP (Launch Control Panel).

It was intense knowing we were about to launch a live, one million dollar missile and send it over 1,500 miles down range, aiming at a small point in the Atlantic Ocean! The good news was it wasn't carrying live nuclear warheads! Things were going normally, and the good ship and crew were well prepared for this task. At about T-8 minutes, things changed quickly. Early FBM missile fire control systems had two general-purpose digital computers called Digital GeoBallistic Computers (DGBCs) developed by Control Data Corporation; the second DGBC was for backup. Their main function is to take current latitude and longitude signals from *Will Rogers'* navigation division and, knowing the fixed position of the target, calculate the trajectory values to be fed into the missile's guidance computer seconds before launch. (Fun fact, these DGBCs had less computing power than your smartphone or tablet today!) The problem we faced at T-8 minutes was that one of the dual feed Lxo and Lyo (latitude and longitude) inputs coming down from Navigation (the pair we were using) started to fail, and their indicator light blinked yellow then red, and an alarm flashed on the console. Chief Villegas quickly turned around and looked at me with a mildly panicked look in his eyes. I had seen the error light on the console and immediately knew how to correct it. I said, "Recommend the Lxo and Lyo inputs from Nav be casualty switched."

The Chief repeated the recommendation to LT. Graham, who in turn looked around at me and said, "Robertson, *are you sure?*"

"Yes, sir!" was my firm reply.

Next, LT. Graham to the skipper in the Conn: "Captain, we've had a failure of the latitude and longitude input from Nav. Permission to casualty switch the inputs." Then from Conn, "Weapons, Conn, aye, permission granted to switch Nav inputs." With the pushing of two buttons on one of the DGBCs, we were again *go for launch*. This may have been the first launch of a T&I configured Polaris A3 missile while in a backup, casualty switched mode on the DGBCs.

Several seemingly short minutes later, we arrived at T minus zero (T-0). There was a loud whoosh, and the boat oscillated up and down just a bit as missile no. 3 left its tube and seawater poured in to replace the missile's weight in the missile tube. The launched missile ignited on schedule while still in the water and was away down the Atlantic Missile Range! A successful launch! Later we learned just *how accurate* that shot was. It's still classified, but the Polaris A3 was a *very* accurate ballistic missile. It had to leave the immediate atmosphere of our earth, reenter, and then accurately hit its target. Great technology, and that was over fifty years ago!

The Captain and crew were ecstatic about the successful A3 missile launch. On the way into Cape Kennedy, someone wrote the words "Another Clean Sweep by the Beaver Patrol" in large black letters on a white sheet, attached it to a broom, and tied that to a raised periscope for all to see as we arrived back in port. It really was an important event. The last of the forty-one Polaris submarines had another successful DASO and something America could be proud of!

There was news coverage when we arrived back at Cape Kennedy, and a famed military journalist and former Naval Officer, Hanson Baldwin from the *New York Times*, came aboard to cover the story. Unfortunately, in a way, Mr. Baldwin eventually made his way to MCC and ran into PO Smith, whom he started to interview:

"So what is the significance of the banner being flown from a broom 'Another Clean Sweep by the Beaver Patrol'?" Petty Officer Smith started into this long dissertation about rivalry between the Blue and Gold crews and how we were giving the Blue crew a ribbing about us successfully launching a missile when the Blue crew didn't. Some say the article Hanson wrote and was published in the *New York Times* was tongue-in-cheek, and Hanson knew the difference. However, I was there, and to this day I believe he had no idea that the Beaver Patrol reference was actually directed to the Fort Montague Hotel escapades of some of my shipmates and not intra-crew rivalry! Great memories with superior shipmates in times gone by! These are memories that everyone, unfortunately, doesn't get the privilege of experiencing. (A copy of Mr. Baldwin's *New York Times* article can be found in the Appendix no. III at the back of this book.)

After DASO, USS *Will Rogers* returned to EB for its Post Shakedown Availability (PSA). To celebrate a successful shakedown period, Captain Kaufman's staff arranged a celebratory ship's party at a local hotel. All Blue and Gold crew members and their partners were invited. It was a great party, but one it seemed was centered around Captain Kaufman to a large degree. Diane and I invited a very nice black couple from the Blue crew to sit at our table when it seemed they hadn't yet met any of his Blue crew shipmates. The cap (or downer) event of the evening that confirmed my initial decision not to join the Blue crew was when Yogi made the boast, "I can do a push-up with a three-hundred-pound man on my back! Swanson, get up here!"

My friend Swanney replied, "Captain, I'm sorry, but I don't weigh three hundred pounds." And he didn't leave his seat. Yogi was noticeably embarrassed, and several months later, Dewayne Swanson, TM2(SS) was transferred to a torpedo retriever in Groton and never made patrols on the USS *Will Rogers* with us. My friend was a good sailor, but his Naval record was permanently damaged by an egotistical skipper. More about Swanney later in this book.

During PSA, the test and instrumentation stacks were removed from the port side of MCC, leaving an excellent spot for a desk and workspace plus a mounting place for the reel-to-reel tape deck required to record WSRTs (Weapons System Readiness Tests). With input from all Gold FTBs, I had designed what we felt was the perfect thing for this space. It was L-shaped with a desk and upper storage cabinets going port and starboard and a cushioned seat with storage doors behind the seat running fore and aft. The tape deck was to be mounted in a location within this area. I drew engineering drawings of the piece with front and side views that could be used by the various shops within EB to construct the work desk. Chief Villegas was again key in helping us with the *comshaw acquisition* project. He started with the sheet metal shop to construct the main parts of the structure. Before we were finished, we had the Formica and upholstery shops of EB working on the project! I believe it was Smitty who actually got those engineering drawings incorporated into SSBN659's official ship's construction records, making it a legitimate and official part of the boat.

After PSA was completed in October 1967, Captain Yogi Kaufman and the Blue crew left Groton for Charleston, South Carolina, and the Naval Weapons Station to load out with sixteen tactical A3 Polaris missiles. Directly after load out, SSBN659 left CONUS for its first patrol. The last of the *41 for Freedom* FBM submarines was now operational. She would remain so for another twenty-six years until USS *Will Rogers* was decommissioned on 12 April 1993, and struck from the Naval Vessel Registry!

USS *Will Rogers*—Cape Kennedy

A3 Polaris missile launch, Cape Kennedy

Hanson Baldwin, *NY Times* military reporter

CHAPTER TWENTY-TWO

MY FIRST TWO DETERRENT PATROLS ABOARD USS *WILL ROGERS*

Diane and I enjoyed the end of the summer of 1967 in Groton. Di was now working at the Holiday Inn in Groton, Connecticut, as a banquet manager. The Innkeeper, Dr. Leo Golub, owned the franchise of the Holiday Inn in Groton, Connecticut, and one in New London as well. Diane reported to the event manager, Ed Byas. The New London Holiday Inn had a great restaurant called the Red Lion, and Diane had developed a close working relationship with its maître d', Dimitri. I remember going over for dinner some evenings and enjoying an unbelievable meal of Chateaubriand Bouquetiere for Two that was flame cooked beside our table by Dimitri. They went all out for Diane. The food aboard US Navy submarines is way above average, but this was *living large*!

We continued to enjoy the beaches of Connecticut and nearby Rhode Island, and the summer passed quickly. We were enjoying our one-bedroom apartment off Shennecossett Rd. and still going to Costa's Lobster Pound on Thames St. whenever we could for *cull lobsters*. There was a very well-equipped woodworking shop on the Groton Sub Base, and I started making items to use in our new home. One of the items was an oak magazine rack that is now in the possession of our daughter, Erin.

In the fall, while the Blue crew was still on patrol, I took some leave, and Diane and I drove to Bethel, Maine, with Jon and Donna Peckinpaugh in their Volvo 230 Sedan to visit my Maine parents.

Dad had built a one-story home on the site where Nana had previously lived at the top of Chandler Hill. The old house had burned down several years earlier. We all stayed there with Dad and my mother. Peck was an avid hunter and had brought along one of his rifles. There were deer on the property, and it was hunting season, so I borrowed one of Dad's rifles and Dad, Peck, and I started down Chandler Hill, each separating away from each other as we walked downhill. We had agreed to meet back at the house in an hour or two. Time passed, and Dad and I were back at the house, but no Peck! More time passed, and we started to wonder if he'd gotten lost. When we were about to come looking for Peck, he came up the hill, all out of breath and huffing and puffing said, "I have two bear cubs treed and have been waiting for the mother to come back! Come take a look."

He led us down the hill to a big pine tree and pointed up to two dark objects very near the top of the tree. I looked at Dad, and he looked at me and we smiled. I asked Jon, "Are you sure those are bear cubs?"

To which he replied, "Yes, I saw them go up the tree."

Then Dad suggested, "Then why don't you bring 'em down and we'll know for sure?" Peck aimed at the first object and *bang*, then quickly pumped another shell into the chamber and fired a second time! Two of the largest *porcupines* that I've ever seen came crashing to the ground! Peck took one look at his *bear cubs*, and I think he was quite embarrassed! The Great White Hunter had duped himself. We spent a day or two more in Bethel and then headed back to Groton, Connecticut. No one mentioned the incident during the rest of the time we were on Chandler Hill.

As December 1967 rolled around, it was time for USS *Will Rogers* Gold to get ready to relieve the Blue crew. We were to meet them in Rota, Spain. Not a problem for me! I was looking forward to seeing more of Andalusia. Our trip via two commercial Boeing 707 jet aircraft was routine by now. We landed at NAS Rota and were transferred to the USS *Canopus* (AS 34) that had relieved the USS *Holland* about a year before. We stowed our gear aboard the sub tender and awaited the return of our boat from patrol the next day.

The Blue crew and SSBN659 arrived on time as scheduled. We had a good turnover and change of command ceremony, then the Blue crew flew home. This would be my fifth deterrent patrol, and it was all getting rather routine. The whole Gold FTB crew was intact from pre-construction, DASO, and PSA and would be embarking upon this, our first USS *Will Rogers* deterrent patrol.

For recreation during this upkeep period, some of us visited a couple of the sherry bodegas nearby in Jerez de la Frontera, Spain. I remember visiting the Tio Pepe and Pedro Domecq bodegas. Another Spanish tradition that fascinated me was flamenco dancing, and there were several bar/restaurants in Jerez that featured some great dancers!

Of course, the main reason we were all in Rota, Spain, was to get the boat ready for another sixty to seventy-two-day deterrent patrol. The FTB team verified that the analog and digital sections of the fire control system were prepared and ready, went on sea trials taking the boat down to test depth, and finally all hands lent a hand as stores were stowed aboard for the patrol duration. We'd get underway in two days. However, a surprise happened the afternoon before we were scheduled to depart. A Russian *fishing* trawler entered the Bay of Cadiz, which was directly adjacent to Rota and our sub tender, USS *Canopus*, and dropped anchor! If you recall, these Russian vessels are *not* fishing boats but spy ships loaded with antennae and electronics.

It just happened that there were two MSTS (Military Sea Transport Service) ships in port at Rota. They had already unloaded their cargo supplying the base and would be heading home soon. Captain Cowhill and his XO, LCDR Wiggley, went over to the tender to talk with the Squad Dog or Commander of Submarine Squadron 16, more commonly known in Navy jargon as simply SUBRON 16. A clever plan was developed. The next afternoon, we got underway, as did the two MSTS ships. The Captain positioned the *Rogers*, which was still surfaced, in between the two larger vessels as we all headed out toward deep water. The Russian trawler was getting underway now too! As soon as the *Rogers* was in water deep enough for us to dive, we *pulled the plug*. One of the MSTS ships turned east and the other MSTS ship turned west out of Rota. We had positioned ourselves directly beneath one of the MSTS ships and remained submerged there for some period of time! Our quiet noise emissions would likely be drowned out by the louder noise of the MSTS ships and difficult for the trawler to detect a submarine. I don't know if our skipper really kept the trawler from knowing which direction we'd be taking and whether we'd be heading east or north, but I thought it was a very clever move on the part of our commanding officers and SUBRON 16! Just another example of the *cat-and-mouse* games each side played with the other during the Cold War.

Not too long after submerging, USS *Will Rogers* was still in relatively shallow water, and there was a lot of traffic around us. I was in the crew's mess, middle-level operations compartment, watching the evening movie. Suddenly, there was a loud noise of probably a big tanker's huge screws rotating that seemed very close to our sail. *Whoosh, whoosh, whoosh!* We were submerged, and I was thankful this encounter didn't result in an incident. Fortunately, it was only a near miss!

USS *Will Rogers*—SSBN659

USS *Canopus* sub tender

Russian trawler (sure, it's a fishing boat!)

MCC workstation that I designed

Fast attack USS *Scorpion* SSN589

The famous Petty Officer Dave Smith!

Di back home at 24 Kamaha St., kitchen

The rest of our patrol was uneventful by comparison! Patrol life for FBM submariners then and possibly now may seem routine to some, but for SSBN's elite crew members, we lived in a different universe. We wore *poopy suits* on patrol. These one-piece garments made of nylon were easy to wash in the ship's laundry and dried quickly. Because we had nuclear weapons aboard, there were frequent EAB (Emergency Air Breathing) drills. The A3 missiles had potential alpha contamination from the warheads and therefore represented a hazard to the crew if there was an accident, thus the drills! I remember spending many hours in uncomfortable EAB masks during the too frequent drills. The masks were attached to a six-foot rubber hose with a special fitting on the end. There were gangs of receptacles carrying low pressure air every so often throughout the boat that the crew could plug their EAB masks into. To move around, you'd have to take a deep breath, unplug, and find another empty receptacle to plug into.

One event that any submariner can relate to is blowing sanitary no. 1 at sea! Submarines have two basic receiving sanitary tanks inboard of the pressure hull. Sanitary no. 1 receives all the waste from toilets in the heads, while sanitary no. 2 gets the drainage from shipboard sinks, the galley, and the like. When a submarine is submerged for prolonged periods, it becomes necessary to expel the waste from these repositories when they're getting full. Sanitary no. 2 is easy as the auxiliarymen only have to *pump* the waste overboard. Evacuating *shite* overboard from sanitary no. 1 is another story. When at any depth while on patrol, sanitary no. 1 has to be pressurized to a greater pressure than the pressure outside the hull so the waste can be expelled. It takes a while to blow out this tank, so the auxiliarymen put up signs Blowing Sanitaries mounted by chains in all the heads. Each toilet has a large ball valve in the bottom of the bowl which is operated with a long lever extending upward almost three feet. It's possible to use the heads while no. 1 sanitary is being blown, but *just do not pull the handle!* Sailors getting up in the middle of their sleep period and still half-awake had to be wary. Whenever a loud *whoosh* was heard from one of the heads while no. 1 sanitary was being blown, other shipmates came running to laugh at the poor guy who just got poop and waste residue blown all over him and the stall he was in! Beside the embarrassment, if you do it, you have to clean it up, and that's a shitty job! Whenever no. 1 sanitary was being blown and I had to urinate, I'd put my hand nearest the flushing lever behind my back for insurance. I never blew sanitary in my face during my eight Polaris patrols!

I had received my four *family grams* from Diane during the patrol, and after some sixty-plus days, we had completed our circuitous route around our patrol area and were ready to return to Rota, Spain and the USS *Canopus*. The Blue crew met us as we tied up alongside the *Canopus*, and after the turnover period, the Goldies boarded a commercial 707 jet for home!

Returning home to Groton, Connecticut, was amazing! It was sooo good to be home at 24 Kamaha St. with my wife, Diane, and sleeping in a bed that didn't roll from side to side. (Actually, for the first week or so, the bed *did* seem to be rolling back and forth until I got my *land legs*!) I think it was on this off-crew period that the six-year-old son of an SSN fast attack sailor nicknamed Bear, who lived nearby in Boardsen Place, would come to our door and ask Diane, "Can your Daddy come out and play?" When fast attack SSNs go to sea, they have trips that last six or more months! SSNs have only one crew. Bear's son missed his Daddy and looked to me as a temporary substitute. Of course, I'd always go out and throw a ball back and forth with him or whatever game he wanted to play!

Our off-crew period went quickly as usual, and at the end of May 1968, it was time for our crew to relieve the Blue crew in Rota, Spain, again. We departed from Quonset Point Air Force Base in Rhode Island. The Boeing 707 was still the workhorse of the commercial fleet during my times transiting the Atlantic Ocean and didn't have the range to fly nonstop to Spain. I recall on this flight to Rota, the aircraft was scheduled to stop in Santa Maria Island, Portugal, to refuel. It was out in the Atlantic west of Portugal and apparently had a volcanic origin. As we approached, I could look out the window and see a cliff and an elevated plateau that the runway was constructed on top of. Also, there must have been a minimal ILS system (or none), and as the aircraft approached the runway, it looked like we would slam into the cliff! The pilot applied power, and we could hear the four engines straining to gain altitude. Fortunately, we did gain altitude, but too much, and landed halfway down the runway! The flight crew applied maximum braking, and as we passed the last off-ramp, we almost went into a fence at the end of the runway before the pilots got the aircraft stopped. Wow! The next maneuver was to reverse thrust on the four jet engines and back up, which Boeing 707s didn't do very well. I was relieved when we finally arrived in Rota.

Our beloved Chief Villegas was transferred off the boat during off-crew; he had transitioned to another duty station. In his place on our team was a *new kid*, Dave Hero, FTB3(SU).

There was the usual change of command, and the Blue crew left for stateside. Directly after the change of command, our Weapons Officer, LT. Graham, took me to one side and said, "Petty Officer Smith is insistent that he is senior to you and is strongly requesting that I make him the LPO [leading petty officer] of the fire control gang. Do you have any problem with that?" Meatball and I did have almost exact times in rank. We had both been promoted to E-6, E-5, and E-4 on the exact same date, but he had been an E-3 or seaman a *very* short time longer that I had been, so technically, PO Smith was senior to me.

I replied to LT Graham, "I don't have a problem with Smitty being the LPO. I can contribute to the team in the background just as well, sir." So it became official. We were all working for *Meat*.

I again volunteered to be the FTB gang's representative on the ship's recreation committee and wasted no time getting in touch with the recreation department on the *Canopus*! There were many trips available to choose from, but the ship's rec committee selected an overnight trip to Torremolinos, Spain. Torremolinos is a resort town directly on the Mediterranean Sea and quite beautiful. We coordinated arrangements with the COB and XO, and a date for the trip was set. As the *Rogers* was on port and starboard duty while tied up beside the *Canopus*, it required that the other section take the duty for twenty-four hours instead of the normal twelve hours. This was agreed, and our section would have the duty for twenty-four hours within a week to reciprocate. (As it came to pass, when the other section had their twenty-four hours off, they didn't do anything special. I couldn't believe it!)

When the day for the Torremolinos adventure came, we all boarded a bus early in the morning for the trip. Meatball and I were there, plus a good representation of sailors from all divisions. Unfortunately for him, Dr. Kerr, our ship's doctor, drew the short straw in the wardroom and was our *officer chaperone*. Actually, he was a junior non-line officer and likely selected by the XO to accompany us. It was summer in Spain, and upon arrival in Torremolinos, we all checked into our hotel and changed for the beach.

Smitty or Meatball, several other sailors, and I headed to the beach at Torremolinos to swim in the warm waters of the Mediterranean. It was a beautiful day in Spain and very different from being on any of our beaches back home. After a brief dip in the Med, we decided to check out some of the food stands lining the back of the beach. We each bought an El Aguila (The Eagle) beer, and I saw some *onion rings* that looked interesting, so I bought a basket. Come to find out, the *onion rings* were actually calamari or squid! I'd never eaten squid before, but they were fried and delicious! After some beach time, our group headed back to the hotel to change then proceeded to check out some of the local bars in Torremolinos. I don't remember all the details, but it was a very fun trip. After checking out of the hotel and more sightseeing the next day, we again boarded the bus. Dr. Kerr took a headcount, and we returned to Rota, the *Canopus*, and SSBN659. A good time was had by all, and there were many good memories of Spain to take on patrol that run!

While we were tied up beside the *Canopus* during upkeep, a fast attack sub, the USS *Scorpion*, SSN 589 tied up nearby at the dock. Jim "Droop" Marvel had served aboard the *Scorpion* previously and went aboard to see some of his former shipmates. The *Scorpion* was a Skipjack-class fast attack sub and much smaller than FBMs. She was 251 feet long with a beam of thirty-one feet. Her crew consisted of eight officers and seventy-five enlisted men. When *Scorpion* departed NAS Rota, no one knew this was the last time she would be seen on the surface again.

Excerpts from the Naval Court of Inquiry regarding the Scorpion's loss:

> "As well as Soviet intelligence trawlers, there were Soviet fast nuclear attack submarines attempting to detect and follow the U.S. submarines going out of Rota; in this case, two fast 32-knot Soviet November-class hunter-killer subs. *Scorpion* was then detailed to observe Soviet naval activities in the Atlantic in the vicinity of the Azores. An Echo II-class submarine was operating with this Soviet task force, as well as a Russian guided-missile destroyer. Having observed and listened to the Soviet units, *Scorpion* prepared to head back to Naval Station Norfolk.

Disappearance: May 1968

> *Scorpion* attempted to send radio traffic to Naval Station Rota for an unusually long period beginning shortly before midnight on 20 May and ending after midnight on 21 May, but it was only able to reach a Navy communications station in Nea Makri, Greece, which forwarded the messages to COMSUBLANT. Lt. John Roberts was handed Commander Slattery's last message that he was closing on the Soviet submarine and research group, running at a steady 15 kn (28 km/h; 17 mph) at a depth of 350 ft "to begin surveillance of the Soviets." Six days later, the media reported that she was overdue at Norfolk."

The Navy's SOSUS listening system on Andros Island had actually recorded the sounds of the destruction of *Scorpion* and provided an approximate vector to the sound. A search was undertaken at the end of October 1968 and the Navy's oceanographic research ship

Mizar located sections of the hull of *Scorpion* on the seabed, about four hundred nautical miles southwest of the Azores under more than 9,800 feet of water. Whether Soviet action sunk the *Scorpion* or whether a mechanical failure of one of the boat's systems caused her to be lost may never be known by the public. In truth, the *cat-and-mouse* games we witnessed while on patrol were more than just *games* and *very* serious. The Soviet Union was an aggressive foe and constantly monitoring US Navy submarine operations, both FBM and fast attack. To this day, I believe the *Scorpion's* loss could have been caused by Russian aggression. None of us ever expressed our true feelings to loved ones and family, but there was a clear and present danger from the Soviet Navy to our mission each patrol. Unfortunately, SSN589 could have been one of the Cold War casualties.

During USS *Will Rogers's* first two patrols, Dr. David Kerr was our onboard physician. He was very aware of crew pressures of isolation, besides primarily being there for medical issues. Somehow, Dr. Kerr and I connected as he learned that I was interested in art. I had started doing charcoal sketches and oil painting during my off-drew periods in Groton. I did an oil painting of Shennecossett Road directly outside our home, a copy of Robert Wood's *Autumn Morn*, and several charcoal drawings, mostly landscapes. Dr. Kerr taught me proportions of the human body and techniques for drawing humans, which I wasn't good at doing. For example, the average body is eight heads high, eyes are usually about halfway between the chin and top of the head, etc. He introduced me to Da Vinci's human wheel of body proportions. We did these *lessons* in the crew's library right outside MCC and the crew's lounge. It was *very* helpful, and I started sketching the human body with more confidence. Incidentally, Dr. Kerr was the medical officer who also authorized a pint of *gilley* (190 proof alcohol) to clean the relays of the fire control system when requested! The relay contacts were hermetically sealed and not accessible, but a trip to the crew's mess's Coke machine and a *small* ounce of gilley tasted good and relieved the tension when off watch! Dr. Kerr knew the purpose, and we didn't abuse it.

Our second Gold patrol played out very normally, each division getting our tactical systems ready for another patrol, going on sea trials, loading stores, and battening down the hatches for another submerged sixty to seventy-two days under the water. The patrol evolved normally; the ship and crew performed well. During the patrol, Meatball was working on me constantly about the Peckinpaugh incident in Bethel, Maine. I resisted *all patrol* from giving him any details. Jon Peckinpaugh was a friend, and I knew what Meatball would do if he got *any* confirmation of the story he didn't know but suspected was a juicy one! About two weeks from surfacing, Smitty's insistence got to me, and I divulged the complete story of the Bear Cub Porcupines. Well, Meatball was ecstatic and passed the story around the boat. I felt sorry that I had basically betrayed a friend. Peck was devastated as he was somewhat vain and told me, "Well, I guess you can tell who your *real* friends are." I did feel bad, but it really was a good story.

Someone heard Peck say after the story was divulged, "Man, I will be out of this [expletive] Navy a week after we get in. You guys can't get to me this patrol. I can stack BBs in the corner of MCC, and when they fall down, I'll just stack 'um up again."

Another time in the crew's mess, MT2(SS) Dave Ward cracked during a dinner meal, "Hey, what's wrong with these bear steaks? They taste like they've got needles in them or something?" Smitty was at the same table, and Peck came across the table at him with a knife and fork in his hands. Sailors can be cruel in their ribbing. That short period of razzing by the crew about the Great White Hunter bothered Peck a lot, and it was a good thing the patrol was almost over. I would have felt responsible had anything else happened.

The second SSBN659 Gold patrol ended as we surfaced in the Atlantic off Rota and made our way on the surface to the USS *Canopus*. After a change of command, we were flying home again! Upon landing at Quonset Point AFB in Rhode Island, Dave Smith mysteriously disappeared and never served aboard the USS *Will Rogers* again. During a ship's reunion in 2019, I learned why he was reassigned. After our Navy discharges, Smitty, Dave Hero, and I had reconnected, but I never knew the family tragedy that had occurred while Smitty was on that patrol and the reason for his quick departure and transfer. Dave Smith is a good man, and only a strong person could recover from the tragedy that he went through upon his return from sea.

USS *Will Rogers*—SSBN659

Robbie cutting Dave
Hero's hair on patrol

Will Rogers, opening main
ballast tank vents

Ralph Pelletier
entertaining on patrol

Dave Hero and Wingnut
at Console in MCC

Droop Marvell and crew's
mess while on patrol

Chief Taylor and XO LCDR
Wiggley, casino night

Note: All photos marked with "1997 Yogi" were approved/provided to the author by ADM R. Y. Kaufman.

CHAPTER TWENTY-THREE

USS *WILL ROGERS* AND THE REMAINDER OF MY NAVY SERVICE

It was late summer 1968 in Groton when we started our next off-crew period. Diane and I drove the Pontiac Grand Prix up to Bethel to visit my mother and Dad. I only had to call in once a week to muster during the first month back home, and that could be done from anywhere stateside! We had a nice visit in Maine and stayed with Mother and Dad at their Chandler Hill home. Dad and Diane had developed a bond of respect and love for each other. My mother was against Dad smoking, and Diane had the habit then as well. Some evenings, Dad would say to Diane, "Hey, Diane, wanna go for a smoke?" Of course, Diane would agree, and they'd slip outside to puff on their cigarettes! I assume Mom knew what was happening as she seldom missed a thing, but she never said anything to Diane or to me.

Dad had many hunting rifles and also had a German Luger pistol that he'd taken from a German officer in France during his Army Engineering Corps service there. We decided one afternoon while visiting to go down to a gravel pit at the base of Chandler Hill to do some target shooting. The banks of the gravel pit made a safe backstop for the rounds after they penetrated the targets. We had brought some bottles and cans along to place on raised boards that had been placed there already. One of Dad's rifles was a Springfield *thirty aught six* (or .30-06) caliber rifle. Its shells were loaded with extra powder, and that rifle *really* had a kick! Somehow, we persuaded Diane that she should shoot that rifle. As she took the piece to her right shoulder, I admonished her to hold it tight into her shoulder and take aim. I positioned myself directly behind her, just in case. When she pulled the trigger, to her great surprise, Diane was pushed back into me quite strongly! Don't think she ever fired that *thirty aught six* again!

After a nice visit in Bethel, Diane and I returned to Groton and 24 Kamaha St. We continued to enjoy our time with me being home. During the last sixty days of off-crew, I had several training classes at the sub base, but otherwise the Gold crew worked five days a week and six to eight hours a day in the *Will Rogers's* spaces on the sub base.

CDR Cowell was relieved by a new Skipper during this period, CDR Marvin Greer. We also had a new Weapons Officer, LT. Alan Hellawell. CDR Greer was a big, burly sort and quickly but affectionately received the nickname of The Bear. I guess partially as a change of command celebration, but also as a tribute to CDR Cowell whom we all loved and respected, the Captains wanted to put on a ship's party. As I was on the SSBN659 rec committee and Diane was associated with the Holiday Inn, I recommended that the venue for the event be the Holiday Inn in Groton! We interviewed a couple of locations in Groton and New London, Connecticut, but selected the Groton Holiday Inn. It was interesting being part of the selection committee for the boat and having my wife on the other side being interviewed! Ed Byas viewed this event as one that would open the door for all kinds of submarine crew business and rolled out the red carpet for us! Everything that was proposed was top-shelf and either at a loss or low profit for the Holiday Inn. Byas really just wanted to attract more submarine crews, and we were the benefactors!

The night of the ship's party came, and everything was more than outstanding! The food was great, there was a band for dancing, and Captain Greer and the XO made a point of thanking Diane for such a great event when it was over. It *was* excellent, although I don't think Ed Byas got that much additional business from the US Navy's Groton Sub Base crews as he would have liked to.

While on USS *Will Rogers's* second Gold patrol, I'd gotten to know second class MT (missile technician) Dave Ward better. (The

"Hey, what's wrong with these bear steaks? They taste like they've got needles in them or something?" sailor from that patrol!) Dave was a nice guy, and we got along well. During this off-crew, Diane and I got together with Dave and his wife, Kay, on occasion. Although a bit younger than we were, they were a fun couple to hang out with. The Wards had an old color TV that they were selling, and we bought it. Our very first color TV! It had vacuum tubes and was a bit *finicky* as far as reliability was concerned. Another downside to color TV was there weren't that many broadcasts in color in those days, but the programs that were in color were amazing! I remember when the TV stopped working. I would remove the back, take out all the vacuum tubes, and take them to RadioShack for testing on the free tube tester. Invariably, there would be one or two tubes that tested *bad*, but replacing them with new ones and plugging in the *good* old tubes would usually fix the problem!

Diane and I continued to enjoy the Groton, Connecticut, area, and as November 1968 approached it was time for us *Goldies* to again cross *The Pond* and relieve the Blue crew. We were again to meet them in Rota, Spain. We arrived at NAS Rota and made the usual bus trip to the USS Canopus (AS-34) who would again be supporting us during our upkeep period. We went aboard, stowed our seabags, and awaited the USS *Will Rogers* and the Blue crew arrival the next day.

After the usual change of command, thirty-day upkeep period, sea trials, and loading stores, SSBN659 Gold departed on our third deterrent patrol, my seventh Polaris *endurance* adventure. This time, once in the Atlantic we passed Portugal and headed to our patrol area. As Petty Officer Smith had left the boat, I was now senior and LPO of the fire control gang. I accepted this responsibility with enthusiasm and put together a series of informal training sessions that I could give my fellow FTBs while on patrol. I had gained a fair knowledge of the Mk 84 fire control system over the years, and I remember drawing some simplified overview diagrams to illustrate the system. Of course, we had BuShips detailed diagrams, but for learning purposes, I liked the overview concept for helping others becoming familiar with the system.

Being in close proximity to Murmansk, Russia's, submarine base, sonar did at least on one occasion during this patrol detect a Russian November class fast attack sub trailing us when we cleared the baffles. We had some outstanding sonarmen aboard! One of them that I've kept in touch with through various SSBN659 Ship's Reunions is Ed Greany. Again, the Russians would follow us for several days, then depart after apparently getting tired of playing *cat and mouse.*

Nuclear submarines can stay submerged for extended periods of time and therefore have to control the atmosphere within the boat. There are two O2 generators to make oxygen from seawater and two CO2 scrubbers to remove that gas from accumulating in the interior of the boat. On an FBM submarine, these pieces of equipment are all located in AMR no. 1, just aft of the missile compartment. While it didn't happen on any of my patrols, the O2 generators have injured or killed submariners maintaining them while on patrol. These large pieces of equipment take in seawater and, by employing electrolysis, separate it into oxygen and hydrogen. The oxygen is compressed and stored in large cylinders within the ballast tanks outboard of the pressure hull for release later within the boat as needed. The H is mixed with the seawater system and pumped overboard. However, when in close proximity to each other, the O_2 generator's two gasses present one of the most explosive combinations in existence—the fuel (hydrogen) and one of the best oxidizers (oxygen). There are safety circuits to prevent accidents from happening, but in the particular incident we heard about, the safety circuits had been overridden by the auxiliaryman doing the repair. Somehow, possibly from a wrench or something, there was a spark that ignited this deadly combination of close gases. The resulting explosion knocked the auxiliaryman across AMR no. 1 and killed him. Patrols usually aren't aborted, even for tragic events like death of a crewmember. In a previous chapter, I'd mentioned that these FBM subs had a walk-in cooler and a freezer to store food for at least ninety days. To accommodate the disaster, the ship's cooler was emptied of whatever refrigerated items were left and the temperature lowered to below thirty-two degrees Fahrenheit before the dead sailor in his body bag was interred for the remainder of the patrol.

In those days, each FBM submarine set sail with a full medical doctor aboard. I did participate in patrols during which one of our crewmembers came down with an infectious disease while on patrol and was quarantined in a separate isolated bunk in the missile compartment until well. During the quarantine period, he had almost no exposure to the rest of the crew, and his eating utensils were washed separately from ours. There had to be a very serious reason to abort the mission then, as I'm sure it is now.

Around February 1969, our third Gold patrol was ending, and probably just in time! Again, crew members' traits that normally wouldn't bother me started to become very annoying. We surfaced off the coast of Rota and made way to our sub tender USS Canopus. The Blue crew was there to meet us. After a three-day change of command, we were flying home again!

I didn't know it until I returned to Groton, but Diane had gone home to Jersey for the Christmas holidays while I was on patrol. She had purchased a roundtrip ticket on Pilgrim Airlines. Pilgrim was a small airline that had two Beach 99 prop aircraft and flew between Groton, Connecticut, LaGuardia Airport in New York City, and Hartford, Connecticut. On the day Diane was scheduled to go home, she decided to stay a bit longer and delayed her departure until the very last flight between LaGuardia and Groton that day. As the event was relayed to Diane later, it's a good thing she did as the flight she was originally scheduled to fly on crashed with a loss of all souls on board! Pilgrim Airlines lost 50 percent of its fleet that day. I almost lost a wife and an unborn child (see next paragraph)!

When I returned home, I received more *very* happy news! Diane was pregnant with our first child! As she had had one previous miscarriage, we took it a bit easy on this off-crew period. 24 Kamaha St. was a one-bedroom apartment, so one of the first things we did was to look for a two-bedroom unit at Boardsen Place. 34 Kamaha St. on the second floor of an adjacent building was available, so we signed a new contract and moved up. This would give us a separate room for the new baby when he or she was born. I still had access to the great woodworking shop on the sub base, so I made a dresser for the new baby. It had two panels that opened, right and left, on the top front with two small pull-out drawers behind them on each side. Below were three full-width drawers for storing big items. I remember I made the pull handles out of plywood and in the shape of friendly animals that I painted in acrylics. The dresser was finished in glossy white enamel, and I placed a white section of Formica as the top piece.

After our thirty-day relaxed mustering period, we reported to our space on the sub base five days a week and attended some formal Navy refresher classes on the boat's fire control systems for the next two months. It was during this period that I fine-tuned my resume and started sending them out (maybe fifty or so) to prospective future civilian employers. Diane and I had discussed it, and it was decided that I'd give civilian life a try. I had learned electronics skills and found that field very interesting. There were many pluses for staying in the Navy—retirement pay, medical benefits for life, commissary privileges, etc. My skippers and XOs had discussed enlisted to officer programs available, which were quite appealing, and they offered to recommend me. However, I had enough of going on sixty to seventy-two-day patrols, plus options for FTB1(SS) shore duty were limited if I didn't get into one of the officer programs. We decided to try civilian life. Looking back at it, the Navy was probably one of the best things that could have happened to me at the time. My career in the hotel business was certainly not going to take me very far, and I know I would have tired of it quickly at some point. The Navy gave me a direction and introduced me to a field that I really found challenging. Something I could excel at!

May 1969 approached, and it was time for my eighth and final Polaris deterrent patrol. We were again relieving the Blue crew in Rota. Our destination was the USS Holland (AS-32) who had relieved the Canopus while the Blue crew was on patrol. We were bused to her, stowed our sea bags aboard and awaited the Blue crew the next day. They arrived on time and we completed the change of command and assumed responsibility for SSBN659.

Our patrol area was again north, but summer seas above the Arctic Circle were not as rough as they were in the winter. For this my eighth and final patrol, I occupied the *goat locker* or chief's quarters for sleeping like I had done for the previous patrol. I was again the fire control gang LPO and one of the senior petty officers aboard. The goat locker was also directly outside MCC, so it was close for me to get to my duty station during *Battle Stations Missile*.

Directly forward of MCC and the goat locker was the crew's lounge. There was usually a poker game going on there with crew members smoking, which was allowed. (I remember seeing the auxiliarymen, on *all* the patrols that I had been on, cleaning the air filters for the boat's circulation system. They were caked with an ochre colored nicotine that had to be cleaned out. I didn't smoke, and it was disgusting to look at the crap that was in the air due to smokers.) Anyway, on this and most of the patrols I'd been on, there were typically several senior enlisted first class or chief petty officers that took home around $1,000 in cash each! It was the junior sailors, who probably least could afford it, that went home with a loss.

During this last patrol, I received a *baby gram* that announced Diane had given birth to a son! I was ecstatic! The sub base had a hospital, but it was small. We purposely waited until other sailors had already registered and the base hospital was booked up before registering Diane's pregnancy with the Navy. With base facilities full and for the sum of twenty-five dollars out of pocket, Diane could have the baby at Lawrence and Memorial Hospitals in New London, Connecticut. The sub base hospital didn't have a bad reputation for childbirths and care, but Lawrence and Memorial Hospitals had a better one for neonatal care. Nothing else out of the ordinary happened on this patrol, and we all returned to USS Holland on time and were relieved by the Blue crew.

Of course, I didn't learn the details until the patrol was over and I returned to Groton, but apparently, getting Diane to the hospital was very eventful! Diane had a friend, Eleanor Scussel, whom she'd worked with at Ogilvy, Benson & Mather in New York City and who was now living in Groton with her husband. Diane had spoken with Eleanor previously, and they had devised a plan. As soon as

Diane started having labor pains, she called Eleanor, who came over to Kamaha St. with her sister, picked up Diane, and they raced across the Thames River to the hospital thinking a baby was going to be born any minute.

As it turned out, Thomas Alan Robertson wouldn't be born for another ten and a half hours (of standard labor) at 7:32 a.m. It was July 9, 1969, during the Feast Week of St. Thomas More, whom Tom was named after. Diane and I had seen *A Man for All Seasons* on my last off-crew period, and we liked the name because of St. Thomas More's strong, upstanding character. We just had a feeling our son would do the name proud (and he has lived up to the challenge).

Tom was only three weeks old the first time I saw him. When I got off the bus and Diane met me with our newborn at the Groton sub base, it was like a miracle!

Dr. David Kerr — Da Vinci Wheel of Life

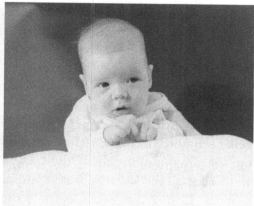

St. Thomas More,
Archbishop of Canterbury

Thomas Alan Robertson, 1969

Living aboard a nuclear submarine with its periodic contamination drills, *field days* to clean the boat, WSRTs, and other interruptions to one's sleep was challenging, but nothing like those presented by one newborn who seemed to be constantly hungry! Diane got up most of the time to give Tom his bottle, but I tried to be a good partner and help out, too, as we were in the *Rogers*'s thirty-day *off-crew* period.

One of my first priorities now was to decide what I wanted to do when my Navy obligation was completed. To give me options, I had applied to Fairleigh Dickinson University in Hackensack, New Jersey, to continue my college education and had been accepted. Diane's sister, Cherilyn, had graduated from Fairleigh Dickinson and touted it highly.

Of the many resumés I'd sent out prior to patrol, the most promising were from Control Data Corporation in Rockville, Maryland; Vitro Corp in Bethesda, Maryland; and Honeywell in Hartford, Connecticut. I only did a phone interview with Honeywell, but I traveled to Maryland at the two other company's expense to interview in person. I was very interested in both companies! Vitro was offering an instructor position for Polaris crews, and I'd be working at their Bethesda, Maryland, headquarters, and Control Data Corporation (CDC) needed customer engineers for their 3300 and 3500 lines of mainframe computers in the Washington, DC, area. Our friend Larry Fetter was now working for Vitro, and he and Diane no. 1 were living in Silver Spring, Maryland, after Larry had made *nine* patrols on the USS *James Monroe*!

While I was leaning a bit toward Vitro, my interview with Chris Michele, the Customer Engineering Branch Manager at CDC, went *very* well. Chris had been a Tech Support Engineer at CDC before being promoted to Branch Manager and was very technical. He asked me specific questions about the CDC DGBC aboard submarines, and I aced all the answers! Both computers, while they had a much different form factor, were logically the same. I knew the DGBC inside and out.

When I returned home to Groton and Boardsen Place, Diane and I discussed our options for the future. We didn't have the funding for my college expenses and living expenses combined, so Control Data Corporation was chosen. All I had to do now was complete my Navy obligation, which I did with pride.

About 26 August 1969, I was transferred from USS *Will Rogers*, SSBN659 to the Squadron staff on the Groton sub base and was assigned to the brig and Shore Patrol duty! I had *never* had Shore Patrol duty in my almost eight years of Navy service. What a way to leave. I was issued a baton and web belt, plus white spats and a big "Shore Patrol" armband! I spent overnight on brig duty and was told I could hit the rack unless needed to go out on SP patrol to bring in an unruly sailor. Oh, joy! As it turned out, I didn't have to leave the brig that night, but I was awakened around 0300 hours to help process a sailor who had been brought in by another detachment. I witnessed a disgusting search (humiliation) technique called a *cavity search*, then went back to my rack and was discharged the next day. Could have done without that final experience. I was formally discharged from the US Navy's Submarine Service on 27 July 1969, a good yet somewhat sad day in my life.

It's interesting to note here that there are stark contrasts between the Navy's FBM fleet and operations of over fifty-five years ago and now! Today there are fourteen SSBN-726 Ohio-Class submarines in the Navy's fleet that are much larger and capable of carrying up to twenty-four Trident II D-5, three-stage ballistic missiles. The forward bases of Rota, Spain, Holy Loch, Scotland, and Guam have been closed and the submarine tenders retired. SUBLANT submarines now operate out of Kings Bay, Georgia, and SUBPAC out of Bremerton, Washington. The increased range of the D-5 missile greatly increases the patrol area over the old A-3 or Poseidon C-3 missiles. Through retrofit and new reactor cores, these Ohio-Class SSBN's life has been extended to forty-two years (two twenty-year deployments separated by a two-year overhaul—period!) Looking forward to the next generation of SSBN-826 Columbia-Class boats, the first submarine is scheduled to start construction in FY2021 and enter service in 2031. China is building SSN and SSBN submarines faster than any country today with Russia again adding to its ballistic missile submarine fleet. Even India is starting to deploy FBM submarines. To maintain our leadership role and defend our freedom, we must not let down our defensive guard.

CHAPTER TWENTY-FOUR

THE START OF A NEW CAREER

Being a civilian now felt different, yet other than not having a submarine as a workplace, it was in many respects similar. One big difference would be my salary. Even with all the extra ProPay, hazardous duty pay, and ComRats, I was making about $6,000 a year in the Navy. My new customer engineer position would pay roughly $9,000 annually, not counting overtime pay!

I coordinated with the Control Data Corporation (CDC) human resources personnel, and I was to report for eight months of training in Minneapolis in October 1969. The Navy paid severance pay and travel mileage back to my home of record (Miami). CDC would pay to transport our furniture and personal effects from Groton, Connecticut. Diane and I took a break and made a trip north to say so long to her parents and my Maine parents during the month of September 1969, then returned to Groton to pack our things and get ready for the trip west!

During this time, I tried to warn Diane, "Di, Minnesota winters are cold. You might want to purchase some extra warm clothes before we leave, items such as long underwear, extra sweaters, and the like. Minnesota's weather is similar to Maine's, and it gets *very* cold in Maine."

Diane's reply was "Oh, I'll be okay. I grew up in the New York/ New Jersey area and can take the cold!"

The first of October came. Our furniture had been picked up, and we packed the Grand Prix for the trip. We'd purchased a portable baby bed to put in the back seat for Tommy. It consisted of a plastic enclosure, mattress pad, two front legs that touched the floor, and the rear of the bed rested on the back seat itself. There was no other connection to the car interior, and there were no rear seat belts at the time to better secure it. By today's standards, it was not very accident safe. We made it safely to the Twin Cities, however! Temporarily staying in a motel room, we found a nice apartment very near the CDC *tower building* on East Old Shakopee Rd. and south of I-494. It was just behind the Minnesota Viking's outdoor stadium. I incorrectly assumed my training classes would be held in the CDC tower building. The new apartment itself was expensive, and we also rented a garage for the Grand Prix to help it get through the winter months. CDC was giving me an allowance for rent during the training period, but we exceeded that a bit. It should have been an omen for the rest of the winter, because the day we moved into our new apartment, it was snowing!

I attended various training classes *all around* the Twin Cities area over the next months, but never a class that was held in the CDC tower building! I learned the internal workings of and how to maintain stand-alone CDC printers, card readers, card punches, disk drives, and other peripherals of the day. Mainframe training was conducted at CDC's Arden Hills facility where CDC's two major product lines of computers were being fabricated. Our troubleshooting sessions were always held during the mid-shift (midnight to 8:00 a.m.) when the manufacturing process was not going on. At the time, CDC had two main product lines of computer systems: the 6000 series and the 3000 series. The CDC 3500 that I was learning directly competed with IBM's 360/30 computers. CDC's 3300 series mainframe computers and peripheral controllers in the 1960s were all designed with discrete components of resistors, capacitors, and transistors on a printed circuit board. There were few integrated chips at the time. The 3500 consisted mainly of early integrated circuits and was a first attempt by CDC to get away from discrete component machines. I was learning something very new to me technically, and life in the civilian world was going fine!

The people of Minnesota were amazing! I'd never lived in such a friendly area and much different from the East Coast. For example,

I'd be standing in line at Sears and Roebuck waiting to pay a monthly bill and someone in the line beside me would strike up a conversation! Diane, Tommy, and I would occasionally go out to one of the many family restaurants in Minneapolis for dinner. The wait staff and other customers couldn't have been friendlier in those places!

Winters in Minneapolis *were* tough, however. The first time it was below zero and there were tiny ice crystals in the air, Diane walked outside, and she had trouble taking a breath. It was then she told me, "It really is *cold* out here! Guess I'll have to buy some warmer clothes tomorrow." There was a lot of snow and ice that year. I ended up purchasing a block heater for the Grand Prix. It consisted of a heated rod that replaced the oil dipstick and was plugged onto an 110v AC outlet on the other end. Our garage stall was designed with an 110v AC outlet directly in front of the Grand Prix, so the block heater got plugged in there during cold Minnesota nights. Plus I had a heavy blanket that I'd place over the hood to help keep the heat in. Only once during that winter, it was so cold that I couldn't get the car started the next morning, and I was late for class!

Another difference with Minnesota for me was one could buy 3.2% beer in grocery stores. Normal *strong beer* (6%) could only be purchased in liquor stores. Diane and I shopped at various grocery stores. One that I recall, Red Owl had a large scale in the produce department for weighing vegetables. Of course, Tommy always came shopping with us, and when he was eight months old, Tommy's first word was *clock*. He looked at the large produce scale, which looked like a clock to him, pointed at it, and said, "Clock." We thought that was quite special! Tommy also started walking at ten months, which we felt, even as first-time parents, was early.

While in Minneapolis, Diane and I became Minnesota Vikings fans. The Viking's stadium was within walking distance of our apartment. The Vikings were having a great year in 1969 under Coach Bud Grant! We got tickets and watched them win both the Divisional Playoff on December 27 and the NFL Championship game on January 4, 1970. We left Tommy with Bill, a CDC classmate of mine, and his wife, who also lived in our same apartment building. It was *cold, sooo cold!* We had a small flask of brandy to help ward off the freezing temperatures, but when we got up at halftime to stretch, our legs were so numb we could hardly move! The amazing thing was that Bud Grant would not allow his team to have heaters behind them like the other teams did. They were going to show their Viking stamina! It was cold for both games, but we were young and enjoyed the experience immensely. The Vikings lost Super Bowl IV to the Kansas City Chiefs in New Orleans that season. While the Vikings have appeared in four Super Bowls, they have never won one.

Spring came (but not *ice out* yet) in Minnesota. It was May 1970, and I had completed my CDC customer engineer training. We packed up our personal things. The movers came for our furniture, and we loaded up the Grand Prix for the trip east to the Washington, DC, area for a continuation of our new civilian life adventure. Life was still exciting!

When I reported back to CDC's office in Rockville, Maryland (ROCOLA), Chris Michele had decided to go back to Tech Support, and I had a new manager, Bob Thorne. I would be reporting to Bob in his Rockville office, but maintaining mainly CDC 3300 series computer systems all over Maryland, Northern Virginia, and the District of Columbia within his branch. While logically the same, the CDC 3500 and 3300 computers had differences that I had to learn on my own.

Diane and I decided on an apartment in McLean, Virginia, and signed a one-year contract. We eventually wanted to purchase a new home but needed time to look around and see what area of Northern Virginia that we wanted to live in.

During the cold winter in Minneapolis, Diane had become pregnant again, and we were very much looking forward to our second child! I settled into a routine of servicing CDC's computer systems in the DC area and soon was assigned to an on-site position at George Washington University Hospital just off Washington Circle on K St., NW. The cardiologist in charge, Dr. Herman Klingenmeyer, was pioneering and developing software applications for a new heart monitoring function on a Control Data 3300 computer. It was groundbreaking, and I felt like I was part of the team! There were data lines coming from the hospital to the Mary Washington Building where our 3300 system was in the basement. The new programs monitored QRS curves of patients in the hospital and sounded alarms if the parameters were exceeded. As you know, today that is done by a small device in each room that is connected to the nurse's station on the floor!

At the end of December 1970, Diane was starting to have contractions, and we drove down the George Washington Parkway to Georgetown University Hospital where Diane's obstetrician, Dr. Amorosi, practiced. Erin Norris Robertson was born at 4:52 p.m. and for a change, I was in the delivery room to witness the blessed event! The day before it was time to drive down to Georgetown University Hospital to pick up Di and Erin, a terrible snow and ice storm passed through our area. The next day, I loaded Tommy into the Grand Prix and slowly started to back out of a parking spot in the apartment complex. Almost immediately, the car started sliding sideways without me applying the gas or brakes! I stopped, took Tommy back to stay with Agnes, a neighbor, and slowly made my way to Georgetown to retrieve the girls. If I was going to get stuck on the way down, I didn't want to place Tommy in that cold, icy situation. Long story short, I did make it down and back safely, and our new enlarged family was safe in our McLean, Virginia, apartment.

Professionally, I felt I'd made a good choice by joining Control Data Corporation. I quickly became Bob Thorne's branch tech support engineer. When there was a critical CDC system component down and the responsible CE couldn't fix it, Bob would call me. This would often be sometimes at 2:00 a.m. to 3:00 a.m. or later! I'd get up and respond to the call and usually have it fixed within a couple of hours or less. I was being challenged and loved it!

During the next phase of my career at CDC, I had the opportunity of becoming a Systems Engineer (or SE) on CDC's *Master* operating system. I knew the hardware inside and out and now had the chance to learn the OS that controlled the hardware and application programs. I believe it was during 1971 and after my SE training that CDC won a $30 million award from the IRS for an IDRS (Integrated Data Retrieval System). This was the first time IRS had distributed databases that could be accessed from terminals in branch and district offices to one of its ten IRS Service Centers around the USA where there would be a CDC 3300 computer system. I was assigned to the test bed system in Arlington, Virginia, as the IRS's System Engineer for software support purposes. Curt Haralson was the CDC Engineer in Charge (EIC) and Rob Swatala our primary IRS customer and contact.

Also during 1971, Diane and I had looked around the Northern Virginia area and signed a contract on a new home in Greenbriar off Route 50 west in Fairfax, Virginia. It was new construction and cost $27,500! We used part of the savings from the allotment that had been building up in my Navy Federal savings account for the down payment! The home was a story and a half Cape Cod design with four bedrooms and two baths. I was concerned about the new mortgage payment of $254 per month! We anxiously watched it being built and moved in during the summer of 1971. The address was 13140 Pelfrey Ln.

I had a long successful career at CDC. Professionally after my SE experiences, I was a Tech Support Manager for about a year for CDC's plug peripheral (IBM compatible) products that CDC was starting to sell. It was the year the first *Star Wars* movie came out, and our tech support team had a good time with the theme! There was a second manager who was responsible for supporting all the traditional CDC hardware. He was shorter than I was, so his team called him R2D2. Being taller, I was C3PO. We all had fun with it. The one downside of this new position for me was reporting to an office in ROCOLA every day. In those days, the Beltway in Virginia had only two lanes going into Maryland. There were three lanes on the Maryland side. Going to work in the morning was fine, but the backup of merging three lanes in Maryland into two in Virginia during rush hour at the Cabin John Bridge over the Potomac River was horrible. Traffic backed up for miles into Maryland. I eventually found some ways around it, but it was still bad.

During my time as CDC Tech Support Manager, I had the opportunity of visiting some classified or *spook* agencies, as we called them. I had kept my Navy Top Secret clearance current specifically so I could be involved in TS projects as part of my job. If you didn't have a clearance, you just were not permitted access to sensitive US Government data and locations. One of the first classified sites I had the occasion of visiting was the National Security Agency (NSA) at Ft. Meade, Maryland. One had to call ahead for clearance and, after being checked out, pass through tight security layers of containment. Two of my Tech Support Engineers were going into the bowels of NSA's many underground computer rooms to do some required equipment grounding checks. I went along mainly to meet our NSA technical customers and make sure we completed the required services.

My second experience going into a restricted US Government agency was at the CIA in Langley, Virginia. This is *the* famous worldwide CIA headquarters operation! CDC literally had rooms full of IBM plug-compatible disk drives known then as *disk farms*. There had been some annoying intermittent drive errors, and the CIA CTO was getting *very* upset with our products. After clearances days ahead to gain access to the building, we met with the customer, and I presented our approach to solving the issues. As my team went to work in one of the vast *disk farm* rooms, several of the CIA people and I retreated to a room deep in the bowels of the CIA to talk. I had been issued a CIA Visitors badge but was required to have a government escort whenever I moved about within the building. I was getting updates on the progress of the troubleshooting from my team, but at one point I had to go to the men's room. I asked my government escort, and he said, "Oh, it's just down the corridor to the left, then take another left at the first hallway, and its right there. The men's room is so close that I don't need to come with you." Well, after doing what I had to do and on my way back, I came around a corner, and there was a big Marine with his right hand on his pistol! He yelled, "Halt. Where is your escort? Why are you in this hallway alone?"

I think one of my orifices puckered up a bit, and I said, "I was meeting in a room just down the hall. My escort told me it was okay to go to the men's room and return." The marine escorted me back to the room. I don't know if my escort ever got reprimanded, but I was fine. Incidentally, while at the CIA, I only met dedicated government career individuals and saw no signs of a secret *cabal*!

Tommy and Erin started school on two different years attending Greenbriar West Elementary that was very near our home. The first summer when they were old enough, we wanted to join the Greenbriar pool, but all the memberships were sold out, and there was a waiting list. We checked around and ended up joining International Town and Country Club as social members. It was located just across Route 50 from Greenbriar. International had a nice pool, and we could go there for dinner or lunch with the family. There were food and snacks sold at the pool, but no cash was allowed. Instead, you bought *chits* in various denominations and used those at the pool for food. I remember when we were at the pool, Tommy and Erin would say, "Mommy, do you have any chits?" when they wanted a snack or drink. International had a great golf course, but we didn't play golf then.

While living in Greenbriar, we became good friends with neighbors who lived across Pelfrey Lane, Bill and Eileen Gavin. Bill was an FBI agent and worked in the FBI's DC labs in hematology. Bill would analyze blood samples from crime scenes across the USA and occasionally have to travel to a city to testify as an expert witness. Bill and Eileen were from Revere, Massachusetts, and both quick witted! We partied at each other's and other homes of mutual friends and participated in a bowling league for several years as *the Bags and Balls*.

During this time, we were members of the National Democratic Club (NDC) that was located just off Capitol Hill in DC. Occasionally, when I'd finished an afternoon meeting in The District, I'd pick up Bill Gavin at FBI headquarters, and we'd drive over to the NDC before returning to Greenbriar. Diane and I attended a St. Patrick's Day party at the NDC one year when Speaker of the House Tip O'Neil was there. At one point, Tip came over to Diane and said, while kissing her cheek, "Happy St. Paddy's Day, Little Miss Irish!" Diane was thrilled (back then, it wasn't taken as sexual harassment). I think Democrats were more moderate then than today's batch. I had voted for Ronald Reagan in 1980 and remember Tommy and I traveling to Freedom Plaza in the middle of Pennsylvania Ave. on January 20, 1981, to watch Reagan's motorcade headed for the US Capital Building and his inauguration. There was a lot of excitement for *change* until years later, it was apparent that *trickle-down econom-ics* doesn't work, and I did not vote for Reagan four years later.

My torpedoman friend, Dwayne Swanson (Swanney), came to visit us in Greenbriar one day. He told me he was up to here with the Navy, had gone AWOL, and was going to Canada. Swanney spent a couple of days with us helping me paint trim and baseboards in our living room. Then one evening, he told us he was leaving the next day. I spent most of the night trying to talk him out of it, but he left the next morning. Swanney ended up in Western Canada, where he would eventually meet his second wife, Diane. He was quite disillusioned with the Navy and life in general. One could say Yogi started it by having him removed from the USS *Will Rogers*, but Swanney had separated from his wife, wouldn't get to see his children regularly, and had other issues. I really felt bad for him. He had been a good Navy torpedoman. We would still keep in touch over the years, however.

For Diane's birthday in 1974, I bought her a white Austin Healey Sprite sports car. My friend, Lynn Windingland, painted cars and sprayed the Sprite Cadillac Fire Mist Silver, adding a twelve-inch black racing stripe with metallic sprinkles down the driver's side hood and trunk. It was a really sharp car!

On May 7, 1975, during my time at CDC, our third child, Dennis John Robertson, was born at Fairfax Hospital in Fairfax, Virginia, at 6:42 p.m. Again, I was allowed to be in the delivery room as Diane was giving birth to our second son. Awesome! When we were able to bring Dennis John (DJ) home, Diane and I were still living in Greenbriar. Our young family was growing!

My next promotion was to a position as the Customer Engineering Program Manager for several US government accounts. I reported to a gentleman named Andy Cronin. He was a great guy to work for and son of the author A. J. Cronin. I had Control Data's IRS, DSA, and DISA accounts, plus a couple more. The IRS account required the most of my time. As the Program Manager, I was involved in meetings at IRS headquarters at 1111 Constitution Ave., Washington, DC, and part of a team of salesman, Larry "Hoss" Campbell, and IRS Project Manager, Paul "PNO" Olson.

We usually met with IRS at its headquarters in DC. However, Larry had sold IRS a multimillion-dollar upgrade to CDC 3500 systems, and as the systems were installed, the three of us traveled to each of the ten Service Centers during acceptance of the new mainframes. We would meet Service Center Directors and management, offering any support necessary for the new installation. It meant a lot of travel and time away from family, but it was professionally rewarding.

During the time all these job promotions and changes were going on, Diane had us moving within the Northern Virginia area every eight to nine years or less! I have to admit, these moves were good financially as the real estate market then was moving upward, and we always had a nice equity built up in the house we were moving from! While on a trip to the IRS Service Centers in Ogden, Utah, and Fresno, California, in 1979 with Larry Campbell and Paul Olson and National Office IRS individuals, I received a call from Diane: "We've just bought a new house!" My shocked reply was "What?" Pat Campbell was a realtor, and the home beside theirs had just gone on the market. The address was 12861 Tewksbury Dr. It was in Fox Mill Estates, Fairfax, Virginia, and right off Reston Avenue. It was a bigger house than our Greenbriar home and had a basement. We ended up keeping the Greenbriar house and renting it out for about three years as an investment. During our time at Tewksbury Dr., I finished the basement in an Old English theme and added a dance floor and a bar. We called it the Pub Room and had many great parties there over the years. There was an elementary school in the neighborhood that was about a mile away. Tommy and Erin transferred there that fall.

During several summers in the late 1970s, we had taken some rugged family camping vacations in Maine. I wanted our family to see the remote parts of Maine that I had come to love when I was growing up there. My mother and Dad were living in Kingfield, Maine, now as Dad was managing a wood turning mill there. We drove up, and after a brief visit, Diane, Tommy, Erin (John was too young for camping so he stayed with Grandma), and I borrowed Dad's boat and outboard motor and towed it up to the remote Allagash Wilderness Waterway area. We put the boat in at the southern foot of Chamberlain Lake and loaded our food supplies, tents, etc. into it. The lower section of the

Allagash Wilderness Waterway is a series of lakes, while the northern section is made up exclusively of the Allagash River, which incidentally flows north. Chamberlain Lake is a big lake being about thirteen miles long. The water is clear and cold! The Maine State Forest Service maintains a series of campsites on both sides of the lake. They are available on a first-come basis. We headed north in Dad's boat until we found one and set up camp, primarily our tent and a dining fly.

We spent several days on the lake and camped at various sites along the way until we reached the northern end of Chamberlain. There by the brook outlet that leads to Eagle Lake were several canoes secured with a chain. There was a fire warden's house nearby where we learned the canoes belonged to a flying service in Greenville and were for rent. A plan was devised! We'd rent a canoe, load essential stuff for an overnight, and spend the night on Pillsbury Island in Eagle Lake. There was an easy portage down the dam at the northern end of Chamberlain and a short canoe trip down a stream connecting the two lakes. The campsite on Pillsbury Island was beautiful. I remember looking up at the stars that clear evening. There was absolutely no ambient light as there was no civilization nearby and we could see tiny stars and the Milky Way more clearly that we'd ever seen it before! The next day, after exploring Eagle Lake a bit, we headed back up the stream to Chamberlain. I got out of the canoe, and while Tommy and Erin were hacking around, rocking the canoe back and forth, Diane slipped on a mossy submerged rock as she entered the stream and did some minor damage to one knee. We were able to walk the canoe and our two children back up against the modest current as the stream was shallow. However, I believe that was the start of the issues that many years later necessitated a partial knee replacement for Diane. One curiosity just off the shore in that area were several abandoned old steam locomotives left over from logging days! One just wouldn't expect to find large steam engines in such a remote location! We then re-boarded Dad's boat and made our way back down Chamberlain to our car. It had been a very nice week!

The following summer, we returned to North Central Maine, but this time to Mount Katahdin. John was three years old now and came along. I had reserved a three-sided log lean-to on Roaring Brook for six or seven nights. There was a raised wooden floor for setting up sleeping bags, a firepit outside, and even an outhouse nearby! (This was an improvement over the horizontal log latrine we'd encountered in the Allagash!) I made the reservations in January as these campsites booked up very quickly. We stayed at Roaring Brook for several days and watched wildlife, including deer and moose, walk right through our campsite like we weren't even there. It was a wonderful location.

I'd also reserved a lean-to up the mountain at Chimney Pond. Diane and I had normal-sized backpacks and Tommy and Erin smaller ones. We packed our freeze-dried food, cooking/eating utensils, sleeping bags, etc. in our backpacks and headed up the trail to Chimney Pond. The trail was 3.3 miles long and looked like an elevated dry stream bed consisting of small rocks and fairly large boulders all the way to Chimney Pond. John had taken along his friend Taddy that he'd placed at the top of my backpack with only Taddy's head sticking out "so he could breathe."

Our hike to Chimney Pond took about three hours, and young John did a super job as a three-year-old hiker in a wilderness environment! We set up camp in another three-sided log lean-to exactly like the one we'd just left on Roaring Brook. Chimney Pond is roughly halfway between the base of Katahdin and the summit. It's a glacial cirque in a feature of Katahdin called the Great Basin, which was created by glacial erosion. We spent an amazing night there. It was *dark* until the moon came up. Again the sky was sooo clear, and one could see more stars, plus the constellations were very discernible. Diane took a flashlight to walk out to the outhouse before turning in. When trying to return, it was so dark that she had no idea which way to go, even with a flashlight, and started getting a bit scared. Fortunately, I was coming out to do the same thing, and Diane was saved.

On a previous trip in an earlier year, when John had stayed with my mother, Diane, Tommy, Erin, and I had taken the Saddle Trail from Chimney Pond to the summit and came down the Cathedral Trail. John was still too young for that adventure on this trip, so after a couple of days at Chimney Pond, we hiked back down to Roaring Brook where we spent one more night before driving back to Kingfield for a brief visit with my mother and Dad.

Baxter State Park—Mt. Katahdin, ME

Our First Trip Climbing Mt. Katahdin with Tom and Erin

3.3m trail to Chimney Pond

Climbing up to Baxter Peak (That's Chinmey Pond below!)

Robertson family at the summit

Our Second Trip Climbing Mt. Katahdin—John Joins Us!

Cool Roaring Brook Campsite—Dad and John

Roaring Brook—Mom and Erin dinnertime!

On the trail to Chimney Pond

Erin and three-year-old John in Chimney Pond lean-to

CHAPTER TWENTY-FIVE

THE BEGINNING OF MY SALES CAREER

Larry and Pat Campbell and Paul Olson had become good friends of Diane's and mine. We kept in touch and did cool things together like opening up summer rentals in Ocean City, Maryland, for a man Larry knew well, serving in the Reston Lions Club, having parties, and just doing things together in general. It was early in 1979 that Larry decided he was leaving CDC to go with a Georgetown, DC, based Federal Government systems integrator. He recommended me for his replacement on the IRS account as the National Salesman! I was making a decent guaranteed salary by then, and when I looked at the CDC sales plan with a *base salary* and *potential commissions*, it seemed like too much risk financially for my family. I said, "No, but thank you." Larry had been talking with the Civilian Agencies sales manager, John Warden, as he was recruiting me. About a week later, Larry came up to my office in ROCOLA about 11:00 a.m. and said, "Listen A-hole, you and I are going to lunch!" We had one of those all afternoon lunches at a DC restaurant, and Larry detailed the business he had in the pipeline for the next year. The financial risk didn't seem as drastic as I initially imagined, so after discussing it with Diane, I decided to give it a try. That was the start of my sales career. I never had any regrets and never looked back!

My new manager was John Warden, Federal Sales Manager for Control Data Civilian Agencies. (There was another separate sales group at ROCOLA that was responsible for all CDC DoD business. One of the team members was a salesman named Erwin Muschter, who you'll hear more about later in this book.) John Warden was a relatively low-key sales manager compared with some, but he was smart and knew what had to be done to make the numbers. For me, he was a good teacher and first sales manager. Basically, I was working with IRS people I already knew and closing the business Larry Campbell had in the *pipeline*. There were third-party classes available to teach salespeople the rules of doing business with the Feds, the FARS (Federal Acquisition Regulations), and FIRMR (Federal Information Resource Management Regulations). I took several week-long courses during my early sales years and got to know the rules inside and out.

I continued working with the IRS individuals responsible for writing the requirements, and in 1979, I made my quota the first year! This qualified me to attend CDC's 100% Club in Hawaii at the Sheraton Kauai resort on Poipu Beach, Kauai, in 1980. I'd never been to Hawaii, and the five-day experience was out of this world! What a beautiful part of America! CDC had a policy of no dependents during the 100% Clubs, only eligible salespeople, so Diane had to stay back in Virginia.

The CDC regional facility on Executive Blvd. in Rockville, Maryland (ROCOLA), had a group on the fourth floor managed by Hank Philburn. It was basically a group of lobbyists that worked Capitol Hill looking out for CDC's government interests. John Warden and I worked closely with them, especially for our IRS account. During my very first year in sales, I remember accompanying one of Hank's lobbyists, John Carter, into DC and into the US Capitol Building's basement. John had arranged a meeting to verify that funding for a major CDC/IRS project was intact for the coming fiscal year. It was a real thrill and further verification that I'd made the right choice getting into sales!

Another key support person for this new salesman was a gentleman named Dick Clover based in Minneapolis. Dick was a CDC Vice President in finance and an expert in government business. He could come up with some of *the* most creative financing options, and I learned a lot from him during my time at CDC. We developed a personal respect for each other, and I'd meet him for dinner the night before in Rosslyn, Virginia, whenever he came in town for an IRS meeting. Great guy!

The IRS was always trying to enhance its data processing capabilities, so there were plenty of opportunities for more recommendations and subsequent sales. I had worked with Jay Pyle (IRS IDRS software support manager), Jerry Evans (IDRS software requirements specialist), and Doug Sanders (IRS IDRS hardware requirements specialist) while supporting IRS as the CDC IRS Program Manager, and it felt very natural to continue working with them to support IRS's future data processing requirements. We helped IRS upgrade the memory of its eleven CDC 3500 systems and some other minor acquisitions. I made quota again in 1980 and qualified for CDC's 100% Club to be held in Acapulco in 1981!

CDC still only allowed employees to attend its quota clubs, so when the time came, I made arrangements for Diane to come down when the 100% Club was over. We joined a friend and fellow CDC salesman Jerry Beazley, and his wife, Melissa. Melissa and Diane had traveled to Acapulco together. The four of us had reservations at Las Brisas, which was a unique resort built on a hill overlooking Acapulco Bay. Each *casita* had its own pool! Jerry had made arrangements with two CDC couples who had driven a VW bus to Acapulco from Mexico City before the club started.

The plan was for the four of us to drive that VW bus back up to Mexico City, then fly to Washington, DC, from there. After five or six nights at Las Brisas, we started our trip north from Acapulco. Taxco, Mexico (the *silver capital* of Mexico) was about halfway, so we booked the Holiday Inn in Taxco for the overnight. The next day, after checking out some touristy silver shops and making purchases, we jumped back into the VW bus for the rest of our journey to Mexico City.

The terrain along the way is quite mountainous in places. Frequently, the road dropped off sharply on the right side, and there were *no guardrails*! On one occasion, we came around a corner about to start down a long grade and saw two large dump trucks coming right at us. One was passing the other, and they were taking up both lanes of the narrow road. We stopped quickly just in time. Getting gas along the way was interesting. Once, when it was Jerry's turn to pay, I heard a frantic, "Dennis, I need help!" coming from the other side of the bus. I spoke a little Spanish, but Jerry spoke none. It seems the attendant hadn't reset the manual pump, and the previous sale price plus ours was on the pump. The attendant was trying to get Jerry to pay double what we should be paying. With my broken Spanish, I was able to get the situation straightened out, and we continued our trip north. We overnighted in the city then boarded a plane for Washington Dulles Airport after a very nice time in Mexico.

Of course, there were system upgrades along the way like the CDC 3500 mainframes, but IRS's Control Data IDRS systems had been installed since 1972 and were candidates for a complete replacement. IRS had been working on a Request for Proposals (RFP) in their offices in Bailey's Crossroads, Virginia, for a new system called the Service Center Replacement System or SCRS. The government employees we'd been working with for years—Dick Grebinsky, Doug Sanders, Jay Pyle, and Jerry Evans—were responsible for writing the RFP technical requirements!

The CDC systems favorability and our relationship with both IRS National Office and IRS Service Center people were excellent! CDC was a well-respected vendor to the IRS. Each fall, the IRS National Office conducted *Readiness Checks* at each of its ten Service Centers, doing two centers a week. They would invite their major vendors like Control Data, Honeywell, etc. to attend. We had a great opportunity to get to know all the IRS people! While government employees and vendors had to be careful about how to conduct business and follow the FARS while the government is writing an RFP, there were subtle things that could be done. Our sales support team and I wrote *whitepapers* that offered new technology concepts with the hope that these ideas would appear in the specifications for the new SCRS system. The strategy, of course, was to get requirements added to the RFP that you knew your competition either couldn't do or didn't do well.

When the SCRS RFP was released in late 1981, we were very pleased. There was hardly anything that our systems couldn't evaluate very highly on. I worked with a very capable Federal proposal support team in Arden Hills, Minnesota, to develop CDC's response to the RFP. These people were absolutely superb! Through a little sniffing around, the *G2* I was getting was CDC only had one other viable bidder, UNISYS Federal. We'd had a lot of bidding experience against UNISYS and had a good feel for their discounting policies. Our proposal support team at Arden Hills scoped out the requirements from a UNISYS perspective and determined they would have to bid a UNISYS 1100/83 system.

Toward the end of the proposal cycle, John Warden and I made weekly trips to Minneapolis to check with our proposal team at Arden Hills and brief Vern Sieling, VP of Worldwide Sales regarding the current status of the opportunity. We felt we needed a specific discount to win and had a number in mind based upon UNISYS's past bidding history. CDC's original IDRS win was worth $30 million, but after support fees and upgrades over the contract life, IDRS had brought in over $100 million in revenue for CDC! There's no reason SCRS wouldn't have the same protracted revenue stream. We recommended a nice discount up front and later would recoup revenue in the out years of the contract at least ten-plus times the initial contract value.

Sales management in Minneapolis, in the end, decided to *no bid* that lucrative IRS opportunity, basically giving the business to UNISYS. CDC was the well-respected incumbent and had an excellent chance of winning! We were told later that CDC executive sales management, with those deep discounts, would risk missing their annual bonuses for Cyber class systems as the eleven going to IRS would be a large percentage of total machines projected to be sold that year. It was apparent to me that the executive sales management's compensation plan was seriously flawed, and I started looking around for a sales position outside CDC. Control Data had been an excellent career experience for me over my twelve years there. I'd progressed up the ladder from Hardware Customer Engineer to Software Systems Engineer to Tech Support Management to Program Manager and finally to sales, but it was time to move on to a more progressive company. The year was 1982.

On March 3, 1982, Edward Norris Robertson (Dad) had a massive heart attack while at work in his mill in Kingfield, Maine. He collapsed on the floor and died. The world lost a gentle and kind man's man that day! While he wasn't my father by blood, he whole-heartedly accepted that role, and while putting up with my teenage antics, he was indeed a father in all other respects for over thirty years. I truly loved him.

CHAPTER TWENTY-SIX

THE JOURNEY CONTINUES

My next sales position was with the Burroughs Corporation's Federal Systems Group in McLean, Virginia, working for John Meshinski (District Manager) and Lee Bartleman (Branch Manager). My responsibilities were the Department of Treasury, which of course includes IRS. It was at Burroughs where I met Julie Bitzer, who was doing a great job covering sections of the IRS that I had not worked with before. I think she was a bit apprehensive of me initially, but we became good friends professionally, worked together well, and still keep in touch today.

The US Customs Service had a large Burroughs mainframe in their San Diego Data Center and wanted to upgrade it with a newer system. I made many trips to San Diego meeting with the data center management and learning more about the requirement. Over the course of remaining months of 1982, I helped Customs with a *sole-source* justification and worked with our Burroughs financial team to develop a financial plan for a Burroughs B6700 mainframe that would fit into Customs's FY1983 budget. We finalized the deal, and I qualified for Burroughs's Worldwide Legion of Merit that was held in Rancho Mirage, California, early in 1983! Diane came with me at Burroughs expense. It was an interesting club as there were literally sales winners from all around the globe. Somehow, I got in with the Australian's one evening and regretted it the next morning due to a massive headache!

I finished the year as the number two salesman in the Federal Systems group. Burroughs had a very low percentage commission plan, so a salesperson's income was mostly their base salary and a possible bonus for good performance. At the Worldwide Legion of Merit, Olin Acres (Federal Sales VP) presented me, along with much fanfare, a check for $24,000. The US Customs Service contract was worth over $3 million to Burroughs. While $24,000 is a lot of money, I felt the bonus was a *very* small percentage of the margin on the business and promised myself I'd move on from the Burroughs Corporation.

As a result of my job search, I had interviewed with a Federal leasing company called Finalco and decided this was my future. I had become very interested in government financial strategies for bidding procurements. Dick Clover at CDC had started it, and my time at Burroughs Federal had cemented my interest! I was going into the government leasing business. Then a headhunter contacted me about a sales position with a new company named Network Systems Corporation. It was a spin-off of my former employer, Control Data Corporation, and started by several CDC design engineers and sales executives. The headhunter had set up an interview, but I really didn't have any interest in keeping the appointment. Diane said, "What have you got to lose?" and convinced me to go on the interview. I was interviewed by Mike Green, who was the Federal Sales Manager. It didn't take me long to come to the conclusion that Network Systems was a company I wanted to be part of! Their Civilian Agencies office was located at 501 Church St. in Vienna, Virginia, and it wouldn't be a long commute from my home every weekday. I started with NSC in 1984, and it was the beginning of a very long mutually beneficial relationship.

During this time, our children were growing up quickly. All three would attend a new Catholic high school in Fairfax, Virginia, called Paul the VI. Tommy played football his first year. Unlike public high schools, there was tuition required to attend PVI. Diane had a position as a medical transcriber and, over the course of the years, paid the PVI tuition for all three of our children from her salary.

Tommy had become a Boy Scout when he was old enough during 1981 and joined Troop 158 of Herndon, Virginia. The Scoutmaster was Don Denisar, a retired Air Force E-9. Don was stern on the outside but had a heart of gold and loved *his* boys. After Tommy was in the troop for a while, Don Denisar recruited me to become the Troop 158 Committee Chairman. Tommy was progressing through the BSA ranks and, when a First-Class Scout, became a Patrol Leader. A group of new WEBELOS Cub Scouts had *crossed the bridge* into Troop 158, and Scoutmaster Denisar put them all into Tommy's patrol. They selected the Eagle Patrol as their name. and Tommy's leadership turned them into one of the finer patrols in the troop!

I became very interested in Scouting and started attending district training sessions and soon was teaching these sessions! Other BSA activities for me as an adult included staff positions for District Junior Leader Training (JLT) weekends, Order of the Arrow, and a Woodbadge training class 82-41 (Antelope Patrol), where I earned my Woodbadge beads (two-bead award), woggle, and neckerchief with the Maclaren tartan patch. Woodbadge is an adult Scout training program started in 1919 in England by Lord Baden Powell, the founder of Scouting.

Early in 1983, when Troop 158 had half a dozen WEBELOS Scouts scheduled to cross the bridge into our troop, Don Denisar came to me and said, "Dennis, our troop is already at sixty-plus Scouts and a manageable size. I'd like you to start a new troop and be its first Scoutmaster!" I was reluctant, but Don said he'd work with me. We took several of the older Troop 158 Scouts, two of their dads (Ed Moore and Don Dolnack) as Assistant Scoutmasters, plus the WEBLOS and formed BSA Troop 159. Tommy stayed in Troop 158 at Don's recommendation. I acted as Troop 159 Scoutmaster from March 1983 to September 1985 then as Assistant Scoutmaster until December 1989. The last time I checked, Troop 159 of Herndon, Virginia, was still well run and going strong!

One of the most personally rewarding events for me during my adult Scouting career was leading three eleven-day trips into the Maine wilderness, two with T.158 and one with T.159. The Scouts did the detailed planning as Scouts are supposed to do, but I provided the "view from ten thousand feet" overall day-to-day plan. Diane and I owned a big GMC Starcraft conversion van, and one of the other adult leaders had a big van also. The travel arrangements were six Scouts and two adult BSA leaders in each van. It was a two-day trip each way following BSA maximum, daily mileage restrictions. We spent four days in the lake section of the Allagash Wilderness Waterway, canoeing fifty miles, and the other three days climbing Mt. Katahdin. Just prior to entering the Allagash area, we'd rent eight canoes, four tied to the top of each van (two canoes facedown and two faceup on top of those). These older Scouts were all from suburbia and had never seen moose or deer up close or the other wildlife that we'd always observe on the trip! Not to mention the sheer beauty of the Maine wilderness! Sons Tommy and John both participated in one or more of these Maine trips.

The only regret I had as an adult Scouter was when I was selected to be an instructor at an upcoming National Capital Area Council Woodbadge training program. This would have allowed me to be a Patrol Leader and introduce other adult Scouters to Woodbadge concepts. It would also allow me to earn my third Woodbadge bead. I started the pre-event planning sessions but was traveling in conjunction with my work, still very involved with Troop 159 and had other personal commitments that simply didn't leave enough time to properly carry out the responsibilities of a Woodbadge Patrol Leader. I very reluctantly had to resign from that year's program.

Professionally, things were going well at Network Systems Corporation (NSC). I was enjoying my customers and selling the products, primarily a product called HyperChannel that allowed dissimilar computer systems to exchange data with each other. I made quota all but one year. The Clubs were held at some very nice beach places like Marco Island, Florida, Puerto Rico, and St. John Island in the USVI where club members took a day trip sailing on a catamaran and participated in a jeep scavenger hunt all around the island! Hawaii was a favorite of the snow-bound Minneapolis execs too! One year we stayed at the Waiohai Beach Club on Kauai. We even had a foreign club at the Hotel Melia Don Pepe on the Costa del Sol in Spain. This was my first trip back as a civilian!

The company didn't pay for spouses or dependents being with the employee during 100% Clubs, but family could be there at the same time, as long as the salesperson paid their expenses. Diane and I met many really good people at NSC. From home office in Brooklyn Park, Minnesota, were Don Haeny, Mahlon Moore, Craig Gust, Marion Patrick, and Admin Jill Avery and Patty Barkley, to name only a few. Of course, local DC area Federal salesmen Mike Wasno, Rich Kent, Dave Butler, and Dan Frigard were always at the 100% Clubs. Dan Frigard was responsible for NSC's National Security Agency (NSA), and Diane and I became good friends with Dan and Ann Frigard and made many trips together. One summer, the four of us took a Western Caribbean cruise. It was great fun! At NSC, in order to qualify for the 100% Club, the salesperson had to make his or her quota, *plus* the company had to make its goal. The 1985 100% Club was planned for Fisherman's Reef Hotel on St. Thomas, Virgin Islands! I made my quota, but that year the company didn't, so there was no Club.

I said to Diane, "Hey, I made my quota. Let's find something special to do in or around St. Thomas!" We had attended the annual sailboat show at Annapolis City Dock and visited a booth that had a lot of brochures for crewed sailboat trips in the Caribbean which we took home. Diane and I selected *Samana*, a 63' Bermuda ketch out of Charlotte Amalie, St. Thomas, US Virgin Islands. It was crewed by a former French paratrooper John Paul and his wife, Annie, who was Vietnamese French. The same dates as the NSC club was to be held were open, so we booked *Samana* for an eight-day sailing trip. We all flew to Charlotte Amalie, stayed there for two nights, and met John Paul in the morning at the dock. After a short trip in *Samana*'s Zodiac tender, we reached *Samana* anchored out in the harbor. It was the start of an adventure that we still talk about today! We had the whole steel-hulled German-made ketch to ourselves. School was in session, so Diane had contacted the teachers who gave all three children their assignments for the week. I'd also made several cassette tapes of music as we'd read that *Samana* had a cassette player on board. We brought cassettes of Dire Straits, *Hooked on Classics*, and such to play while sailing.

We sailed all over the US Virgin Islands and British Virgin Islands. Annie was an outstanding French cook, and the three meals a day that she prepared in her small galley were amazing. After anchoring for the afternoon/evening in an exotic bay near Norman Island, John Paul opened a section of the handrail surrounding the deck topside and said, "The pool is open!" This would be repeated many times during the cruise. The fish in these waters were unbelievably gorgeous: Sergeant Majors, Angelfish, Parrotfish, and an occasional barracuda. After a swim, we'd climb back in the boat, and Annie would be serving cocktails for Diane and me in the cockpit area before bringing out a scrumptious dinner! Some nights, John Paul would turn on spotlights high on the mainmast, and we'd dance on part of the deck under the mainsail area. Occasionally, when we were near a town, we'd take the Zodiac in to a restaurant. One place that I recall was in Spanish Town on the north side of Virgin Gorda, British Virgin Islands.

During the day, we'd be sailing. All five of us had a turn or more at the helm, even John, who was ten at the time. One thrill was sailing down the Sir Francis Drake Channel on the way to Road Town, Tortola, British Virgin Islands, with the wind behind us, all three sails filled, green water coming over the gunnels, and *Hooked on Classics* playing from *Samana*'s topside speakers! It didn't get much better than that! (John Paul liked that cassette so much that we left it with him when our cruise was over.) The kids would study for an hour or so every day in a lounge area next to the galley. Annie had a stuffed parrot on a perch hanging above the table named *Prosper*. Prosper watched over them as they did their homework. Our sleeping accommodations were great too. We had three separate cabins: one for Di and me, the boys shared one, and Erin had her own. When our great adventure on *Samana* was over, we returned home to 12861 Tewksbury Dr. and resumed our normal routines.

In 1993, one of my last Network Systems' 100% Clubs was held at the Hyatt Regency Grand Cayman Resort. We again hung out with the Frigards during free time, snorkeling off Seven Mile Beach, kissing the stingrays at Stingray City, and even visiting the post office at Hell, Grand Cayman. Our CEO, Lyle Altman, was an *all-business* type of guy, but his wife, a former flight attendant, was all party! Several evenings, while we believe Lyle slept, one could see Mrs. Altman partying around the pool area with our European club attendees! These NSC 100% Clubs were definitely fun times! Shortly after returning home to Northern Virginia, Diane and I saw the movie *The Firm* starring Tom Cruise. Some of the movie scenes had been filmed at the Hyatt Regency Grand Cayman, and we recognized several of the Hyatt staff members from the movie!

The last couple of years at Network Systems, we had a new VP of Sales, Rick Heller. He was a dynamic goal setter and handed out small hourglasses at various meetings to remind everyone that *time was money*. He had some whacky and expensive incentive programs each quarter to motivate the sales team. One time it was a Formula 1 race car driving class in Le Mans, France, if the salesperson made their goal for the quarter. A real gem was a four-day trip on the Concorde to Paris. If you made your quarterly quota the first quarter, you qualified. If you made your quota the second quarter, your wife or significant other (SO) could attend with you. I was working a big, slow developing deal with IRS at the time, missed my Q1 number, but qualified in Q2. This meant Diane wouldn't be riding the Concorde or going to Paris. Of course, *all* the salesmen in the Columbia, Maryland, office covering NSC's "spook business" made it—Dan Frigard, Rich Kent, Mike Wasno, etc. The two-hour-fifteen-minute ride from JFK to Charles de Gaulle Airport in Paris was amazing! Even though we all flew home on a normal wide-body aircraft, my airfare alone cost the company over $6,000. I felt bad that I missed my Q1 quote and that Diane couldn't attend with me, and I knew she was disappointed too.

During our first few years living at 12861 Tewksbury Dr., there was a big field behind the house with grazing cattle. It was sort of amusing, but one time the cows broke through the fencing, and when we woke up the next morning, they were grazing in our front yard! Then suddenly one year, we started noticing construction bulldozers leveling that field. A new housing community was going in. Fast-forwarding a bit, we purchased a new construction house in Franklin Oaks that backed up, through woods, to our original Tewksbury Dr. home and watched the new house being built. The address was 12801 Sunnyvale Ct., Herndon, Virginia. We moved in during May 1987. Tom was eighteen, Erin seventeen, and John twelve years old.

I had been talking with Mother for a while about leaving Kingfield, Maine, and moving down to Bethel where she had friends. Dad had been gone since 1982, and it was getting harder for my mother to take care of herself during the cold winter months. Mother did move to a retirement home in Bethel, Maine, The Bethel House, for a while, but eventually we convinced her to move nearer to our family. Several years earlier, my brother Dave had converted to Mormonism, spent a two-year mission in Brazil, and ended up converting Dad, Mother, and brother Ned too. We sold her home in Kingfield, Maine, quite easily, and with the proceeds, we put a down payment on a new town house in Sterling, Virginia, close by our home. It was within walking distance of a Mormon church, which fit the bill perfectly for Mother. During her time living there, Mother became close to our son John. He would stay overnight, keeping her company, and during weekends, they would take daily eleven-mile walks on the W&OD trail. The Washington and Old Dominion had been a railroad bed at one time but now was a popular hiking/biking trail, and it was right next to Mother's town house. As John had become very close to his grandmother during that time, he remembers those days as being "very magical!" Sometime later, Mother met a nice man her age, Chet Clemens, at her Mormon church, and they were subsequently married. In a way, it broke my heart. On the one hand I was happy that she had found someone to love, but on the other hand, I somehow felt abandoned when they bought a fifth-wheeler RV and left the area forever. Diane and I rented the town house for a while, but tenants who didn't pay the rent on time and other maintenance hassles soon caused us to sell it.

Tom was still involved in Scouting as a Life Scout and had completed all the requirements for Eagle Scout except his Eagle Project. We had all gone to Acapulco for an NSC 100% Club in May, and Tom had taken SCUBA lessons in Acapulco Bay. Unbeknown to us, the city dumped raw sewage waste directly into the water. When we got home, Tom was *very* sick with hepatitis for months. He was so sick that he was unable to finish the Eagle Project before his eighteenth birthday and had to take his final high school exams at home before graduation on June 11, 1987, because he was too sick to go to class. Had we known about the raw sewage, we wouldn't have allowed the SCUBA lessons.

At sixteen years of age, Tom wanted to take a flying *intro ride* from Squadron Aviation out of Dulles Airport. Diane put her foot down and said, "No, I prefer that you wait until you're eighteen years old." Not long after July 9, 1987, arrived, Tom took his *intro ride* at Squadron Aviation and was hooked! He continued flying lessons, and it wasn't long before he passed his FAA private pilot license exam. Tom went on to CFI (certified flight instructor) and CFII (certified flight instructor, instrument) FAA ratings. During that time, we purchased a 1976 PA140 Piper Cherokee single-engine aircraft. It was fully instrument rated, and we leased it back to Squadron Aviation to help defray the expenses. We parked it at Dulles Airport in GA parking where the B-Gates are located today. My thought was that owning an aircraft would be an economical way for Tom to build up *single-engine time* for future FAA ratings. It was fun, but I was wrong about the economy of it all! As a rental, it had to be completely inspected every hundred hours, and there were maintenance costs plus the steep monthly parking fees at Dulles. When a navigation instrument called an ADF (automatic direction finder, basically AM radio technology) failed, it cost $3,000 to purchase a reconditioned one! Tom did get excellent experience flying out of a major airport under the control of the Dulles tower. We'd be in the line to take off behind larger planes like 727s, 747s, Embraers, Beach-99s, and the like, and talking with the tower and ATC was a good early experience for Tom.

In addition to Tom building his single-engine hours, our family had a lot of fun with the Cherokee! While it had four seats, it was practically a two-person aircraft if you were flying very far. Total weight of the aircraft, fuel, baggage, and passengers determined the range. We did take it to nearby destinations like Annapolis and Ocean City, Maryland. At one point, Dulles Airport wanted to reduce its General Aviation or *GA* traffic and increased the parking fee exponentially to discourage it! We moved the Cherokee to the Manassas Airport. I'd take the controls of the aircraft on many occasions and enjoyed flying her. Tom was a Certified Flight Instructor (CFI) and encouraged me to at least get my private license. One event that had happened discouraged me from that goal. Tom and I were flying the Cherokee in the *practice area* just west of Dulles one day. I had control of the aircraft. It was a beautiful day, and I was looking out ahead of us, but probably watching the instruments more as I was inexperienced and wanted to maintain level flight and altitude. Suddenly, I looked up, and another small aircraft was approaching at a forty-five-degree angle, maybe 1,500 feet below us. I hadn't seen it coming! I said to Tom, "Did you see that plane?"

Tom replied, "Sure, I've been watching it for a while." I decided then and there that I shouldn't trust myself to be comfortable in a three-dimensional environment, and I never pursued my private flying license!

In order to get his Commercial Pilot FAA rating, Tom needed, I believe, five hundred multi-engine hours. We put the Cherokee up for sale, and Tom bought one-fifth share of a dual-engine Piper Aztec that was kept at Dulles Airport. We sold the plane, and our Cherokee ownership days were over! Whew!

The late 1980s were a busy and fun time for our family. We had purchased an airplane! I had purchased a new 1986 Lincoln Town Car and soon installed a $1,200 *car phone* in it. Wow, being able to talk on a phone while driving was really *rad*. It did help me keep in touch with customers as I traveled to various government sites in DC and needed to coordinate multiple meetings.

To round out our transportation and recreation options, we purchased a 21' Chris Craft, Cutty Cabin boat that we docked in Occoquan, Virginia, at Hoffmaster's Marina. She had a single screw driven by a powerful 5.7-liter inboard V-8 engine that would propel the boat in excess of fifty knots when on *the step*. Hoffmaster's was on the Occoquan River, which led into Belmont Bay and the Potomac River. Our children named her *Simply Awesome!* Over the years we owned her, we made many enjoyable trips. Close by was Mattawoman Bay, just south and across the Potomac for swimming and water skiing. Going north was the District of Columbia. One of our favorite places to tie up was Washington Harbour and Tony and Joe's Restaurant. We'd travel up for lunch or during the Washington Redskin's season to watch a football game on TV before getting back on the boat and returning to Occoquan. We made the trip only one year but went north and into the Tidal Basin for a Fourth of July celebration. The view of fireworks on the Mall was outstanding; however, getting back into the river after the fireworks, and considering most boaters had been drinking heavily, was a bit risky. We waited for the crazies to leave first, but even then it was hairy. The way back down the Potomac to Occoquan in the dark was also challenging. We had a bright spotlight, but it wasn't strong enough. Tom sat on the bow with a supplemental light and warned when we were approaching a half-submerged log. We slowly made it back down the Potomac to the marina safely, but it was late, and we were all tired. We never attempted a Fourth of July by boat in DC again!

I had made a lot of small improvements to *Simply Awesome*. One was the addition of LORAN-C for navigation. Diane was driving a Mercury Topaz at the time that we'd installed a *car phone* in. The phone electronics were in the trunk, but they could be removed and placed in a *battery bag* that came with a handset. We bought one and used it whenever we went out on the boat. The range was decent, and coverage along the Potomac where we boated was quite good.

To the south of the Occoquan was Fairview Beach which had a nice restaurant and a sandy beach to hang out and swim. Farther south and just beyond the Rt. 301 bridge was Robertson's Crab House (no relation!) that had crabs that were out-of-this-world delicious. On one occasion, the five of us made a weekend trip to Solomon's Island on the Chesapeake Bay. We had to stop both ways at Cobb Island to refuel, and after rounding Point Lookout and into the Chesapeake, we traveled about five miles north to Solomon's Island. I had reserved a B&B room for Diane and I and dock slip, but the *crew* stayed on *Simply Awesome* overnight. The next morning, it was a bit rough on the Chesapeake Bay, and we had a following sea with big swells all the way to Point Lookout. It was good to get back into the much calmer Potomac River!

In the summer of 1988, we were invited to a free five-day vacation in the Outer Banks of North Carolina. All we had to do was listen to a sales presentation! (You can probably still hear the line reeling out as I say this!) We decided to attend, and all five of us drove to Kitty Hawk, North Carolina, to the SeaScape properties. We ended up buying unit I3 and the next year unit K5. We were timeshare owners! We did use our SeaScape units most years, but one year we traded for a week at a place called Vistana in Orlando, Florida. Probably the perfect timeshare owner *fish*, we liked Vistana so much that we purchased Christmas week no. 25 in that resort.

As the 1980s came to a close, I considered myself a very fortunate man! Diane and I had made a decent life for ourselves, had opportunities to travel, and had made great friends, both through my work and with our neighbors. More importantly, we had three children we were very proud of, for different reasons. Life was good!

Tom and our PA140 Piper Cherokee—N8619E

CHAPTER TWENTY-SEVEN

THE 1990S IN NORTHERN VIRGINIA

Our daughter, Erin, had graduated from Paul VI Catholic High School in 1988 and entered Marymount University in Arlington, Virginia, that fall. Erin's roommate in her sophomore year turned out to be her future sister-in-law, Suzy Mullins! Erin has always been a driven person and started working at the early age of fourteen at Pet Hotel in Great Falls, Virginia, in the veterinary industry. This required parental permission to allow her to work that young.

In the spring of 1992, Erin was scheduled to graduate from Marymount University but hadn't taken her final exams yet. I qualified for yet another Network Systems 100% Club, this time in Maui. I wanted to take our whole family, but Erin's final exam schedule was an issue. We settled on a trip that would take all of us to San Francisco for two nights, then Erin would fly home to take her finals, and the rest of the family would go on to Maui. We *did* enjoy San Francisco with its cable cars taking us everywhere: from breakfast in the morning to lunch at the Buena Vista and to dinner at Scoma's Restaurant on Fisherman's Wharf! After a great time in San Francisco, Erin took her flight back to Washington, and the rest of us went on to Hawaii. I don't think Erin ever let us forget leaving her, but she did the right thing by placing a college degree over a fun vacation in Hawaii.

My rewarding journey at Network Systems continued, and sometime early in the 1990s, Mike Green was promoted to District Federal Sales Manager. The company was expanding its Federal Operations. Mike promoted Bruce Fox and me to Branch Sales

Manager positions for Civilian Agencies. Our IRS business was increasing rapidly, and Chuck Hathaway, our Professional Services Manager, recruited an ace SE he knew that was then working for Boeing in Seattle, Washington. His name was Ed Gidzinski. Ed came on board and soon proved himself to be an extremely valuable asset on the IRS account. He and I not only worked well together but also became close friends! Ed had an amazing depth of knowledge of IBM operating systems and a very logical and creative mind. He would become responsible for much of the IRS business we closed for over four years. Later, when support requirements for IRS slowed down for NSC, Ed joined Cisco Systems, where he continued to excel! Fast-forward to May 31, 2009. Ed was watching TV with his wife and son at their home in Reston, Virginia. He had a massive heart attack and was pronounced dead shortly after the EMTs arrived at his home. I can honestly say Ed was loved by everyone who had ever worked with him, and we were all devastated.

Having entered PVI in the fall of 1989, younger son John (DJ) was thriving in the academic environment there. He had taken a Spanish class and really seemed to be a natural with the language. Paul VI HS participated in a Spanish exchange program, and in his sophomore year, John spent a month in Madrid, Spain, with the Morales family and their son, Javier, who was John's age. Another year, John was selected to attend the Virginia Governor's Academy for Spanish and spent a week in Danville, Virginia, learning advanced Spanish. It was a nice honor for him to be selected!

Early in 1992, my father, Larry Holt, was diagnosed with advanced prostate cancer that had metastasized. Prior to that time, the PSA test was not readily available. When his PSA was taken, I believe it was 1,100! I traveled to Miami to visit with him and do whatever I could to make the remainder of his life as comfortable as possible. I installed handrails in his shower so he could get in and out. At that point, there was little else I could do to extend his life. I returned home to Northern Virginia, and on September 19, 1992, I lost my father to prostate cancer. Our whole family traveled to Miami for the funeral, of course. At his wake, I got to meet many of the people Father had worked with over the years and heard some *very* interesting stories that I won't detail here! My father had a led a full life! His remains are currently in a mausoleum in SW Miami in the area that became *Little Havana* after he and Evelyn purchased the mausoleum vaults.

On July 29, 1992, our daughter, Erin, graduated from Marymount University with her BA in Communications and *no* student debt! Diane and I are very proud of her and happy to have been able to provide the financial assistance.

By 1993, Tom was working in the aviation industry that he loved and taking evening classes at George Mason University in Fairfax, Virginia. Erin was working as the practice manager at Alexandria Animal Hospital for the Hospital Administrator, Karen Bates. John graduated from Paul VI HS on June 6, 1993, and was entering James Madison University in Harrisonburg, Virginia. John's roommate his freshman year was a really cool student named Darby Jones! Diane and I met his parents during student move-in. Richard and Joan Jones and Darby have remained friends of our family ever since!

Events for the last part of the 1990s decade became *very* busy! In 1995, Diane and I decided to downsize, sold our home on Sunnyvale Ct., and bought a town house on Lowe's Island in Sterling, Virginia. Again, we watched it being built and moved in. There was a brook bubbling just behind the house, and the screened-in porch we had built was a very peaceful place in which to relax. Later, Congressman and House Majority Leader Dick Gephardt and his wife, Jane, moved into the building next to us. It was interesting to see the black government SUV parked in front of their town house in the morning, waiting for Congressman Gephardt to come down to be transported to the Rayburn Building and Capitol Hill for work. As neighbors, we had previously met the Gephardts, and when he was out walking their dog, Spot, he'd say, "Hi, Dennis." And I'd reply, "Hi, Dick!"

During the 1990s while at NSC, I was working on an opportunity at the Navy Annex in Arlington, Virginia, for BUPERS (Navy Bureau of Personnel). It was a large building on a hill overlooking the Pentagon and the central location where all Navy assignments and reassignments were made worldwide. BUPERs was in need of a high-speed network to connect workstations throughout the building to its database computers. We were proposing a proprietary 50 Mbps network NSC called HyperBus. Our customer and COTR (contracting officer's technical representative) was Chief Petty Officer Mike Langan. Mike and I became friends and eventually socialized outside working hours. I remember a trip one weekend to Annapolis where Mike, his son, my son Tom, and I camped out and did some fishing. Mike was originally a Mid-Westerner and very easy to get along with. It was almost a two-year effort and involved a protest by another bidder, but in the end NSC prevailed, and we closed and successfully installed a $3 million dollar network in the Navy Annex for BUPERS! When PO Langan retired from the Navy several years later, we hired him as an SE.

In the later part of the 1990s, my IRS account really picked up activity. The IRS had awarded a contract for an IBM mainframe-based Communications Replacement System called CRS to bidder Sysorex Inc. This contract would provide a vital function that connected to multiple local IRS workstations in the ten Service Centers and numerous IRS Regional Offices on the front end and the UNISYS mainframe's database on the back end. The proposed CRS contract's connectivity solution between mainframes didn't provide the bandwidth that was required, but Network Systems had the answer in HyperChannel. I spoke with Mike Green and offered to resign my Branch Sales Manager position so I could pursue the IRS opportunity on a full-time basis. He agreed, so I rolled my sales group under Bruce Fox's Branch, and I went after the IRS business. We were ultimately successful and over the years brought in over $10 million revenue for NSC!

I again made my quote in 1994, and during April 1995, Network Systems held its last 100% Club at the Stouffer Wailea Beach Club on Maui. It was a fun club as always, and Diane and all the usual top NSC performers were there. The Frigards and Diane and I drove up 10,000' Haleakala and another day drove the forbidden back road around the mountain from Hana. A guest speaker at the business meeting was Ryal Poppa, Chairman of Storage Technology Corp!

In 1995, StorageTek acquired Network Systems Corporation. STK closed the Vienna, Virginia, office and I got the pleasure of traveling the Beltway to Silver Springs, Maryland, every day for work! Things had changed culturally for us NSC employees as STK had a more formal way of conducting business, not necessarily for the better in my opinion. It was during our STK/NSC sales kickoff meeting during January 1996 in Minneapolis that my friend and NSC home office executive, Craig Gust, pulled me aside. We were all watching NFL Super Bowl XXX in a large meeting room. Craig told me about a reorganization that would be taking place and an opportunity he recommended me for, SE Region Business Unit Director (or BUD) for the Network Systems Group. The STK GM for the region was Erwin Muschter, whom I'd worked with at Control Data and knew quite well.

When I returned home after the kickoff, I discussed the opportunity with Diane. Craig had set up an interview with Erwin in his Atlanta office after our kickoff, which I kept. My sales manager, Bruce Fox, had already traveled to Atlanta to interview for the position, and I later learned Bruce told some of our sales people, "He'll never get that job." My interview with Erwin went well, and I was offered the position on the spot! Erwin had two stipulations, however: (1) I had to move to Atlanta as he wanted all his direct reports to be in the same office, and (2) I had to fire Bruce Fox. OMG, I really didn't want to be placed in that position!

After talking it out with my partner, Diane, we decided to make the leap. It was supposed to be a two-year gig, so we put our home at Muddy Harbour Square in Sterling, Virginia, on the market, and in 1997, we found a really nice home in Alpharetta, Georgia. The location was in the Chartwell community at 9745 Rod Road, Alpharetta, Georgia. Our son John was living with us in Sterling at the time, so he came down to Atlanta with us.

Atlanta was a totally different environment for both Diane and me. The office building I was now working in was quite nice. Entering the building from the parking lot, one could hear music playing outside with beautiful flowers along the walkway. My office itself was quite nice, and the other STK people there were pleasant to work with. One person I soon came to respect was our HR manager, Kathy Madalino. One of the first things we worked on together was a nice severance package for Bruce Fox. My challenge as the SE Region BUD was to organize three groups that had been functioning separately at Network Systems. There was the US Government Civilian Agencies Group that I had been a part of for so many years; the *spooks* or Government Intelligence Group working out of Columbia, Maryland; and the Commercial Group headquartered in Atlanta. The territory included states from Florida to Texas and Maryland and The District. We all had different cultures, customers, and skills. It was my challenge to make a cohesive team of the three groups.

I initially had eighteen direct report salespeople and seventeen systems engineers, all former NSC employees. The first thing I needed was a Systems Engineering Manager that knew the internal workings of STK. I worked with Kathy Madalino and interviewed and subsequently hired RB Hooks, a longtime STK'er. The seventeen SEs now reported to RB. It proved to be an excellent move as RB knew exactly how to operate within STK's support environment. Adding a Financial Manager to track opportunities and closed business was my final organizing move. I spent the next five or six months traveling around the SE Region getting the team focused and working together.

Son John was living with us in Atlanta then, and we had Erin's dog, Jake, with us as well. It's a good thing John was there as I was traveling so much and seldom home during the week. When I was home, Diane and I learned to drink Bourbon Manhattans. Erwin and wife, Beverly, and Kathy and Richard Madalino both lived in Country Club of the South. Our three couples would take turns hosting and generally got together once a week on a rotating basis at our homes for cocktails and hors d'oeuvres. It was fun! Richard Madalino was a US Naval Academy graduate and a *very* funny guy!

As 1998 arrived, STK management in Louisville, Colorado, decided that the five Regional Network Systems Group BUDS weren't needed anymore and folded the former Network Systems sales and support people into STK's existing organizational structure! So much for the two-year BUD position! *Until an abrupt reorganization, this was one of the most challenging and fun positions I've ever held!* I was offered a sales position selling STK and NSG products from

Atlanta but decided it was perhaps time to seek other opportunities back in Northern Virginia.

Mike Green was now the National VP of Sales for FORE Systems, a new startup company in Pittsburgh. I called Mike, and after an interview with the Federal Sales Manager, Richard Bibb, I accepted a position in FORE's Tyson's Corner, Virginia, office as Civilian Agencies Sales Manager. In the hiring incentive package were twenty thousand options of FORE common stock vesting over four years.

After a little more than a year in Atlanta, Diane and I sold our nice home on Rod Road in Alpharetta, Georgia, and moved back to Northern Virginia. We rented a town house in Sterling, Virginia, on Lowe's Island not far from the Lowes Island Country Club, which today is Trump National Golf Club.

On my Civilian Agencies team was a former NSC'er, Bob Sowell, who was a consistent performer at Network Systems and was killing it at FORE as well! Another winner in the rough was Dave DeBuhr in California. STK management was pushing me to replace Dave, but I made a trip to California, visited with his major prospects, and he had outstanding opportunities. He just needed a little more time to close this business, which he did! I enjoyed my time at FORE. It was a great company with leading edge technology called ATM for Asynchronous Transfer Mode. ATM was capable of data transmissions of up to 155 Mbps and 622 Mbps, which was unheard of before that protocol became available. FORE was a company started by four Carnegie-Mellon University graduate students: *F*rancois Bitz, *O*nat Menzilcioglu, *R*obert Sansom, and *E*ric Cooper—*FORE*. It was located in Warrendale, Pennsylvania, just north of Pittsburgh. The headquarters buildings were unique as they weren't symmetrical. It looked like a group of building blocks that had been stacked randomly. Some appeared not to be even level.

Our son John had stayed in Atlanta and was working at a branch of Sun Trust Bank. While I was starting at FORE Systems, Diane was looking around Northern Virginia for a permanent home. One Sunday, a large ad appeared in the *Washington Post* advertising a new community in Leesburg, Virginia, called River Creek. It was located at the confluence of the Potomac River and Goose Creek and was going to be a gated golf course community. The golf course had been built and was operational, but there were less than a dozen homes finished when Diane first took me up there to see the property. We both realized the potential of the area, and after visiting all the builder models in the community, we decided on a Michael Harris home on Crystal Lake St. and signed a contract. Construction on our new home didn't start until November 1998, and we moved in during May 1999.

The FORE Civilian Agencies Group brought in a lot of new business, but the expectations and goals had perhaps been set a bit high, and we didn't make our numbers my first year. During 1999, my second year at FORE, the company was acquired by Marconi, a communications company in the United Kingdom. My twenty thousand options and everyone else's immediately became vested! When I sold my shares, I did well financially, but others who had been at FORE for years and had accumulated many more options became overnight millionaires! In October 1999, I resigned from FORE Systems and took a sabbatical for several months.

Not too long after moving back to Northern Virginia, Diane and I were looking for a dermatologist. We had both spent probably too much time in the sun without sunscreen. Baby lotion mixed with iodine for color was all the rage when we were young in the 1950s and 1960s, and our skin was now reacting with basal cell and squamous cell carcinomas. Dr. Sebastian, who had a practice in nearby Reston, Virginia, was recommended, and we began to see him on a regular basis. One day, when we were living in River Creek, I had a sebaceous cyst on the back of my right shoulder that I asked Diane to look at. As she was checking that out, she said, "Dennis, there's something else on your back that I don't like!" A visit to Dr. Sebastian confirmed it was indeed a dangerous melanoma skin cancer. He removed it during another visit. Fortunately, it had not metastasized, and I've had no recurrence of a melanoma since!

CHAPTER TWENTY-EIGHT

Y2K ARRIVES

After much activity by major government agencies, commercial companies and IT departments worldwide plus a whole lot of worrying, January 1, 2000, arrived, and everything proceeded to go on normally! Data processing and computers didn't grind to a halt as some had predicted they would.

Diane and I were settling into 43332 Crystal Lake St. in River Creek and getting to know our neighbors. One of the first couples we met at mixers sponsored by the River Creek builders was Carl and Evelyn Morin. Carl was a retired Brigadier General and one of the finest people I would ever meet. ClubCorp, a Texas company, had built the River Creek golf course. There was a small building on the property that served as a clubhouse, golf pro shop, and community events room. ClubCorp planned to build a suitable clubhouse when the community was built out sufficiently to support it financially. Diane and I decided to join the River Creek Club as full golfing members and paid the up-front initiation fee. An additional initiation fee would be assessed several years later when the clubhouse was built. We were now *golfers!*

At the beginning of 2000, Tom was flying professionally for Atlantic Coast Airlines under the United Express banner. He had earned his Commercial Pilot's license and Airline Transport Pilot (ATP) ratings and was now flying two-engine propjet Jetstream 32 and Jetstream 41 aircraft, initially as an FO and later as Captain. Erin, as previously mentioned, had been the Practice Manager at a very large veterinary hospital with eighteen veterinarians and seventy-five support staff in Alexandria called Alexandria Animal Hospital from 1992 to 1998. After about a year selling vet supplies in the DC area for Burns, she completely changed professions and was now a Regional Account Manager (RAM) selling web hosting services for UUNET. I was very proud that she could make that radical a career move and still be successful! Son John had kept in touch with his early childhood friend, Mike McDonald, back in Northern Virginia. Mike's father, Brian, was then President of Navy Federal Credit Union. During this period, Brian said to John while he was on a visit with us in Leesburg, Virginia, "John, you need to move back to Virginia and get out of the banking business." Brian McDonald created a position in NFCU's Vienna, Virginia, offices, and John moved north from Atlanta and in with us at River Creek. Diane and I were happy to again have his smiling face around!

Toward the end of my sabbatical that spanned the months of late 1999 to early 2000, Diane said to me one day, "Aren't you ever going back to work? All you do is hang around the house and play golf!" So much for our thirty-six years (at the time) of blissful marriage!

Craig Gust had spun off the maintenance and sales responsibilities for StorageTek's Network Systems Group (NSG) business and was CEO of a new company he'd formed called Network Executive Software Inc. (NESi). I gave Craig a call! I believed I could help him expand the business. After all, he'd recommended me for the StorageTek SE Region BUD position, so we joined forces in June 2000, and I became a NESi Regional Sales Manager. Craig had assembled a good team! Ron Rains, Bob MacIntyre, Jill Avery, Dave Reiland, Marion Patrick, Jim Signorelli, and other top-notch former NSC people were all there on Craig's team! Jill Avery and I were soon putting our heads together and devising a series of winning proposals to upgrade IRS's systems from older technology NSC hardware and software to current technology. This took place over a number of years! The IRS had always needed help keeping up with current Information Technology, and to make it more challenging for them, their workload was increasing rapidly every year. The other challenge that IRS had was the United States Congress. Congressmen and Congresswomen and Senators didn't want to get audited any more than we ordinary citizens, so (for some strange reason) funding for compliance programs seemed to be cut more and more every year!

We had numerous other customers that I consulted and worked with. One of them was New York City Health and Hospital Corporation (HHC). Their offices were in Manhattan at Forty-Fourth Street. I'd take an early Amtrak Acela for the two-hour and thirty-five-minute trip to Penn Station! Then walk north the ten blocks to HHC's offices and meet with James Major and other users of NESi products. After lunch with Director Gene Ferraioli, I'd hop back on an Acela for the return trip to Union Station in DC. It was always a nice day trip! Another customer that was fun to visit was QVC in West Chester, Pennsylvania. Dave Reiland, NESi Vice President of Engineering, and I made a trip there one year to discuss an upgrade of our products that QVC was contemplating. Several months later, we closed the deal! NASA Goddard was another good account, and our primary contact there, John Garten, was excellent to work with.

We had phenomenal success at other former NSC accounts and provided the support that our customers all needed to keep current technology in their data processing solutions. It was a good *marriage!* I was contributing to NESi's bottom line, making my *numbers,* and having fun! I've always had three rules for salespeople: (1) Leave your mother in the car, (2) Don't answer any unasked questions, and (3) Don't be afraid to ask for the order! It has worked for me for over thirty years! If you're in sales, you should be having fun or looking for another profession. When I was in the US Navy Submarine Force above the Arctic Circle or on a seventy-day Med deterrent patrol, I never thought I'd be having so much fun when I left the passion that I felt while serving my country!

Our family really took advantage of and enjoyed our SeaScape timeshare weeks in Kitty Hawk, North Carolina, in the Outer Banks and Vistana in Orlando, Florida. I guess so much so that Diane and I decided we no longer wanted to be limited to a week at each resort, so why not purchase a property we could enjoy all year long? High-tech stocks were booming at the time, and we'd invested in Cisco Systems (CSCO) many years before. The stock was going crazy, increasing in value exponentially, splitting then increasing in value again! We decided to take some profit and invest it in a 20 percent down payment for a beach house in the Outer Banks of North Carolina. We made several trips to the area looking at properties and purchased one at 761 Lakeview Ct., Corolla, North Carolina. It was July 9, 2000.

That date was the beginning of roughly ten years of enjoying this beach retreat, but unfortunately it was also the day that Evelyn Middleditch Holt passed away in her assisted living home at the Atrium in Atlanta, Georgia. Our whole family traveled to Atlanta for her funeral services then on to Miami for interment in the mausoleum she would share with my father, Larry Holt. Evelyn had always joked, "If I go first, I want you to pull me out when your father dies, put your father in, and then return me to the vault. That way, I know he won't be going out and messing around!" It was a horizontal vault for two caskets. As things turned out, my father passed away first, and Evelyn didn't have to worry about us switching the casket positions!

Diane's selection of River Creek for our new home when we moved back to Northern Virginia couldn't have been better. We had never lived in a community where we met so many genuinely nice people. Besides the Morins mentioned previously, there were Jack and Janet Fox, Steve and Sherol Taylor, Joe and Marj Motheral, Al and Ginny Gravallese, Barry and Debbie McDaniel, Woody and Carol Wrable, Bill and Cathy Cross, only to mention a few. Diane and I were playing golf two to three times a week and were enjoying it! One March, the Taylors invited us on a trip to Palm Beach Gardens for three days that Sherol had won. Another time, we went on a golfing trip with the Foxes to their beach house on Rehoboth Beach, Delaware, then drove up to Corolla, staying at our beach house. We played mostly ClubCorp courses on the trip, only paying twenty-five to thirty-five dollars cart fees per person!

Many of the *River Creekers* owned Marriott timeshares at Shadow Ridge in Palm Desert, California. There was an annual migration for a week or two in February/March by eight to ten couples from River Creek. Our first year going, Diane and I were invited by Ed and Chris Gould. We stayed at a very nice timeshare in the Desert

Willow area of Palm Desert and played golf with the other eight River Creek couples at each of the four ClubCorp Country Clubs in that area. Subsequent years, we shared a two-bedroom condo with the Taylors at Shadow Ridge, doing that for four or five years in a row. Diane and I enjoyed this break from Northern Virginia winters so much that we bought a week at Shadow Ridge and continue using that for these annual junkets! All in all, during our time living in River Creek, we made winter golf outings to Palm Desert ten out of eleven years. Life was large!

Additionally, several summers while living in River Creek on Crystal Lake St., a group of us decided to play the three ClubCorp courses on Hilton Head Island, South Carolina. Diane and I were the guests of Warren and Jill Stromberg one summer, and Al and Ginny Gravallese another year at their Marriott timeshare villas. Many of the usual River Creek golf gang was there with us at the same time.

Our son John was living with us on Crystal Lake St., but during the 2001–2002 period, both Tom and Erin bought town houses and stopped spending money on rental apartments. The real estate market was escalating nicely in those days in NOVA (Northern Virginia) and owning your own home was an excellent investment.

There was a lot to do living in the Washington, DC, area. There were many very nice restaurants in DC, and along with another couple or two, we'd frequently drive into town for dinner. We also had season tickets at the Kennedy Center or *Ken Cen* with Carl and Evelyn Morin for several years. Marvin Hamlisch was featuring a show that changed weekly. Marvin was a great entertainer! Sometime after 9-11-2001, Mayor Rudy Giuliani had put a program together to attract tourism back into New York City. It was called *Paint the Town Red, White, and Blue*. Broadway shows, restaurants, and hotels were offering big discounts as an incentive. Carl and Evelyn and Diane and I took Amtrak to The City, booked rooms at the Roosevelt Hotel, and stayed for three days and two nights. We saw a play, ate in fine restaurants, and generally had a great time!

Another fun thing Diane and I did several times was fly to Portland, Maine, for the day on United Express (ACA). Direct relatives, which include parents, can fly *non-rev* on a space available basis. We could check the loads on a particular flight and would catch an early flight out of Dulles Airport to the Portland, Maine, "Jet Port" then rent a car. We'd usually include a stop at LL Bean in Freeport, then a nice lobster dinner either in Boothbay Harbor or at DiMillo's Restaurant in Portland, Maine. Catching one of the last flights back to Dulles would round out a very enjoyable and not too expensive day! We did this more than once while Tom was at United Express and later.

Tom left Atlantic Coast Airlines in 2001 to become a First Officer or FO flying America Trans Air's (ATA's) Boeing 737 aircraft. He was based out of Chicago Midway, which meant he had to commute to work. Tom had been dating Erin's former Marymount roommate, Suzy, for a while. When the time was right, he proposed to her, and on September 1, 2002, Tom and Suzanne Mullins were married in St. Luke's Catholic Church with a reception following at a close-by country club in Westport, Connecticut. Several of our neighbors traveled to Connecticut to join in the festivities. It was a really nice venue, great wedding, and everyone had an excellent time!

A couple of years after we moved into River Creek, I decided to finish the approximately one thousand square foot basement. After drawing up the plans and getting building approval, I started construction. The design consisted of a full bathroom with jetted tub, a large party area with wet bar, a small relaxing area with comfortable leather couch and reclining chair, a card room, and last but not least, a full theatre with reclining chairs and state-of-the-art video and sound electronics. I did most of the construction work of framing, minor wiring, hanging drywall, etc. but acted as general contractor for running six electrical *home runs*, the plumbing, tile work, granite bar countertops, and dry wall mudding. It took me twelve months to complete, but on November 8, 2003, the Lower Deck was completed, and we had a grand opening with all our good friends from River Creek. We also enjoyed the space for the rest of the time we lived at 43332 Crystal Lake St., especially the theater!

In 2003, our daughter, Erin, left her position at Cable & Wireless where she was selling web hosting services and returned to the veterinary field where her heart had been for many years. She interviewed and accepted the position of Practice Manager at Old Mill Veterinary Hospital in Leesburg, Virginia. Erin had been dating Mark Melton, a veterinary imagining equipment salesman, while she was working in veterinary sales. Mark subsequently proposed to her, and on August 23, 2003, they were married in Leesburg, Virginia. The venue was Raspberry Falls, which was a quaint old farmhouse and attached banquet facility. Friends and family from both sides gathered for the wedding ceremony and reception that were both held at Raspberry Falls. It was a beautiful day, although a bit warm for August in Virginia, and the wedding ceremony was held outside. I have to admit, while I was happy for Erin on the one hand, on the other I felt sad that I was giving away my only daughter! There were genuine tears in my eyes as Erin and I walked down the aisle. Overall, I believe a good time was had by all!

It was around this time that my mother's marriage to Chet started getting strained. They were living in their fifth-wheeler RV on one of Chet's daughter's properties in Ohio. Apparently, Mother had been suffering more and more from Alzheimer's and was getting out of control on occasion. She had allegedly been yelling at Chet. This exceeded Chet's daughter's tolerance, and she requested that our family do something. My brother Ned picked up the ball and found a special facility in the Cleveland area that would provide loving care for Alzheimer's patients.

I remember our family traveling up to Cleveland, Ohio, from Northern Virginia and us visiting Ned then my mother while we were there. Ned said to Mother, "Mom, Denny is here to see you!" My mother replied, "Oh, I have a son named Denny." It was so sad. This woman who always ate healthy foods and walked eight or more miles a day when she was healthy had absolutely no idea who I was. I quietly cried inside. Ned had done a great job finding a place that gave our mother a good home nearby his dental practice for the remainder of her time on this earth. For this, I'll be eternally grateful to him. Mom passed away on January 2, 2005, at age eighty-eight. The world lost an exceptional pioneer woman on that day, and I lost my best friend from my childhood days.

Outer Banks, NC and Beach House
Just Breezin' Inn

761 Lakeview Ct., Corolla, NC

Just Breezin' Inn's pool,
many fun times!

Tom, Suzy, and family, OBX, NC

John and Luke, OBX, NC

Diane, Cherilyn, and Claire,
Carova Beach, 4WD

Area wild horse, North
Banks on 4WD Beach

CHAPTER TWENTY-NINE

THE *GOLDEN YEARS!*

On October 12, 2003, our first grandchild, Hollyn Norris Robertson, was born at Fair Oaks Hospital in Fairfax, Virginia. Tom called us with the good news. I was driving my 2000 BMW 528i at the time. Diane and I jumped into the car and quickly headed south to the Fairfax County Parkway. When almost at the turnoff for the hospital, I was stopped by a Virginia State Trooper. I pulled over, and this very big African American trooper with his State Trooper hat on came over to the car and said, "Where are you going in such a hurry, sir? Do you know you were speeding?" I replied, "Sorry, I was in a hurry to see our first grandchild." His next admonition was "Slow down, sir. I'm not giving you a ticket, but if you don't slow down, you'll never see your grandchild!" As intimidating as he initially appeared as he was approaching our car, he was actually a very compassionate person!

During the 2000s, our whole family enjoyed our beach house on the Outer Banks in Corolla, North Carolina! It was a five- to five-and-a-half-hour drive from Leesburg, Virginia, depending upon the season and traffic. We had named it *Just Breezin' Inn*. It was designed with an inverted floor plan and had the kitchen, living room, and master bedroom on the third floor. On the second floor were two bedrooms and a third bedroom with two double bunks for children. On the bottom floor was the fifth bedroom and a rec room with pullout couch and featured a slate pool table. The pool was just outside the rec room.

Diane and I hosted many golf outings from *Just Breezin' Inn* over the years for our close friends in River Creek. Besides the general beach attraction of the location, there were two ClubCorp golf courses nearby, Nags Head Links and the Currituck Club, which was only two miles south on Route 12. *Just Breezin' Inn's* five bedrooms would easily accommodate four couples, which conveniently made up two foursomes on the golf course!

We did rent *Just Breezin' Inn* during peak summer months to help defray the costs associated with ownership. Besides routine maintenance (which I did most of myself during our many trips to Corolla), there were real estate taxes, utility expenses, pool upkeep charges, etc. To go there off-season, Diane and I had to plan well as many area restaurants would close from just before Christmas to around first part of March, but we would still go down during the winter months on occasion. We spent many Thanksgiving holidays there with our whole family, sometimes freezing while cooking a turkey in peanut oil outside under the house! However, we also took advantage of visits poolside or on the beach during spring or summer weeks when it wasn't rented and the fall September/October period, which is very pleasant in the Outer Banks. It was a great family gathering spot, and we all loved it!

In 2005, our son Tom and his wife, Suzy, had decided to move to the Atlanta area. Tom was still flying Boeing 737s for American Trans Air or simply ATA airlines at the time. The airline had started out as a government charter business and subsequently expanded also into a low-cost commercial airline carrier. Then as ATA's commercial airline business was starting to deteriorate, Tom began interviewing with AirTran Airlines and came onboard in August 2005 flying their Boeing 717 aircraft. Tom and Suzy made several trips to Newnan, Georgia, looking at houses and decided to purchase one on Northcrest Drive in the White Oak community of Newnan. In May 2005, Tom had sold his town house in Sterling, Virginia, for about 272 percent of its original cost! The housing market in Northern Virginia was still going crazy!

Prior to moving day, Tom and Suzy had done the tedious job of packing boxes, but they hired a moving company to load the big rental truck professionally. However, when moving day arrived, the movers never showed up! Tom went to a local 7-Eleven and hired day workers to pack the truck. What an experience! Diane and I helped clean up last-minute items in the town house while Tom and Suzy started the ten-hour drive to their new home in Newnan, Georgia! Eighteen-month-old Hollyn and their greyhound, Gracie, stayed behind with us. The next day, our son John, Diane, and I drove the Robertson's manual shift Honda Civic and their Honda Pilot vehicles along with Hollyn and Gracie to their new home in Newnan. It was a relatively uneventful trip, and young Hollyn was a great little traveler! One event that does stand out in my mind was as we were passing Lake Norman just north of Charlotte, North Carolina, we hit *heavy* stop-and-go traffic that was backed up many miles north of the city. I was driving the stick shift Civic, and my left leg started cramping badly due to multiple stops and starts. We didn't have cell phones to communicate then, but we did have short-range walkie-talkies. I contacted Diane, and we switched drivers at the next possible time. It was quite an adventure!

In the mid-2000s, River Creek was starting to become built-out, and more and more families were moving in. The River Creek declaration was the official document that defined how community management would transition from developer control to resident control. The percentage of resident-owned homes to developer-owned lots had reached the level that allowed various committees to be formed. I was interested in helping form the Safety and Security Committee and became its first Chairman. The declaration also defined a five-member Board of Directors. Initially, all five members represented the developer, Marc Montgomery, but now the number of resident-owned homes allowed two Board members to be residents. A community-wide election was held, and I threw my name in the hat. Residents John Thornell and Stu Curley were first and second respectively, and I came in third of a field of six or seven. They joined the Board immediately. Then in 2005, another resident threshold was reached, and a third resident could be added. Because I was third in the previous general election, I was added to the Board, and the residents now had control three members to two for the developer. It was interesting getting involved with influencing how the River Creek community would grow and mature, but resident complaints, especially frivolous ones, took a lot of joy out of the experience. I served my one-year term and then went back on the Safety and Security Committee.

On June 30, 2005, our second grandchild, Luke Holt Melton, was born at Fair Oaks Hospital in Fairfax, Virginia! In addition to a granddaughter, Diane and I now had a grandson! Our daughter, Erin, was still the Practice Manager at Old Mill Veterinary Hospital in Leesburg, Virginia. About one year after Luke was born, Erin had sold her Leesburg town house for over 260 percent of the original cost, and she and Mark bought a big four-bedroom single-family home on Cooper Run in Lovettsville, Virginia.

In the summer of 2005, Diane and I booked a Western Caribbean cruise on the *Star Princess* with the Motherals, Wrables, and McDaniels! We all flew to Miami and boarded the ship. It was a great cruise, and our group really had an exciting seven-day adventure! There were interesting ports of call, good food, and a "Little Girl" progressive slot in the casino that was very good to Carol Wrable and Diane. Joe and Woody played ping-pong with two Russian guests and beat them so badly the first match that the Russians were *no-shows* for the second match! One fun event was the putt-putt course on the upper deck; however, each time the ship rolled from one side to the other, it presented a new element into lining up the hole for the putt! It was a good time with good friends! After the cruise, we all stayed on Miami's South Beach at the Whitelaw Hotel for a couple of nights to extend our trip.

I continued to have fun pursuing NESi business at IRS and other Federal accounts, and our family continued to grow and prosper. In 2006, we were invited on a Notre Dame University sponsored trip to Italy by alumni Dr. Jack Fox. Diane and I had a wonderful time touring Tuscany for ten days. The only downside was Alitalia Airlines had lost my suitcase, and it didn't catch up with me until five days into the trip. I fell in love with Tuscany. Outstanding trip!

After the Notre Dame trip, several of us extended in Rome for several days. Diane and I booked two nights at the Excelsior Hotel on Westin Star Points. We were shocked at the size of the room. It was luxurious and very large! Ernie and Roberta Carpico, the Foxes, and the Wrables were all staying at a Marriott Hotel just around the corner from the Excelsior. Ernie's family had been from a small town named Fonte Chiara, Italy. Ernie wanted to connect with some of his relatives, so he rented a small bus with a driver/interpreter, and eight of us drove out of Rome in search of the Italian Carpicos! We met some very friendly people, some of whom gave us bottles of wine, but the best we could do was find the house Ernie's relatives lived in. There was a little old man living there who remembered Ernie's dad standing in that very doorway on a visit during WWII. Ernie's dad was a US Army soldier on his way with his unit to attack the Nazi stronghold atop Monte Cassino. For some reason, the little Italian man fell in love with Diane, and when our bus was pulling out, he came over to Diane's window and put his hand on the glass outside, holding it there as long as possible! Returning to Rome, our group went to dinner that evening and generally enjoyed each other's company and the sights and tastes of the food of Rome for a couple of days until it was time for Diane and me to board our plane for the trip back to the USA.

While Diane and I didn't have any grandchildren for the first several years that our two older children were married, 2006 turned out to be a banner year, and suddenly we had many! On April 2, 2006, Claire Elizabeth Robertson was born at Piedmont Atlanta Hospital! And shortly after that, on October 11, 2006, Mark Ryan Melton (or Ryan) was born at Fair Oaks Hospital in Fairfax, Virginia!

During the late 2006 and 2007 period, we had our Corolla beach house on the market. It was still very much a place both Diane, our family, and I enjoyed going to, but we were contemplating a move to the Newnan, Georgia, area and downsizing from our home in Leesburg, Virginia. We were trying to do an IRS *1031 Exchange* with the Corolla property. This gives a capital gains tax break if one sells a rental property and purchases another like property. After a year, we weren't able to sell the beach house and finally exceeded the 1031 exchange period, so we just purchased a house in SummerGrove, Newnan, Georgia. Because we had exceeded the period of time for the 1031 exchange, we had to forgo the tax advantage. In 2007, Diane and I had three healthy mortgages: the River

Creek house, the Corolla beach house, and our new future residence in SummerGrove, Newnan, Georgia. It was a bit scary!

During that period, daughter Erin and her husband, Mark, got caught up in the housing bubble burst that started in early 2007. Their builder at Cooper Run, in Lovettsville, Virginia, was having severe financial issues, and when he pulled out of Cooper Run, prices on his homes in that development dropped $100,000 in a very short period. We were all devastated! Housing in the greater Washington, DC, area had always been increasing exponentially for many, many years. How could this happen? In 2007, Mark and Erin Melton decided to move south to a more stable housing environment and moved into our vacant home in the *Cottages* subdivision of the SummerGrove community in Newnan, Georgia. It helped the Melton family get back on their feet and helped Diane and I to defray part of the mortgage on the property. Diane and I made several *non-rev* trips on AirTran to visit our families, who had moved out of the Northern Virginia area. We would be reunited soon.

Diane and I continued to travel during this period. In January 2007, we joined Erin and family in Orlando at their Sheraton Vistana Villages timeshare and visited several parks at Disney World for a week.

Later in 2007, we took a trip to Hawaii with Barry and Debbie McDaniel. We spent a week at their timeshare in Kauai, playing golf and just having fun. I remember all the roosters around their condo that would start *cock-a-doodle-doing* at dawn very early and waking everyone up! We had a couple of golf tee times at Kauai. One very rainy day, we drove up to the pro shop at Kauai Dunes and asked for a rain check. It was raining *very* hard. The pro behind the desk said, "Oh, the course is open. It's okay to play." We were shocked, but they wouldn't budge! We discussed it and finally decided to play. I had a rainsuit with me, but we had to buy one for Diane at pro shop prices! The course was basically flooded in places, and when you tried to hit your ball, there would be a huge splash of water that left with the ball! That lasted maybe twelve holes, and we finally decided our $175 pp greens fee weren't worth it and quit! We had reservations at a very nice restaurant called Capiche nearby. We had brought a change of clothing to shower and change after golf. Kauai Dunes had a locker room, but only an open gym type shower. Barry and I took a shower, but it seemed like we were back playing sports in school and not in a country club environment! The girls gave us unimaginable grief! Anyway, we made it to Capiche all cleaned up, enjoyed several ninety-five-dollar bottles of wine, and had a great meal! After Kauai, the four of us traveled to Maui, staying at our Westin Ka'anapali Resort timeshare, played more golf, and ate at Diane's and my favorite restaurants (one was the Hula Grill where you could put your feet in the sand, watch the sunset, and listen to Hawaiian entertainment) before flying home to River Creek. It was a very enjoyable two weeks.

During 2009, we had decided to move south to Newnan, Georgia, and put the River Creek house on the market. In anticipation of our move south, Erin and Mark Melton started looking for a home to purchase. They found a nice one in the White Oak community very near where son Tom and family lived. The cousins now would be able to play together; they only had to walk around the corner!

Thanks to Marlene Baugh and her team, our River Creek home sold quickly. Marlene wasn't only a friend but was also an excellent realtor. An added benefit for us was that the buyer was a golfer, and we sold our River Creek full golf membership to him. Our mover had spent several days packing us up, and on August 17, the moving truck arrived. If you've ever gone through this experience, you know how nerve-racking it is! Well, our good friend Al Gravallese arrived in the morning to help. He made a run to the bank for us, took down fixtures in the garage I hadn't had a chance to do yet, drove home to his house, brought back lunch, and in general provided invaluable assistance during this stressful time for us. Al is one of the finest people I've ever met and a great friend. I thought we had everything under control for moving day, but Al stayed with us all day, and I don't know what we would have done without his help!

In 2010, Diane and I attended a USS *Will Rogers* (SSBN659) ship's reunion in Groton, Connecticut, where our boat had been *born* at Electric Boat. It was a great chance to reconnect with former (and now *old*) shipmates!

On September 14, 2010, our fifth and probably last grandchild, John Thomas Melton, was born at Piedmont Hospital, Fayetteville, Georgia! We now had three grandsons by our daughter, Erin, and husband, Mark Melton, and two granddaughters by our son Tom and wife, Suzy Robertson! Life was large!

Summertime activities continued into 2011 with a week in Kitty Hawk, in the Outer Banks of North Carolina at SeaScape. Son Tom's family, Di's sister Cherilyn, and her SO Jack, plus Diane and I had a great time. There are so many things to do there and nice restaurants to go to that we always enjoy our time in the Outer Banks, and a week goes *way* too quickly.

Later that year, Diane and I and Cherilyn and Jack booked a ten-day river cruise on Uniworld's *River Baroness* from Paris to Normandy and back. It was a fun ship with many interesting stops along the way to places like Giverny, my favorite impressionist Monet's home, Les Andelys, Richard the Lionheart's Castle ruins, and many others. Being a veteran, my favorite was the Normandy Beaches where our brave allied military forces landed on June 6, 1944, and the American Cemetery. It was a very moving experience visiting both of these locations, especially seeing what those brave men went through during that massive invasion to insure our freedom!

Life on board the riverboat was interesting too! There was a group of twelve widows from Las Vegas on the river cruise who were a hoot! They partied each night and simply were a fun group to be around. Jack is a retired submarine designer who had worked at Electric Boat in Groton, Connecticut, for many years. Being curious, he and I would go up to the wheelhouse from time to time and talk with the officer of the deck. We learned much about the operation of the *River Baroness*. There was something like nine locks that she had to navigate each way from Paris to Normandy because the Seine dropped in elevation substantially going to Normandy. Additionally, the *River Baroness* was taller above the waterline than the clearance under the many bridges coming out of Paris. To compensate for this, the whole wheelhouse was hydraulically lowered so it was low enough to pass under the bridges, and steering was shifted to a panel on the portside rail just outside the wheelhouse structure. Very clever! After the cruise, we spent several days in Paris seeing the sights. The four of us attended Easter Mass at Notre Dame, not knowing then that this magnificent structure would many years later be substantially damaged by fire.

Diane had been encouraging me to take an Alaska cruise for years. I felt that cruises should have destinations of tropics, beaches, and palm trees, not cold weather, glaciers, and grizzly bears. Well, in 2012, Diane finally convinced me, and we booked an Alaska Inner Passage cruise on *Princess* from Anchorage, Alaska, to Vancouver, British Columbia. We flew from Atlanta to Anchorage, and by the time we got to the hotel, it was approaching 11:00 p.m., and the sun was still up! I'd never seen anything like that! The cruise itself was far better than I could ever imagine and actually one of the better cruises I had ever taken. I was sorry I had dragged my feet so long! We saw several glaciers up close and observed the *calving* of the ice. The ship made stops in (1) Skagway, where we boarded the White Pass and Yukon Route railroad and chugged up the side of a mountain to a point in Canada where the Klondike gold prospectors had to climb by foot; (2) Juneau the capital (BTW, we could not see Russia from Sarah Palin's house); and (3) Ketchikan, where it rained the whole time we were there. Again, a great cruise!

Diane and I had never been to Vancouver, so we had booked the Westin there for two nights and explored the beautiful city for three days. We could see the bay from our room and many de Havilland Otter seaplanes taking off and landing constantly. One of those days just happened to be July 1, 2012, Canada Day. Everyone was decked out in Canadian flags and patriotic dress and were celebrating. The city had lighted the Olympic Torch for the occasion. We really enjoyed Vancouver and its people! Our flight home to Atlanta was from Seattle, Washington. So the next logical thing to do was to reserve an overnight Amtrak train for the trip. It was a fun decision. Finally, we stayed two additional nights at the Seattle Westin Hotel on Star Points and enjoyed that city, too, before flying home.

For our 2013 adventure, Diane and I booked the cruise of a lifetime on Regent *Seven Seas Mariner*! The eight-day itinerary was Barcelona to Rome with stops along the way in France and Italy. We had been upgraded at no extra cost to a suite with a huge outdoor balcony at the rear of the ship. The cruise was all-inclusive, and that level of suites included a butler, who in our case was a young man from India. He turned out to be great. The stops were excellent: Palma de Mallorca, Marseille, San Tropez, Monte Carlo, Portofino, and Florence/Pisa (Livorno). We arrived a couple days early for the cruise, staying at a Le Méridien Hotel directly off Las Ramblas. We used public transportation and visited many Barcelona sights such as Gaudi's Sagrada Familia Basilica. Construction had begun in March 1882, and completion is estimated to be finished in 2026! After the fabulous cruise was finished, we extended our time, as we frequently like to do, with a stay at the San Regis in Rome. It is a classic old hotel with a lot of charm, but I think we liked the Excelsior better. Finally, there was the long flight back over the Atlantic that Diane does not like.

Southwest Airlines had purchased AirTran in 2011. The integration took several years, but in February 2013, son Tom became a SWA First Officer, changed uniforms, and started flying Southwest routes. He couldn't hold Atlanta as a domicile, so he had to commute to PHX or HOU.

Later that year, we made a trip to a timeshare on Maui, the Westin Kā'anapali Ocean Resort Villas. We both loved Maui and especially the old whaling village of Lahaina that was close by. There were many great restaurants in Lahaina, like Kimo's, and we visited the Lahaina Galleries where we had bought several fine art pieces over the years. We especially liked paintings by Dario Campanile and sculptures by Frederick Hart. It just happened that Dan and Ann Frigard were in Kā'anapali at the same time, and we had dinner with them several times.

The year 2014 arrived and turned out to be a very significant and busy one! It started with a week in Cancun in January at the Westin Lagunamar Ocean Resort with Diane's sister Cherilyn and her SO, Jack Grapp, plus son John and his SO, Stephen. We all love that resort. The staff is very friendly to Americans. It's a great location, and the weather was great that year. Later that year, Diane and I made a trip to the Massachusetts shore at Acoaxet, Massachusetts, with Cherilyn and Jack. It's a nice area, southwest of Cape Cod, with plenty of casual restaurants and places to see (like Elephant Rock).

Alaska Cruise—*Sapphire Princess*, 2012

Anchorage (Whittier),
AK—Departure port

Watching glacial caving, Alaska

White Pass and Yukon
Route RR, Skagway, AK

Di and Den on the way to
White Pass and Canada

Skagway, AK—a former brothel

Princess concierge, wine
tasting evening

Diane visiting an Alaska glacier

Olympic torch (for Canada
Day!), Vancouver, BC

Mediterranean Cruise 2013—Barcelona to Rome

Regent *Seven Seas Mariner*

Our two-room stateroom
with walk-in closet!

Sagrada Familia, Barcelona, Gaudi

Yachts of Saint-Tropez, FR

Monte Carlo

Portofino, Italy

Trevi Fountain, Rome

Diane, St. Peter's Basilica, Rome

The big event this year was on June 21, 2014. Our son D. John Robertson was joined in matrimony with Stephen McCollum in Washington, DC. John's aunt Cherilyn plus family friends Father Gus and Sister Mary Claire came down from upstate New York. The ceremony was originally scheduled to take place on the steps of National City Christian Church on Thomas Circle, but inclement weather threatened, so it was moved inside the church. After the ceremony, we all traveled up to the Barcelona Bar on Fourteenth Street, NW, where a fabulous reception followed! Relatives from both families were in attendance. Entertainment was provided by a new young jazz pianist and vocalist Champian Fulton, who had just released an album. She was great, and everyone had an excellent time!

Not that 2014 wasn't busy enough, but Diane and I rented our old beach house, Just Breezin' Inn, for a week in August. Diane and I flew to Richmond, Virginia, where we rented a stretch Chevy Suburban SUV and drove to the Outer Banks. Son Tom and family drove up from Newnan and joined us for the week. Hollyn was now ten years old, and Claire eight years old. We were disappointed to see that our old pride and joy wasn't kept in the same good repair as when we owned it. It had been painted a different color, which is fine, but there were many minor repairs that needed to be done. We did the usual things that we always did there: driving north on Rt. 12 to the end of the road then onto the four-wheel drive section of the beach for about five miles to swim and cook lunch on a charcoal grill, going to our favorite restaurants, enjoying the pool at the beach house, and in general just enjoying the North Banks of North Carolina!

Diane and I were still making our annual golfing trips to California's Coachella Valley in the February/March timeframe and staying at our Shadow Ridge timeshare in Palm Desert, but the group was getting smaller.

In 2015, our big trip was to Ireland. Diane had always wanted to visit the country where her ancestors had come from. She had previously had her DNA analyzed, and it indicated she was of 93 percent Irish heritage! I did a lot of research on the Internet and came up with a plan to start in Dublin, drive a semi-circular route south near the eastern coast in a clockwise direction, then work our way west and end up at Shannon Airport to fly home from there. With the help of a travel agent in Ireland, we booked three B&Bs for the trip. I secured our air travel and reserved a BMW 520d for transportation. The cost of the automatic BMW going through Costco Travel was much less expensive than the manual shift Fiat van the travel agent had recommended. We had driven cars on the left side of the road in Freeport and the UK, and I just couldn't imagine having to shift a car with your left hand (because the steering wheel was on the right side of the car and everything is reversed) and at the same time watch for traffic from a direction you're not used to. The BMW *seemed* like the logical and less expensive choice.

We flew all night and landed at the Dublin Airport early the next day. After retrieving our bags, we were transported to our hotel, the Westin Dublin. Diane and I were again staying on Star Points, and Cherilyn and Jack had booked another hotel close by. We enjoyed touring Dublin for a couple days, seeing sights like the Guinness Store House and Jameson's Distillery (sense a pattern here)? We really enjoyed Dublin, and I'd go back in a heartbeat! The people were very friendly and welcoming.

As Diane's sister Cherilyn and Jack Grapp were with us on the trip, the plan was that Diane and Jack would split up the driving, and I would navigate. While I can drive okay on local roads, I get a vertigo type of feeling when attempting to drive on interstate highways and have to slow down a lot. This has been gradually getting worse over the years, so much so that I didn't feel comfortable driving in Ireland. The day we picked up our BMW 520d in Dublin, Jack had the occasion to drive it from one building to the place where Diane and Cherilyn and our luggage was located. I thought he was going to scrape some barriers on the left side of the BMW and warned him. He was obviously struggling, and after we reached our destination, he told me, "I can't drive this thing." So Diane drove 100 percent of the rest of the trip! I really felt bad that I couldn't assist with the driving.

We spent the first night in Kilkenny. The B&B there was very basic. It was way out of the way and quite small. The owners weren't very friendly, and the breakfast the next morning was minimal. This was not a good start to the accommodations arranged by our Irish travel agent! The next day, we drove to the coast to visit Waterford on the way to Cork. In doing research on the web, I had kept seeing raves about a B&B in Cork called Fernroyd House, so I booked it for several nights. The innkeepers, Tony and Avril, couldn't have been nicer! It was Diane's birthday the day we arrived, and I had mentioned that fact previously when booking the room. Avril's daughter had made cupcakes and added birthday candles to them. When Tony brought it in, we all sang happy birthday to Diane. Tony also furnished a celebratory bottle of wine for us on the house. The four of us had rooms in a separate building that also had a small kitchen and lounge area with a TV. The accommodations were great, and Avril's breakfasts were simply amazing!

My overall plan was to book B&Bs in key locations for several nights and make day trips from the B&Bs like spokes on a wheel. There was a lot to see in and around Cork—the University College was within walking distance, there were great pubs in downtown Cork, and a short drive to the village of Cobh where the Titanic stopped offshore to board more passengers before disappearing over the horizon. We also drove out to Mizen Head from Cork, which was a mistake. The road out to Mizen Head is very narrow, like about one and a half car widths for a two-lane road. To make things worse, there were short hedges lining each side of the road. While it appeared to be a soft ivy hedge, there were stone walls immediately behind the shrubbery! The width of the BMW would prove not to be very practical for these narrow roads, and there were many of them. The other challenge that the BMW presented to the driver was going through the various small Irish towns. Typically, the sidewalks didn't have high curbs on the street side, and cars would park half on the sidewalk and half in the street, on *both sides*! The resulting available width for two cars going in different directions was minimal at best. Sitting in the front seat on the left side of the BMW, I could see how close we were to the parked cars and probably bugged Diane as I'd frequently say, "Di, you've got to move right!" The BMW was fine for the motorways, but the narrower van the travel agent had proposed would have been less nerve-racking for our driver!

After leaving Cork, we stopped at Blarney Castle on the way to our next B&B, which was in Killarney where we'd stay for two days. The B&B was owned by an older lady who set her tables every morning with fine silverware and china, and it was quite nice overall. While in Killarney, we took a Barrett bus tour of the Dingle Peninsula. We decided on a guided bus tour so Diane could relax and better see more of the countryside.

The next B&B was in Ennis. The innkeepers here, Domhnall and Sheila, were also very warm and gracious, and Sheila made the best breakfasts also. Domhnall was a riot and was always talking about *the board of directors* when referring to his wife and her staff! He also spoke a lot about *the Irish language*, and in this part of Ireland, we were seeing more and more signs in Gaelic or *the Irish language*. We drove out to the Cliffs of Moher, but they were covered with fog, so we basically didn't see a thing! Another trip in the BMW took us up to the Galway area, which is beautiful. We took one more Barrett tour, and this time the bus conveniently picked us up right in front of the hotel.

We had a very early flight back to the USA from Shannon Airport, so the day we left, we got up at 0' Dark Thirty and drove to the airport for departure. This was easily at the very top of trips I've ever taken! I have just four words to describe Ireland: "beautiful country, beautiful people." Those words say it all. I hope someday I can return to this beautiful place on earth!

Ireland Trip—2015

Checking into the Westin Dublin

Beautiful River Nore, Kilkenny

Reginald's Tower, thirteenth century, Waterford

Diane's birthday cupcakes (September 13) with Tony, owner of Fernroyd House, Cork

Poll na Bron, five-thousand-year-old burial tomb, Ennis

Irish pub fun!

Cathedral in Cobh

Blarney Castile

Beautiful Dingle
Peninsula

Diane and Dennis on Dingle Peninsula!

Anne Moore and her brothers,
going to America

BMW 520d and its travelers

Impromptu Irish pub band   Small-town streets are *narrow*!

Ireland's windy west coast!

Our next vacation adventure was a three-week stay in the Hawaiian Islands in 2016. If one travels that distance, you might as well stay for a while, plus Diane and I had the idea in the back of our minds that this might be our last trip to Hawaii. We invited Newnan golfing friends, Dr. Bill and Linda Glass, to come along. They traveled extensively but had never been to Hawaii. After an overnight stop in San Francisco, Diane and I took off for Honolulu, Oahu. Bill and Linda met us there. The four of us did the touristy things for several days visiting the USS *Arizona* Memorial at Pearl Harbor, having mai tai cocktails at the Royal Hawaiian Hotel on Waikiki Beach and driving around the island to the North Shore, including sampling food trucks along the way. Next, we island hopped to Kauai, where we stayed at our Westin timeshare at Princeville for three nights. It was a good time, and I believe Bill and Linda enjoyed the islands!

They departed for the US mainland, and Diane and I flew over to Maui, our favorite Hawaiian Island, to continue our vacation.

Once on Maui, we checked into the Westin Ka'anapali Resort for ten days. Diane and I did the usual things we do there. We ate at our favorite restaurants, drove to some of our favorite locations on the island, and just enjoyed the tropical splendor! One thing we did differently that year was to make a trip to Lana'i. We'd booked the trip through our Westin concierge and caught the ferry from Lahaina for the forty-five-minute trip to Manele Harbor, where we met our guide Bruce and his four-wheel drive vehicle. We were impressed with the differences in various parts of Lana'i. Lana'i City was like going back in time to the 1920s. Original homes had been restored to the period, and Larry Ellison (who owns 98 percent of the island) has restored the movie theatre and other municipal buildings to the same period. Bruce took us to many places on Lana'i. One favorite was the Garden of the God's. It made you feel like you were on the moon. Going out on a point of land there, the trade winds blew through the venturi created by Molokai and Maui so strong that it almost blew us over. Bruce also took us to Shipwreck Beach and other interesting parts of the island probably not seen by many visitors. We returned to Lahaina on the return ferry. All in all, a very nice day! At the end of our ten days on Maui, we boarded our flight back to the mainland and eventually to Atlanta.

Son John had been promoted to AVP by Navy Federal Credit Union (NFCU) and moved to Pensacola, Florida, where he would be managing a large portion of NFCU's call center there. In September 2016, John and Stephen rented a very nice condo in a building known as The Rivera. It was a three-bedroom unit right on Pensacola Bay. Living there was like living on a cruise ship and looking out at the ocean all the time! During their period renting, a unit one floor below on eleven became available. They purchased it, completely renovated it, and moved in the fall of 2017. Pensacola is only about four and a half hours from our home in Newnan, so Diane and I visited whenever we could. On one trip, John, Diane, and I drove over to New Orleans for a couple days. Diane had never been to NOLO. She wasn't too fond of Bourbon St. but liked several of the nicer restaurants in town (GW Fins, Commander's Palace, Café du Monde, etc.). We had a drink at a cool jazz club called Fritzel's and listened to the jazz band. One of the main reasons for the trip was to visit the National WWII Museum, which took us a day and a half to see most of it. Highly recommend this museum! It's very well done, and veterans or history buffs would especially enjoy it.

During this period of 2016, son Tom was still flying for Southwest, and daughter Erin was VP of Sales and Marketing for a company called Dog Leggs. Both Tom, Erin, and their families (and our five wonderful grandchildren) were living in the White Oak section of Newnan, Georgia. As for me, on January 1, 2015, my status at Network Executive Software (NESi) had changed from a company employee to a sales agent. During 2016, I was still involved with interfacing with our customers and sales, but on a less frequent basis. It was good for me in that I felt it helped me keep up with current technology and stimulated my brain.

Over the period of June 18 to 27, Diane, Ryan Melton, and I joined son Tom and family at SeaScape in the Outer Banks. Diane, Ryan, and I had flown into Washington National Airport and drove a rental car to Kitty Hawk, North Carolina. This was the first time Ryan had been on vacation without his family, and he did fine. There is so much to do in the Outer Banks with good restaurants, putt-putt golf, and other attractions besides the great beaches. We had a great week!

In March 2017, I had a pain in my lower back, right side. Diane took me to the ER, and I ended up staying eight nights due to a severe kidney infection! The Newnan Piedmont Hospital nursing staff was great, but I thought the hospitalist, Dr. Savage, was going to kill me before I was released! I went through more tests than I ever could imagine, was receiving unmonitored IV fluids ordered by Dr. Savage, and developed atrial fibrillation before being released. When I left the hospital, I was on oxygen for three or four weeks and not able to take deep breaths very well. I had excess fluid in my lungs and body. Over a period of seven to eight months, doctors tried various procedures to get my heart back in normal sinus rhythm again, but it always slipped back into aFib, so I'm just living with it.

I was feeling more *normal* by June 2017, so Tom's family, Erin's family, and Diane and I went on our planned trip to Cancun and the Westin Lagunamar Resort. It was fun having all five grandchildren present and watching them having fun! There is so much to do at that particular resort that you really don't need to leave the premises. We did make the obligatory trip to Costco in Cancun for supplies, and the Robertson family and Diane and I took a bus tour to Xel-Ha, which is a huge water park just north of Tulum, Mexico. It was another memorable week in paradise.

On December 12, 2017, a sad event occurred for our family. Diane and her sister Cherilyn's younger sister, Jamie Lynaugh, passed away from cancer in Schenectady, New York. Jamie had been sick for a while as the cancer had slowly spread throughout her body. It was difficult emotionally for the two older sisters. Even when one knows something is coming, it still doesn't make it any easier when the event actually happens.

The year 2018 started ominously. In March, Diane's sister Cherilyn drove south about one hour from her home for a routine doctor's appointment in Englewood, New Jersey, but she never made it. She apparently drove around for hours looking for his office, which she normally knew well. When Cherilyn was stopped going down a one-way street the wrong way, the police officers realized something was seriously wrong and took her to the closest emergency room. She had a brain tumor that had ruptured and was bleeding. Cherilyn was in serious trouble.

The year 2018 was another busy one for us. In January, we had planned a trip to Chicago over April 10 to 13, 2018, to see the play *Hamilton*. It was playing in New York City and coming to Atlanta, but the ticket prices in Chicago were roughly half the cost of tickets in the other two cities. We both thoroughly enjoyed *Hamilton*. I thought the choreography, acting, and the message were outstanding! Diane had never been to Chicago, so we booked three nights on Star Points at the Sheraton Grand, which is right on the Chicago River. We ate some Chicago deep-dish pizza, did an architectural river tour, and spent several days seeing other Chicago sites before returning home to Atlanta.

We had no more than returned from Chicago when it was time for another scheduled trip from April 23–30, 2018. This time, it was back to Cancun and the Westin Lagunamar Resort with son John and Stephen for our third time. It was another great week! We enjoyed the beaches and restaurants at the resort as usual. One thing a bit different this time was the four of us took a bus tour booked through the Westin Concierge to see the Cirque du Soleil production "Joya" south of Cancun. It was of the usual Cirque du Soleil quality and very enjoyable!

Diane's sister Cherilyn was not getting any better. After many months of treatment and desperately trying several different specialists, Cherilyn Nicholson passed away on May 24, 2018. Within a period of less than six months, Diane had lost both of her younger sisters. Cherilyn was a good person and loved by all, including what she considered her nine grandchildren. Our five grandchildren called her AC for Aunt Cherilyn. Our families all traveled north to Saugerties, New York, for the funeral services. I had put together a slide presentation that was shown in the funeral home during her viewing, depicting her life during the many, many great times our families had shared with AC and, for the past ten years, her companion, Jack Grapp. Cherilyn was interred in the Nicholson family cemetery plot in Englewood, New Jersey. It was a very sad time. We all miss AC!

As February 1, 2019, approached, John and Stephen had consulted with Diane as to a venue and were planning the *80-40* event of the century! Stephen McCollum and I share February 1 as our birthday, my eightieth and his fortieth. First, a little background. As you may recall, my grandfather Robert Kirk was stationed in Charleston, South Carolina, while in the Navy, plus my mother was born there. He and my grandmother Mabel would go to the beach on the nearby Isle of Palms in their *swimming costumes*. When Diane and I were first married and I was stationed in Charleston aboard SSBN622, we would also go to the Isle of Palms to swim and soak in the sun. Therefore, it was decided that there would be a grand *80-40* birthday celebration based around Charleston and specifically the Isle of Palms! Stephen is an event planner by occupation, and between him and John, they planned an event *par excellence.* They rented an eleven-bedroom house right on the beach. The home had an elevator, a heated pool, and a practice pitching/putting golf hole next to the ocean. The home was amazing! Stephen's mom, Robyin, and husband, Mark, were there, and his brother traveled from as far away as Bellingham, Washington, with his girlfriend, Lacey, to join in on the celebration! Son Tom and family and daughter Erin and family came up from Newnan, Georgia. My brother Ned drove down from Maine in a snowstorm (took him three days) and stopped in Saugerties, New York, to pick up Jack Grapp on the way. Mutual friends Darby Jones came down from Boston, and Mike and Katie McDonald attempted to fly from Washington, DC, but when flights were canceled because of the snowstorm, they ended up renting a car and driving to the IOP!

It was an amazing dual celebration. There were 80/40 tote bags filled with goodies for each guest when they checked in, 80/40 sweatshirts, 80/40 plastic cups, and too many other 80/40 articles to mention! Before dinner, the night of Stephen and my birthday, an outdoor reception was held on the grounds behind the house near the beach. After cocktails al fresco, a gala-catered dinner was planned in the large living room of the gigantic house where each guest had a choice of their meal. The invitation jokingly said "black tie optional" for the dinner. One only turns eighty once, so I brought my tux and showed up for the grand event in it! Stephen had rented two small buses for one of the free days, and 80/40 revelers had their choice of shopping in Charleston or a trip to Patriot's Point. Tom, all five grandchildren, and I chose Patriot's Point! It was a birthday celebration like no other, and I'll never forget it!

USS *Will Rogers* SSBN659 held its biennial reunion in Tulsa, Oklahoma, the birthplace of Will Rogers, over June 12–16, 2019. Shipmates Dave Smith and Dave Hero and their wives Katie and Paula traveled from Boston to be there. We all toured Will Rogers's ranch and later the Will Rogers Museum, plus we enjoyed various get-togethers and banquets. It was fun visiting with various past shipmates and enjoying the camaraderie! We also had a memorial service for all those shipmates on eternal patrol.

The summer of 2019 passed with its usual Georgia heat, but we were all doing fine. When fall arrived, it found granddaughters Hollyn playing soccer and Claire playing lacrosse for their school, Trinity Christian. Diane and I loved to go to their games whenever we could to cheer them on! The three Melton grandsons were playing baseball, either for Trinity or rec travel ball. John was just learning and playing organized ball, but both Luke and Ryan had been playing for a while and were getting very good at it! Luke was becoming an excellent left-handed pitcher and also played right field with the determination to not miss any ball that came his way. In July 2019, Ryan was selected to be on the Peachtree City Little League team as first baseman and was a dynamite hitter. Our family traveled to Toccoa, Georgia, and watched Ryan's team win the Georgia Little League state title for 2019! This gave them the right to compete in the Southeastern Regional competition held in Warner Robbins, Georgia, in August. I'd never been to a Little League tournament at that level, but the stadium was very impressive and resembled a small professional baseball stadium. There were eight teams from the southeast that competed over a two-day period. Ryan's team did well and retired the first three teams they played. When they met the team from Virginia, however, they suffered their first loss. The Georgia champs won two more games, but ended up in second place in the regionals after playing Virginia twice. There was nothing to be ashamed of. The Georgia boys played well and did the very best they could. We were very proud of Ryan as he hit some very long balls, scored runs, and posted several RBIs! It was a Norman Rockwell moment when after the SE Regional Championship Game that they lost, two young boys came up to Ryan and asked him for his autograph. He was down because his team had lost the championship game, but somehow I think that moment of recognition cheered him up a bit!

Diane and I took two more trips toward the end of 2019. The first one over the period October 10–15 in Orlando at our Vistana Villages timeshare with the Robertson family and Erin and her family. We always enjoy this resort and area, and of course being with all our grandchildren is always a treat.

The second 2019 vacation over Thanksgiving, November 23–30, was to the Westin Kierland Villas in Scottsdale, Arizona, with John and Stephen and Stephen's family. Scottsdale is great place to visit that time of year. We all enjoyed a fantastic Thanksgiving Day dinner at the Four Seasons Resort Scottsdale at Troon North. The resort is up on a hill overlooking Scottsdale, and the food was very good. Diane and I arranged to meet our friend Dan Frigard for breakfast one morning. His new wife couldn't make it, but it was great seeing Dan again after several years! We also enjoyed a great dinner with Di's high school buddy Jacquie and husband, John, at their home in Chandler, Arizona.

We spent the Christmas holiday in Newnan, Georgia, with our family, and 2019 came to a close. At that time, we were all oblivious to what would be in store for the world early in 2020.

Grand 80/40 Birthday Celebration!

Eleven-bedroom venue,
Isle of Palms, SC

Family, Isle of Palms Beach

Impressive birthday dinner table!

80/40 dinner with family

Dennis's birthday cake

80/40 birthday
dinner, full table

Stephen's birthday cake

CHAPTER THIRTY

THE FINAL CHAPTER

The year 2020 started out quite normally. My wife, Diane, will have her eightieth birthday this year in September, so I planned a special trip to celebrate. Son John and Stephen would enthusiastically join us. I booked a ten-day Princess cruise. We'd start the trip by flying to Montreal where we'd stay overnight. The next day, we'd board a train to Quebec and another night's stay there before embarking on the ship on September 11. Once aboard the *Caribbean Princess*, we'd make stops in ports along the Canadian Maritime Provinces, continuing along the New England coast with termination in New York City where we would fly home. The leaves should be in full force during that time of year, and Diane and I had talked about a cruise like that for many years! Diane was excited!

Very early in 2020, Americans started hearing about a new virus that had been initially reported in Wuhan, China, on December 31, 2019. Subsequent to that date, the new virus, COVID-19, started appearing in European countries and Down Under. The first case in the US was reported on January 22, 2020, from a man who had just returned from Wuhan. The number of reported cases here began to increase, and the first US death from COVID-19 occurred on February 29, 2020. Even though cases and now deaths were also occurring in the EU and other countries around the world, it was an election year, and the then current administration decided to ignore and play down the danger with statements like "It will disappear when we get into April with the heat." Then on February 26: "You have fifteen15 people, when in a couple days it will be down to close to zero." The real facts are that from February 10, 2020, until August 31, 2020, we were told untruthfully that "it will go away" or "it will disappear" over *thirty-two times*!

The recommendations of infectious disease experts Dr. Anthony Fauci and Dr. Deborah Birx and the rest of the CDC were largely ignored, and the expert scientist's opinions were pushed into the background. The US had no national plan to combat and minimize the pandemic. It was up to the individual states to develop their own plans instead of a set of national guidelines that would have given states coordinated guidance. Additionally, instead of the Administration taking responsibility for acquiring masks, PPE, and ventilators for our health-care providers in *all* states and having the advantage of volume discounts, each state had to compete individually for these critical items, resulting in shortages and much higher prices due to the states having to bid against each other. Other countries like New Zealand, Germany, and a few more that had rolled out unified responses to a pandemic and implemented restrictions immediately had seen drastic declines, had pushed their curves downward, and began opening up their countries again. Failure to act quickly has resulted in the numbers continuing to climb rapidly here in the US.

As a direct result of the above failure to address COVID-19 and its rampant spread here, Princess Cruise Lines canceled the Canada/New England cruise that was to be Diane's special birthday celebration. Another factor that would have prevented us from taking that particular cruise is that US citizens are currently prohibited from entry into Canada due to the uncontrolled spread of the virus here. The then current administration's arrogance toward Prime Minister Trudeau soured this relationship too.

My big concern in 2020 is what kind of a country will Diane and I be leaving our three children and five grandchildren? I've always considered myself an Independent and not firmly attached to any major political party. I classify myself politically as a fiscal conservative and slightly right of center. I voted for JFK in 1960 in the first election that I was eligible to participate in. I also voted for Republican Ronald Reagan when I thought he was best for our country. However, I did *not* vote for Reagan four years later when it became apparent that *trickledown economics* didn't work!

We live in the greatest nation in the world, and it *has been* for a very long time. Our Constitutional Republic form of government, while not perfect, has served Americans well for over 244 years. Don't be distracted by naysayers and the disillusioned, uninformed minority who say otherwise. This is a great nation today! We can do anything we collectively set as a national goal. Over fifty years ago, the USA put twelve astronauts on the moon over a period. To this day, no other country has achieved that feat! Think about it. We accomplished that with 1960s technology that is now fifty-plus years old! Some other nations are still trying to catch up!

Over the years, and especially in 2020, Diane and I have had the pleasure of watching our five grandchildren grow and mature. The two older Melton boys, Luke and Ryan, have been playing travel baseball this summer, and their teams have been winning championships. Both older boys are now taller than their mother and will be taller than me soon! All five grandchildren are currently enrolled at Trinity Christian School—Hollyn a high school Junior, Luke a Sophomore, Claire a Freshman, Ryan in eighth grade, and John in fourth grade. They all are good students, and we're very proud of them. Trinity has started back with on-site learning. We hope the virus can be prevented from spreading in school. All five grandchildren missed their friends and wanted to physically return. Time will tell.

Only God knows how long it will be before I'm on Eternal Patrol, but when that time comes, I'll go with the satisfaction that I did the very best that I could during my life here on earth. I've always tried to be honest, sensitive to others' feelings, followed the Golden Rule, and otherwise very much enjoyed both the blessings and challenges placed in my path along the journey. I feel very fortunate for the love and dedication of my wife, Diane, over these many years and the blessings and love of three wonderful children and five special grandchildren. What more could one ask for?

While perhaps Green Beret Special Forces, Army Rangers, and Navy SEALs faced more dangerous missions over the years than my shipmates and I did on SSBN622 or SSBN659, I'll forever be proud of my service on a total of eight sixty to seventy-two-day dangerous and deterrent FBM submarine missions as part of the Nuclear Triad keeping the USA safe during the Cold War!

As I mentioned at the beginning of this book, the COVID-19 virus and *sheltering in place* at home, along with Diane's encouragement, prompted me to start writing this narrative. It's been fun remembering and reliving these past eighty-one-plus years. Diane and I have dug through the family photo archives and found some representative images to illustrate and perhaps amplify the words themselves a bit. I hope you enjoy reading *Teddy Bears to Dangerous Missions (An Autobiographical Journey from Teddy Bears to Submarines and Beyond)* as much as I have enjoyed writing it!

Grandchildren Sports—2019–20

Ryan signs autographs
after SE LL Tournament

Luke the Great Lefty!

John Thomas at bat

Hollyn, Trinity Varsity XC

Claire, Trinity
softball

I. DIVE DIVE

I served on the Holland over a century ago.

I still serve to this day on the Trident, Los Angeles & Seawolf class boats and look forward to shipping on the Virginia, Texas, and Hawaii SSNs.

Places like Fremantle, Rota, LaMadd, Chinhae, Pattaya, Sasebo, and Subic stir my soul.

For I am a Submariner.

I rest in peace beneath many seas across this earth.

I was on the Barbel off Palawan, the Scorpion off the Azores and the Bonefish in the Sea of Japan.

We gave them hell in the harbors at Wewak and Namkwan.

I am a Shellback, a Bluenose, a Plank Owner, a MCPO of the Navy, a CNO, and a President.

For I am a Submariner.

I heard Howard Gilmore's final order, "Take Her Down." I heard the word passed, "Underway on Nuclear Power."

I have done every job asked of me, from Messcook to Torpedoman to Motormac to COB to Skipper.

I know "Snorkel Patty" and Admiral Rickover.

For I am a Submariner.

I have twin Dolphins tattooed on my chest and twin screws tattooed
  on my ass.
I know the difference between a Lady and a Hooker but treat both
  with equal respect.
I know Georgia Street and Magsaysay drive.
And although the Horse & Cow keeps moving I will always find her.
I know the meaning of "Hot, Straight, and Normal."
For I am a Submariner.
I have stood tall and received the Medal of Honor and been thrown
  in the Brig for being Drunk & Disorderly.
I know the reverent tone of "Diesel Boats Forever" and the Gudgeon's
  "Find em, Chase em, Sink em."
I was on the Spearfish evacuating nurses from Corregidor and Skate
  when she surfaced at the North Pole.
I have spent time in the Royal Hawaiian.
For I am a Submariner.
I have gone by names like Nimitz, Cromwell, O'Kane, Ramage,
  Breault, "Mush" and Lockwood.
I have served on boats like the Nautilus, Thresher, Parche, Squalus,
  Wahoo and Halibut.
On December 7th I was onboard the Tautog at Pearl Harbor.
I was also on the Tusk in '49 and sacrificed myself for my shipmates
  on the Cochino.
For I am a Submariner.
I have stood watches in the cold of Holy Loch and the heat of the
  South Pacific.
I know what the "41 For Freedom" accomplished.
I was on the Sealion at Cavite in '41 and the Archerfish in Tokyo Bay
  in '45.
I have endured depth charges and POW camps.
I was on the Seafox when we lost five sailors to a Japanese ambush
  on Guam.
For I am a Submariner.
I tip beers over sea-stories with my shipmates at yearly reunions.
We toll the bell and shed a tear for our buddies who are on eternal
  patrol.

Many pilots have been glad to see me, including a future president.

I have completed numerous highly classified missions during the Cold War.

Because "Freedom Is Not Free," be assured that I am out there at this very moment.

For I am a Submariner.

II. A 9902's Prayer

Oh dear and great Father Polaris,
Make me as sharp as Roger Maris.
Help square me away and just like many,
I'll stay in the Navy from six to twenty.
Send me to Groton and your submarine school,
And I'll ascend from the depths of your 100 foot "pool".
When I complete the rigors you have for me there,
I'll go on to Dam Neck—in the Old Dominion fair.
I'll study the missile, computer and "block",
Never to worry about painting a chock.
When this course of instruction I successfully complete,
I'll be a shinning member of your nuclear fleet.
We'll descend into depths not to be found,
And there like the dolphin we'll live and abound.
Seventy days later, we'll surface worn and pale,
And head for a tavern and some life-giving ale.
But, lo and behold, the time will arrive,
For another few months on a long G.D. dive!

By D. A. Robertson, FTMSN, PF(SU), Circa Summer 1963

III.

Nuclear Submarine Missile Program Shows Gains

Nuclear Submarine Missile Program Shows Gains
By HANSON W. BALDWIN Special to The New York TimesU.S.
Navy
New York Times (1857-Current file); Aug 6, 1967; ProQuest Historical
Newspapers The New York Times pg. 18

By HANSON W. BALDWIN
Special to The New York Times

CAPE KENNEDY, Fla., Aug. 2
—The Will Rogers, latest of
the nation's fleet of 41 nuclear-
powered ballistic missile submarines, hoisted a curious-
looking pennant to the stub-
mast above her superstructure
this week.

It bore the insigne of a
beaver, with its great flat tail,
and the inscription:
"Another clean sweep for the
Beaver Patrol."
The Gold, or second crew, of
the newly commissioned Will
Rogers had just launched successfully a long range M Polaris
missile down the eastern Atlantic test range.
The beaver has become in
the almost seven years since
the first ballistic missile submarine assumed its patrol station beneath the surface of the
Norwegian Sea the symbol of
the Gold crews of the two-
crew submarines, and the pennant was a mild form of gibing
triumph at the expense of the
Blue, or first crew.
Yet in a larger sense the
"banner with the strange device" that flew above the Will
Rogers signified the culminat-
ing triumph of the sea-based
missile system and promised
development of a wide variety
of blue water "Buck Rogers"
launching devices.

Fired Below Surface
The Will Rogers fired her
test missile from a depth of 50
to 60 feet beneath the surface
off Cape Kennedy seven years
and 11 days after the George
Washington, first of the nuclear-powered ballistic missile
submarines, successfully completed the first submarine
launching of a ballistic missile.
The Polaris program, with
its three types of nuclear-tip
missiles varying in range from
1,200 to 2,500 nautical miles,
has scarcely been completed;
yet already new sea-based missiles and strange new submarines and surface ships to
launch them are either under
development or in the "think

A Polaris A-3 leaves sea
more powerful missile called
the Poseidon.

the range of enemy ground de-
fenses, and by increasing active
defensive strength by the construction of an antiballistic
missile system.

But if any of these measures
is taken—if, for instance, new
silos are built to withstand 300
pounds or more per square inch
of pressure—tomorrow's sea-
based launching systems become cost-competitive, at least
in the view of the Navy, in
addition to offering many ad-
vantages that land launchings
do not permit.

Thus, as the Russians in-
crease their inventory of stra-
tegic weapons and as Commu-
nist China acquires a long-
range nuclear delivery capa-
bility, the nation's interest in
new and expanded sea-based
weapons mounts.

In terms of land area for dis-
persal of missile sites and in
in terms of concentration of
population in urban centers, the
United States is at a sharp disadvantage vis-á-vis the Soviet
Union.

Sea-based missiles, which can
be launched from nearby anywhere in the world of water
that comprises most of the
earth, have the tremendous advantage of dispersibility; by
putting United States missiles
at sea, we compensate, the
Navy argues, for our restricted
land area and concentration of
population.

Advantage of Mobility

Most, though not all, of the
sea-based missile systems now
being considered also have the
advantage of mobility, which
means that no enemy can "zero
in' on the launches ahead of

284

IV. *When God Created a Submariner*

15 May 2012

When the good Lord created a Submariner, it was almost 2300 on the sixth day. An angel appeared and said, "You're having a lot of trouble with this one. What's wrong with the standard model?"

And the Lord replied, "Have you seen the specs on this order? It has to be able to think independently, yet be able to take orders; have the qualities of both a scientific mind and a compassionate heart; be able to mentor juniors and learn from seniors; run on black coffee; handle emergencies without a Damage Control Manual, respond competently to critical incidents, decipher cryptographic codes, understand pneumatics, hydraulics and sonar, have the patience of a saint and six pairs of hands, not to mention the strength of three its size."

The angel shook its head slowly and said, "Six pairs of hands—No way!"

And the Lord answered, "Don't worry, we'll make other Submariners to help. Besides it's not the hands which are causing the problem. It's the heart. It must swell with pride when a Shipmate earns his Silver Dolphins—which above all else signifies the crew members trust it with their lives, sustain the incredible hardship of life at sea in a steel tube, beat on soundly when it's too tired to do so, and be strong enough to continue to carry on when it's given all it had."

"Lord," said the angel touching the Lord's sleeve gently, "Stop! It's almost midnight!"

"I can't," said the Lord. "I'm so close to creating something unique. Already I have one whose hands blend knowledge with skill to perform the most intricate procedures, yet are strong enough to patch a ruptured seawater pipe; whose ears can discern the sonar sounds of a myriad of ocean life, yet detect the slightest shift in ventilation; whose mind can practice the science of nuclear submarining, yet not lose sight of the art of teamwork; and whose eyes can peer through a periscope to identify a hull down ship, yet search within to embrace and personify honor, courage and commitment."

The angel circled the model of the Submariner very slowly. "It's too serious," the angel sighed.

"But tough," said the Lord excitedly. "You cannot imagine what this Submariner can do or endure."

"Can it feel?" asked the angel.

"Can it feel! It loves Ship, Shipmates and Country like no other!"

Finally the angel bent over and ran a finger across the Submariner's cheek. "There's a leak," pronounced the angel. "I told you you're trying to put too much into this model."

"That's not a leak," said the Lord. "It's a tear."

"What's it for?" asked the angel.

"It's for joy, sadness, disappointment, pain, frustration and pride!"

"You're a genius!" exclaimed the angel.

The Lord looked pleased and replied, "I didn't put it there."

Filled with pride, the Lord continued, "Great things are planned for this Submariner. It will be one of many and together they will lead a legacy of excellence like none has known before."

And with that the Lord rested. It was the seventh day.

CAPT Jane F. Vieira

Chaplain Corps, United States Navy

ABOUT THE AUTHOR

 The author is a graduate of New England college prep school, Gould Academy, in Bethel, Maine. He also attended the University of Maine.

Many of the experiences retold in *Teddy Bears to Dangerous Missions* come from his eight years of active duty on Polaris missile missions as a member of the US Navy Submarine Service.

After the Navy, Dennis had a successful career in IT with positions in hardware and software engineering, program management, and sales and sales management. He says his most favorite yet challenging position was managing a $43 million a year business unit consisting of thirty-six sales and technical employees for a major data storage company!

He currently lives in Newnan, Georgia, with his wife of fifty-six years.